NO LONGER PROPERTY OF
ANYTHINK LIBRARIES/
RANGEVIEW LIBRARY DISTRICT

BIG DIRTY MONEY

BIG
DIRTY
MONEY

THE SHOCKING INJUSTICE
and UNSEEN COST *of*
WHITE COLLAR CRIME

JENNIFER TAUB

VIKING

VIKING
An imprint of Penguin Random House LLC
penguinrandomhouse.com

Copyright © 2020 by Jennifer Taub
Penguin supports copyright. Copyright fuels creativity, encourages diverse voices,
promotes free speech, and creates a vibrant culture. Thank you for buying an authorized
edition of this book and for complying with copyright laws by not reproducing, scanning,
or distributing any part of it in any form without permission. You are supporting
writers and allowing Penguin to continue to publish books for every reader.

LIBRARY OF CONGRESS CATALOGING-IN-PUBLICATION DATA

Names: Taub, Jennifer, author.
Title: Big dirty money : the shocking injustice and unseen cost of white
collar crime / Jennifer Taub.
Description: [New York] : Viking, [2020] | Includes index.
Identifiers: LCCN 2020024366 (print) | LCCN 2020024367 (ebook) |
ISBN 9781984879974 (hardcover) | ISBN 9781984879981 (ebook)
Subjects: LCSH: White collar crimes—United States. |
Commercial crimes—United States.
Classification: LCC HV6769 .T38 2020 (print) | LCC HV6769 (ebook) |
DDC 364.16/80973—dc23
LC record available at https://lccn.loc.gov/2020024366
LC ebook record available at https://lccn.loc.gov/2020024367

Printed in the United States of America
1   3   5   7   9   10   8   6   4   2

DESIGNED BY MEIGHAN CAVANAUGH

For Emily and Arella

CONTENTS

॥॥॥॥॥॥॥॥॥॥॥॥॥॥॥॥॥॥॥॥॥॥॥॥॥॥॥॥॥॥॥॥

||||||||||||||||||||||||||||||||||||||||||||||||||||||||

CRIME SCENE

Big cheaters often prosper, and they do it right in front of our faces. You can see them almost daily on the front page of the paper, in your Twitter feed, and on broadcast and cable news programs. Rogues-to-riches stories are common now. Cheating the public—and getting away with it—is the new normal.

Turn on the television today and you're more likely to see wealthy, well-connected white men secure presidential pardons than watch one get convicted and sent to prison. Just after Valentine's Day in 2020, President Donald Trump granted clemency to a slew of affluent felons.[1] Their offenses? Bribery, investment fraud, tax evasion, Medicare fraud, public corruption, computer hacking, an extortion cover-up, money laundering, conspiracy to defraud the federal government, obstruction of justice, mail fraud, wire fraud.[2] No white collar crime left behind. The official White House announcement used the word "successful" four times to describe these elite outlaws, but made no mention of the ordinary people they victimized.[3]

Meanwhile, here on the ground, we can clearly see the villains and the victims. Take the secretive Sackler family who cashed in on the opioid crisis. Their pharma business collected $35 billion[4] peddling OxyContin, the supposedly addiction-proof painkiller released to the public in 1996. While the Sacklers personally amassed a reported $14 billion fortune and joined the ranks of our nation's twenty richest families,[5] more than 232,000 fellow Americans died of prescription opioid overdoses between 1999 and 2018.[6]

Pacific Gas & Electric paid out nearly $5 billion in dividends to shareholders instead of using the money it collected from customers to upgrade miles of aging high-voltage power lines that executives knew could spark fires. The decision by PG&E to defer maintenance of a century-old transmission line caused the Camp Fire in 2018, the most deadly blaze in California history, which leveled the entire town of Paradise, killing eighty-five people and destroying more than 18,000 buildings, most of them homes.[7]

As early as 2002, several employees at General Motors, including a lead design engineer,[8] discovered that the company was selling cars with faulty ignition switches.[9] The defect, which caused engines to shut off suddenly and prevented airbags from inflating, killed at least 124 people and injured an additional 275 before a 2014 recall.[10]

It's not just big business. We see these get-rich-corruptly schemes in government as well. In 2009, Robert McDonnell was elected the seventy-first governor of Virginia on the populist promise "Bob for Jobs." Once in office, he accepted an engraved silver Rolex watch, luxury vacations, cash for his daughter's wedding, and loans from a wealthy businessman in exchange for access to state bigwigs.[11] The governor's big benefactor got access, but during his four-year term, Bob's new jobs did not keep up with the growing population of Virginia.[12]

It's hard to stop once you start counting them up. In 2010, billionaire hedge fund manager Leon Cooperman and his investment firm "earned" nearly $4 million in profits by unlawfully trading on confidential insider information about the promising prospects of a natural gas company.[13] Cooperman's victims were in the dark and sold their investments to him on the cheap. When the secret came out, the gas company's stock price jumped up more than 30 percent.[14]

Pressured from the top, from 2009 through late 2016,[15] employees at financial giant Wells Fargo opened potentially 3.5 million checking, savings, and credit card accounts without customer consent, slamming them with overdraft fees and other unauthorized charges. Instead of immediately stopping the ongoing fraud, Wells Fargo retaliated by firing honest employees who tried to blow the whistle, including one manager who told his supervisors and contacted the bank's internal ethics hotline about the suspected fraud.[16] In 2016, after the truth came out, CEO John Stumpf resigned in "shame." Yet the Wells Fargo board of directors awarded him a $134 million exit payment.[17] Years later, in 2020, the Office of the Comptroller of the Currency (OCC), the primary regulator of national banks, fined and banned Stumpf from working in the industry ever again.[18] By then, the still quite wealthy sixty-six-year-old had already retired.

Elizabeth Holmes, a 2003 Stanford University dropout, built

her blood-testing firm Theranos to a $9 billion market valuation by 2015 on a shaky foundation of lies, fawning funders, falsified patient blood test results, and fraudulent financial reports.[19] Her claims included that the U.S. Department of Defense was using Theranos blood analyzer products on the battlefield in Afghanistan and that the company would bring in more than $100 million in revenue in 2014. In reality, the Defense Department never deployed the Theranos products, and the corporation generated just around $100,000 in revenue that year.[20] After an intrepid journalist exposed the truth, Theranos crashed and closed down in 2018, causing Holmes's backers to lose their investments and leaving untold numbers of people with a false sense of good health after receiving phony lab results. Holmes is still a free woman living in a luxury apartment in San Francisco, where, as a close associate explains, "Elizabeth sees herself as the victim."[21]

In 2019, after getting pushed out of the struggling startup WeWork, "disgraced" cofounder and CEO Adam Neumann secured a nearly $1.7 billion (yes, billion-dollar) golden parachute from behemoth buyer SoftBank. He cleaned up, but thousands of WeWork staff were left with no work and worthless underwater stock options. Some layoffs came with offers of four months of severance pay for those who agreed not to sue the company.[22]

WE THE PREY

Everywhere you look, prominent predators are profiting off countless targets and then striding away with their catch. They might lie low for a brief period while waiting for the predictable public outcry to fade, and then they go out hunting again. It's how they survive and thrive. The rest of us are victims, directly or indirectly, even if we've never invested in their companies or bought their shoddy products. We associate the word "victim" with crimes of violence and theft. But corrupt and sometimes criminal acts by trusted business and government leaders can hurt us more frequently and extensively than street crime does. White collar crime in America, such as fraud and embezzlement, costs victims an estimated $300 billion to $800 billion per year.[23] Yet street-level "property" crimes, including burglary, larceny, and theft, cost us far less—around $16 billion annually, according to the FBI.[24] But we cannot know the full extent of white collar crime, as the FBI does not report an annual total.[25] Really. In fact, there is no government agency that measures and reports full white collar crime statistics. Not on an annual basis and not even on a regular basis. Individual private researchers try to piece it all together. Think about that again. No one at all actually measures or knows the amount or cost of white collar crime in the United States.[26]

Of course, the damage to society goes beyond counting up the number of offenses or measuring victims' financial losses. Unpunished and underpunished high-profile criminal offenses by the top echelon in the business, government, and nonprofit sectors undermines our trust in both the rule of law and these institutions that support our democracy.

It's easy to find concrete examples of the grave consequences that stem from this eroding trust. Consider the growing antivaccine movement. A national health crisis emerged because medical experts could not persuade a critical mass of parents in certain geographic regions that vaccines are safe and help prevent disease, suffering, and death. The antivaxxers' irrational skepticism stems in part from an understandable mistrust of Big Pharma.[27] Who isn't discouraged by headline-grabbing stories of once respected pharmaceutical companies and retailers hiding side effects of popular products? Tales of repeated trickery make many wonder whether both childhood vaccines and the health care providers who recommend them can be trusted. Now harmful diseases like measles, once thought to be eradicated, have reemerged.[28] Instead of relying on experts, too many turn to hucksters. Shameful, but not surprising; in March 2020, as the novel coronavirus spread, folks like Alex Jones peddled phony cures. He promoted a "Superblue Toothpaste" that his InfoWars website said would kill "the whole SARS-corona family at point-blank range." There was no medical evidence backing this claim. Fortunately, the New York State Office of the Attorney General sent him a cease and desist notice.[29]

We can also see what happens when trust in all of government weakens due to the unchecked corruption of individual government leaders. Voters can find it hard to distinguish between ordinary, sometimes fallible candidates trying to serve the public, and those outright scoundrels who run for office to line their own pockets and take advantage of the power these institutions convey to them. This mistrust also undermines the efforts to grow public funds through our tax system. When incidents of government corruption go unpunished, it's easier for businesses and the wealthy to rationalize not paying their taxes. Too many engage in criminal tax evasion with the false belief that it is a victimless crime. But we all suffer. While it's hard to pinpoint specific victims,[30] when the very rich decide not to pay the taxes they legally owe, real people suffer. Roads go unrepaired; schoolteachers and nurses lose their jobs. Hospitals run with insufficient medical equipment. We often only notice these starved resources in moments of crisis, when it's too late to remedy.

All of society is injured by these and other unacknowledged by-products of a crime spree—often by prominent members of the business community and government—who go largely unpunished.

RETURN TO THE SCENE OF THE CRIME

So far, not a single person has gone to prison for any of those serious offenses set out above. Not one. How can this be, here in the United States, where we have nearly 2.3 million people incarcerated?[31] Where a man on his way to work can be detained and handcuffed for merely eating his breakfast sandwich on a commuter train platform?[32] Some of the acts described were never even prosecuted as crimes. Yet for those that were, for which felony convictions or pleas materialized, still there was no prison time.

Let's start with the Sacklers' company, Purdue Pharma. The first time the family business had a major run-in with the law was over a decade ago. In 2007, the company and three top executives (none of them Sackler family members) entered guilty pleas for illegally misbranding OxyContin in violation of the Federal Food, Drug, and Cosmetic Act.[33] At one point, this opioid represented more than 90 percent of Purdue's sales. The company pleaded guilty to a felony and paid a fine, but the three managers pleaded only to misdemeanors and served no prison time.[34] After the felony plea, undeterred and backed by the Sacklers, Purdue continued on its crooked path, pushing OxyContin for more than a decade longer. Today, both the firm and (at last) the family members face a crush of fresh litigation. Yet no one is going to be locked up. Whatever settlements are struck will most likely preserve significant family wealth, which likely has been safely squirreled away outside the reach of both prosecutors and private plaintiffs.

The PG&E story is similar. Like Purdue, it is a repeat big-business offender. In 2016, a jury found PG&E guilty of six felonies, including obstructing the government's investigation into a 2010 natural gas explosion in San Bruno, California, that killed eight people and destroyed thirty-eight homes.[35] But no one went to prison, not even for the pipeline safety violations. Not for obstruction. Instead, the federal judge put PG&E on probation for five years, ordered the corporation to pay a fine, and required corporate employees, including officers and directors, to perform a total of 10,000 hours of community service. But even after the San Bruno disaster, the PG&E leaders continued to put greed ahead of safety. The firm paid shareholders billions in dividends while that criminal pipeline case moved forward, and while they knew that the century-old power lines and towers needed repair. In 2018, after the Camp Fire in California, the *Wall Street Journal*, through a Freedom of Information Act request, discovered internal PG&E documents that linked the cause of the fire directly to the deferred maintenance. Then came the 2019 Kincade Fire that destroyed more than 374 structures. All told, as the federal judge who is now overseeing PG&E's probation noted in court, the fires caused by PG&E over recent years have burned more than 3 percent of California.[36] In late March 2020, the company pleaded guilty and agreed to pay $4 million to settle involuntary manslaughter charges in connection with the Camp Fire. The district attorney for the California county where the town of Paradise is located brought the charges against PG&E.[37] The firm hoped to pay this fine out of a proposed $13.5 billion victims fund it planned to set up through its bankruptcy reorganization.[38]

In 2015, to settle the federal criminal and civil charges, General Motors admitted it misled consumers and regulators about the ignition switch defect, forfeited $900 million, and entered into a deferred prosecution agreement, or DPA.[39] Three years later, both felony charges against GM, for wire fraud and concealment of a deadly safety defect, were dismissed. No individuals from the corporation—not even the ones in the know who did nothing for years to prevent these tragedies—were charged with a criminal offense. Sadly, though, some truly blameless GM drivers were. In 2007, twenty-one-year-old Candice Anderson pleaded guilty to manslaughter after she lost control of her Saturn Ion and it crashed into a tree, killing her boyfriend. For years, Anderson, who was also severely injured in the accident, believed that she was responsible for his death. But GM knew the truth. Five months before her guilty plea, the company completed an internal review of the crash and came to the conclusion that the ignition switch, not Anderson, was at fault. But the company did not tell her or local law enforcement. Instead, GM wrote a letter to the National Highway Traffic Safety Administration falsely stating it had not assessed the crash. It was not until 2014, when she learned what had really happened, that a Texas judge cleared Anderson of those criminal charges.[40] All in all, including the Department of Justice settlement and a $600 million victims' compensation fund, the cover-up of the ignition defect cost GM nearly $2 billion.[41] Yet the very same year the auto giant settled with the government and victims, it still managed to earn a record $9.7 billion profit.[42]

As for the Virginia governor, after trial and conviction, Bob Mc-Donnell successfully appealed to the U.S. Supreme Court. With a unanimous decision in 2016, his bribery conviction was overturned and the public corruption laws undermined. To close the loophole, Congress could have amended the bribery statutes, but years later it still has not done so. In 2017, billionaire Leon Cooperman and his firm settled the insider trading case with the Securities and Exchange Commission without facing criminal charges by the Department of Justice. Under the SEC settlement, he and his firm agreed to pay $4.9 million in fines and forfeitures. This included $1.7 million in disgorgement (meaning surrender) of his ill-gotten gains.[43] Nearly meaningless in comparison with the $225 million he'd pulled in the previous year.[44] Instead of banning Cooperman from the industry for life, the SEC subjected him to outside monitoring by a consultant for around five years. While still being monitored, this apparently unrepentant lawbreaker railed against the wealth tax proposals put forward by Democratic presidential candidates in the fall of 2019: "Stop portraying billionaires as criminals," he said.[45] He's not alone. In 2013, fellow billionaire hedge fund manager Steven A. Cohen escaped indictment even after his own namesake investment firm, SAC Capital, pleaded guilty to insider trading charges and paid a $1.8 billion fine and his portfolio manager was sent to prison. After SAC closed down, Cohen still had more than $11 billion in assets under management.[46]

And how did the victims of insider trading make out? Can they get some of the SEC's recovery? It's complicated. Congress has never endowed the SEC with clear authority. While the SEC has for decades used a "Fair Fund" to compensate victims of investment fraud and insider trading, this practice soon may be undermined. In March 2020, the Supreme Court heard oral arguments in a case challenging the right for a court to require disgorgement of ill-gotten gains as part of an SEC enforcement proceeding. Yet letting a cheat keep these unlawful profits will only encourage more lawlessness. And victims will be harmed. This is because a good part of the money in the Fair Funds comes from these surrendered gains.[47] If the court bans the practice, Congress could step in to provide the SEC with the explicit authority to claw back these dirty profits. But will Congress act?

As for the fake accounts fiasco, in 2016 Wells Fargo settled with the Consumer Financial Protection Bureau (CFPB), the OCC, and the city and county of Los Angeles, paying $185 million. The bank expressed regret, but did not admit to any wrongdoing.[48] But that was just the beginning. After CEO John Stumpf was gone, the truth came flooding out. It was hard to keep track of the scandals. In 2017, Wells Fargo got caught overcharging members of our military for auto loans and then illegally repossessing their cars even while the owners were serving in active duty.[49] Then, in 2018, the CFPB and the OCC hit Wells Fargo with a $1 billion fine. What was it this time? The bank admitted that it had charged hundreds of thousands of its car loan customers for insurance they did not need. Nearly 25,000 borrowers who could not pay these extra fees and defaulted had their cars wrongfully repossessed.[50] And Wells Fargo also admitted to charging extra fees to customers to extend locked-in interest rates for home mortgage loans when the bank had caused the delays.[51]

These were civil, not criminal, settlements. There are some big differences between them. With criminal investigations, prosecutors can use grand jury subpoenas to obtain documents and witness testimony to gather evidence. And with a criminal case—in addition to requiring asset forfeitures, fines, and penalties—a judge can impose a prison sentence if a defendant pleads guilty or the jury delivers a guilty verdict. In contrast, in a civil settlement with the government, or if a jury finds the defendant liable, prison is never a punishment. Instead, the sanctions are mainly financial. Typically, the defendant will enter into an agreement or face a court order requiring them to hand over money and abide by the law.

Federal agencies like the CFPB, SEC, and OCC do not have authority to bring criminal cases. All they can pursue is civil enforcement. Some of the laws they enforce, though, have both civil and criminal sanctions available. So if these regulators suspect a person or business committed a crime, they can refer the case to state or federal law enforcement, such as the FBI, to investigate. And ultimately, it's up to prosecutors at the Department of Justice to press charges for federal criminal law violations. But with Wells Fargo, the DOJ blinked. In February 2020, Wells Fargo and its bank subsidiary agreed to pay $3 billion to resolve all "potential" criminal and civil liability with the DOJ and several other federal agencies, including the SEC, related to opening the millions of unauthorized accounts from the time managers knew about the fraud in 2002. Seems big, but that was just short of the bank's quarterly profits. None of that money will be given to the victims.[52] So far, no executives have been indicted. None are going to prison. The

And finally there is Elizabeth Holmes. In March 2018, the Securities and Exchange Commission announced it had settled an investor fraud case with Holmes. Yet under the terms of the settlement, she did not admit to any wrongdoing at all. Holmes just agreed to give up voting control of Theranos, pay a $500,000 penalty, and return to the company the shares she'd gained as a result of the alleged fraud. She also agreed to a ban on serving as an officer or a director of a public company for a decade.[61] A few months later, in June 2018, a grand jury indicted Holmes on numerous counts of wire fraud and conspiracy. The indictment alleged that one scheme involved defrauding Theranos investors, and another defrauding doctors and patients. Holmes pleaded not guilty on all counts.[62] In December 2019, she filed a motion to get the charges dismissed. In response, the Department of Justice highlighted the harm of her alleged criminal fraud. One patient received a lab report falsely stating that he was HIV-positive. A woman struggling to become pregnant was wrongly informed she would miscarry. Another received a test result from Theranos that said she was not pregnant, only to learn from another lab that she had a life-threatening ectopic pregnancy.[63] In February 2020, the judge narrowed the scope of the federal case against Holmes. U.S. district court judge Edward Davila ruled that while the felony counts related to investors could go forward, the allegations that she had defrauded doctors could not. And when it came to patients, the judge said prosecutors could only count as victims those people who actually paid for their blood tests. If their insurance companies footed the bill, he reasoned, then they were not the ones defrauded of "money or property," under the statutes. Not the doctors. Not patients if they did not pay. Judge Davila concluded that "the right to accurate information," even about your health, was not a property interest.[64] Elizabeth Holmes's criminal trial was scheduled for after this book went to press.

Much of the smash-and-grab action described here took place quite recently, in the years following the toxic-mortgage-backed financial crisis of 2008, when the American public had surely seen enough unchecked predation. Maybe that's not an accident. When the bankers got away with it, perhaps others with weak moral compasses saw little potential constraint in the criminal justice system. Yes, there was fraud in every link of the toxic mortgage supply chain, but much of the harm was caused by decades of deregulation and lackluster law enforcement.[65] Instead of punishment, recall that with the mortgage meltdown, behemoth banks received trillions in government bailouts and backstops, and bankers themselves went on to earn billions of dollars in personal bonuses.[66] So after a global catastrophe came little personal accountability, and some American bankers even got trophies. Yet nearly 7.8 million families lost their homes to foreclosure by 2016.[67] In the decade since the 2008 financial crisis, we saw the biggest financial firms not just survive, but thrive, with tremendous profits. A decade after the crisis, in 2018, the banking industry scored record annual profits of more than $270 billion.[68] Even before the country had turned the corner, bank lobbyists were seeking to roll back and repeal the reforms put in place to avoid another crisis.[69]

It didn't have to be this way. Over in Iceland, as of 2018, judges have sent thirty-six bankers to jail in connection with the 2008 crash of the Icelandic banking system—prison sentences of ninety-six years in total.[70] The convictions were at the highest level, including several top bank executives and the former CEO of a giant international bank in Reykjavík, who was sentenced to seven years in prison for financial crimes related to the crisis.[71] Instead, in the United States, while a few notable CEOs of failed giant banks paid civil penalties to settle with federal regulators, they were never criminally prosecuted.

EXTREME WEALTH IS CRIMINOGENIC

In 1887, in a letter to a fellow historian, John Emerich Edward Dalberg (Lord Acton) penned this now familiar sentiment: "Power tends to corrupt, and absolute power corrupts absolutely."[72] In our society, extreme wealth often confers tremendous power. So just as power tends to corrupt, so does excessive wealth. Today we witness how outsized wealth can be criminogenic. In this way, white collar crime in particular is a tool with promising possibilities for those who won't get caught or punished. When powerful people plunder with impunity, they grow even wealthier. And they can use this wealth to change the laws and their enforcement so that they favor those at the top like themselves. This is not a theory. It's reality. The big-money crowd can and does use plundered wealth to help ensure that those elected to positions of power in the government will protect them and further their interests. At the top of the list is cutting taxes, promoting industries they invest in or control, and keeping them (and their dear friends and offspring) out of trouble, out of prison, and in the money. This furthers the wealth divide in America and undermines notions of fairness and meritocracy, paving the way for kleptocracy—government by thieves.

As law professor Harry Manuel Shulman observed in 1952, in our complex society, "large segments of criminal behavior represent some of the means taken by groups to ensure their survival, even though these means are in conflict with larger values of the culture." He believed that white collar offenses flourished due to "strong social pressures that sanction and conventionalize them."[73] Such is the case today with much of the uber-wealthy in America. Now, more than a half century later, with the concentration of wealth and power in giant corporations, money management firms, and the 1 percent, we create the perfect conditions for the unscrupulous. The numbers tell the story. In short, elite crime pays. It pays very well. The cost, if caught, is too small to deter serious misconduct. Sure, the expenses can add up, but they are outweighed by the benefits. Getting caught is more of a loathsome inconvenience than a shameful penalty. For businesses, there can be annoying civil lawsuits brought by individuals or federal and local governments. Then come verdicts or settlements, with some mixture of monetary consequences. Sometimes as part of these resolutions, victims receive a modicum of compensation. On occasion, victims win big settlements, which, if really big, are subsequently greatly reduced. When it comes to business firms, these payouts by offenders are often far less than the initial winnings. Or if all is lost due to one illicit pursuit, then it's just one of many eggs in multiple baskets. A mere cost of doing business. And as for the individual executives presiding over the fraud and abuse? They rarely if ever lose a night's sleep or a week's pay for their transgressions. At best, they get promoted. At worst, a bit of their pay is "clawed back" for the sake of optics and they depart with a cushy exit package.

And criminal punishment for offenders in the upper echelons of the corporate world or elite society? Surely you jest.

IMPLICIT IMMUNITY

We also have a double standard in the American criminal justice system that reflects and perpetuates inequality. Cutting legal corners is a tool for advancement only available to the already affluent. The wealthy not only increase their power by evading punishment, but also benefit from a criminal justice system that incarcerates those with lower social status who also attempt to use crime to get ahead. Selling loose cigarettes on a New York City sidewalk can lead to a choke-hold arrest and death. Eric Garner, a middle-aged black man, was surrounded by police officers, tackled, and suffocated for what was just a small-time tax dodge. Garner was selling cigarettes purchased cheaper by the pack out of state and selling them one by one to passersby. Tax evasion. Depriving New York State and City of nearly $5.85 per pack.[74] The Department of Justice decided not to prosecute the police officer who killed Garner. The reasoning? The powers that be believed he had not used excessive force under the circumstances. Racism is baked into that conclusion. Can you imagine cops circling, tackling, and choking a white woman who was poised to drop her fraudulent tax return in a city mailbox? How would that not be considered excessive force?

Scale that up to a multinational corporate enterprise dodging the law, and the disparities are even more stark. For years, giant London-based HSBC laundered big money for murderous Mexican and Colombian drug cartels.[75] In 2012, the U.S. government punished the bank and its U.S. subsidiary with a five-year deferred prosecution agreement, the equivalent of probation. But not a single executive was imprisoned, let alone indicted. For a bank that would earn $22.6 billion the following year, the $1.9 billion paid to resolve the criminal and civil cases was equal to around one month's profits. After that scandal, CEO Stuart Gulliver, an Oxford-educated white man who was using a Panamanian shell company to hide personal assets, insisted that the bank he ran was not "too big to manage."[76] Should it shock us that units of HSBC reoffended but avoided indictments thanks to two additional deferred prosecution agreements, in 2018 and 2019?[77]

Even when the exception proves the rule, and a high-status individual is prosecuted and convicted, the double standard carries into sentencing, where statutory guidelines require judges to give serious weight to a convicted felon's past contributions to their community. Such leniency fails to acknowledge that preemptively spreading around ill-gotten funds to charities is a con artist's trick to gain public trust, manipulate community do-gooders, and inoculate themselves.[78]

Even the federal prison system allows wealthy offenders better conditions than ordinary convicts, with low-security camp settings for the former and dangerous caged conditions for the latter. Often, when top-shelf felons—like 1980s junk bond king Michael Milken, 1990s lifestyle guru Martha Stewart, and recently released Enron CEO Jeff Skilling—complete a prison sentence, they rejoin high society with sufficient funds to rehabilitate themselves and relaunch their careers with little lasting stigma.[79] In 2019, the actress Lori Loughlin, indicted in the college admissions scandal known as Operation Varsity Blues, reportedly sought to hire a crisis management firm that might fashion her redemption in Martha Stewart style.[80] Model citizens. In contrast, the impact of incarceration on the poor and working class can be irreversible for both the defendant and their children for years, if not generations, to come.

Even when it comes to behavior beyond financial shenanigans, the rich and well connected transgress in private homes and schools with impunity, with criminal consequences the exception, not the rule. Those of lesser means and lower status are more often slapped with prison sentences and tarnished records after engaging in the equivalent types of illegal activities available in their realms. From cradle to grave, there is an implicit immunity from criminal consequences for the megamoney set.

A PATH FORWARD

In this book, I contend that our current framework for discussing, measuring, prosecuting, and punishing white collar crime is aging and needs to be reimagined. By making this move, we will be honoring the legacy of Edwin Sutherland, the sociologist who introduced the concept of "white collar criminality" in 1939 and a decade later defined the term "white collar crime" to mean an offense committed by "a person of respectability and high social status in the course of his occupation."[81] Sutherland focused his full attention on corporate crime, and he got it right eighty years ago: we must pay attention to the status of the offender. This means shifting away from treating all economic crime the same. When we measure the extent and impact of white collar crime, we need to stop bundling together multimillion-dollar corporate fraud with small-time nickel-and-dime crime like writing bad checks or low-level employee embezzlement. If prosecutors are rewarded for the number of convictions they secure, then the quality of the cases won't matter and the public will not be safe from the most powerful predators who can literally defraud millions of people for years with impunity.

After presenting a clear picture of what's broken, in the final chapter I propose six fixes. Taken together, these suggestions could set us on a path to stop the spread of white collar crime and help clean up our public corruption problem. In brief, I believe we should: (1) establish a new division within the Justice Department to focus on prosecuting, convicting, and incarcerating big money criminals; (2) empower federal prosecutors by strengthening laws that target bribery of public officials and responsible corporate officers, money laundering, and shell companies; (3) protect victims by establishing a nationwide registry of white collar criminal offenders; (4) expose more corporate crime by funding independent journalists, by banning forced arbitration of workplace legal disputes, and by expanding our *qui tam* laws, which give special standing to whistleblowers to bring legal cases on behalf of the government against corrupt businesses; (5) close loopholes in the tax code and staff up the IRS so it can audit tax evaders and collect billions of dollars of already identified tax receipts; and (6) establish a nationwide database at the Justice Department that tracks the outcomes of all white collar offenses reported to federal agencies.

THE ELEPHANT IN THE ROOM

One last note. This is not a book expressly about Donald Trump. However, to write about white collar crime and corruption and not mention him would be like discussing the accounting fraud scandals of the 1990s and early 2000s without covering Enron or explaining Ponzi schemes without mentioning Bernie Madoff. Trump took advantage of a system that gives first, second, third, and seemingly infinite chances to the elite. He had many brushes with the law and with lawless associates but came out ahead time and time again.

These legal entanglements date back nearly a half century to when he was a young man in his twenties, a few years out of college. From there, decade by decade, following the rules never appeared to be a top priority. First was a 1973 race discrimination lawsuit against twenty-seven-year-old Trump, his father Fred Trump, and their company Trump Management Inc. involving rental apartments in Brooklyn, Queens, and Staten Island. When the civil case settled in 1975, the Justice Department claimed victory. A government lawyer recalled that the thirty-one-page consent decree was "one of the most far-reaching ever negotiated" under the Fair Housing Act of 1968.[82] Minimizing its importance, Trump later wrote that "we ended up making a minor settlement without admitting guilt."[83]

Over in Manhattan in the early 1980s, Donald Trump, by then in his thirties, built Trump Tower on a foundation of stolen wages and mob-sourced concrete. To knock down the Bonwit Teller building and make room for his tower, Trump paid hundreds of undocumented workers from Poland less than half what union wages were and failed to pay some at all. Some worked twelve-hour days, seven days a week. Members of the House Wreckers Union sued Kaszycki & Sons, the contractor Trump used to find workers to demolish the Bonwit Teller building in 1980. The union members argued that by hiring undocumented workers, Trump had avoided contributing to the union pension fund. Years later, Trump wound up paying more than $1.3 million to settle that federal lawsuit.[84]

When the glitzy tower opened in early 1983, Trump sold or rented condominium units to folks with links to organized crime. This included Verina Hixon, a friend of Teamster boss John Cody, who purchased three duplex apartments in the tower. While Hixon herself has never been accused of wrongdoing, Cody, who was an alleged close associate of the Gambino crime family,[85] was a repeat offender. Cody spent years behind bars on state burglary charges before he became president of Teamsters Local 282, a union that represented thousands of truckers, including those who delivered concrete to construction sites in New York. In January 1982, Cody was indicted on federal criminal charges, including racketeering, all unrelated to Trump.[86] While Trump Tower was under way that July, Cody's union went on strike. Without trucks moving, building in the city was on hold most of that summer. Somehow, though, Trump still continued to receive deliveries of the concrete he needed to build during the three-month strike. As John Cody's son Michael reflected, "My father wasn't that generous, unless there was a reason."[87]

In September 1982, Cody's trial on federal racketeering charges began. The jury found Cody guilty of engaging in a pattern of racketeering dating back to the late 1970s. The criminal behavior included demanding gifts from building contractors,[88] and a judge sentenced him to five years in prison.[89] While Cody was locked up, Trump reportedly helped his friend Hixon obtain a $3 million mortgage, though she had no visible source of income.[90] Then there was Robert Hopkins, a man with ties to organized crime, who brought a briefcase filled with $200,000 in cash to the closing. Hopkins used his several Trump Tower apartments as headquarters to operate one of the city's largest illegal gambling operations.[91]

Closer to Trump was Joey Weichselbaum, a helicopter company operator who made a living importing cocaine from Colombia. After he was indicted on drug trafficking charges in 1985, he began renting an apartment in Trump Plaza and paid in part by providing helicopter services to Trump. After Weichselbaum pleaded guilty, before he was sentenced, Trump wrote a letter to the judge requesting leniency, calling Weichselbaum "a credit to the community."[92] When released from prison after the drug trafficking conviction, Weichselbaum moved into Trump Tower in a double unit previously purchased in cash by his girlfriend, though there is no public record that the money changed hands.[93] Another shady character was David Bogatin, a member of a Russian émigré crime family. When he purchased five apartments in Trump Tower in 1984 for $6 million, using several shell companies, Trump apparently attended the closing.[94]

Speaking of tax evasion, while there's no evidence Trump knew of Bogatin's scheme, he was involved in a scam to cheat on sales tax. In 1986, he testified against employees at Bulgari, a high-end Fifth Avenue jewelry business after he made $65,000 in purchases and then arranged for the store to mail an empty box out of state to avoid city and state taxes. While the Bulgari executives and the company that operated the Manhattan store pleaded guilty and paid fines, they did not serve time in jail.[95]

Legal headaches followed Donald Trump to his casino businesses too. In 1988, when he was in his early forties, Trump agreed to pay the U.S. Federal Trade Commission a $750,000 civil penalty for violating the antitrust laws after he failed to notify the FTC, as required by law, of stock purchases he made in his attempted takeovers of two casino companies.[96] Then, in 1991, the Trump Castle in Atlantic City agreed to pay the New Jersey Division of Gaming Enforcement a $30,000 fine related to an unauthorized loan to the casino. Fred Trump had tried to bail out his son's struggling business by purchasing $3.5 million in poker chips from the Castle without placing any bets.[97] That same year the New Jersey Casino Control Commission leveled a $450,000 fine against the Trump Plaza, another of his Atlantic City casinos, for giving nine luxury automobiles to Robert LiButti, a frequent gambler with reported ties to the Gambino organized crime family, who immediately exchanged the cars for cash, triggering the state law that banned casinos from comping high rollers in cash.[98]

Not to be left out, his third Atlantic City casino, the $1 billion Trump Taj Mahal, struggled to stay afloat and filed for bankruptcy in 1991, followed by the Castle and Plaza in 1992. After that reorganization, where his creditors took substantial haircuts, Trump took his casino businesses public in 1995 with the new name Trump Hotels & Casino Resorts, and now in his fifties, he was in hot water again. The SEC found that THCR had committed securities fraud by issuing a "materially misleading" press release that made the company look healthier than it really was. The consequence? Merely a cease and desist order.[99] Trump brushed it off, calling the press release "just a statement that was too verbose."[100] With yet another bankruptcy in 2004, Trump gave up his CEO position but stayed on as chairman of the board. He did not relinquish that role until another bankruptcy in 2009.[101]

After his exit, more trouble surfaced, dating back to his time running the casinos. The Financial Crimes Enforcement Network (FinCEN), a bureau of the U.S. Treasury Department, imposed a $10 million civil penalty on the Trump Taj Mahal Casino Resort in 2015 for "willful and repeated" violations of the Bank Secrecy Act. This anti–money laundering law targets those who help criminals make illegally gained funds, or "dirty money," look clean. The government's press release mentioned a 1998 $477,000 civil penalty for currency-transaction reporting violations and noted that the "Trump Taj Mahal has a long history of prior, repeated BSA violations cited by examiners dating back to 2003." The director of FinCEN said the casino for many years left our financial system vulnerable to being "exploited by criminals, terrorists, and other bad actors."[102] Though the Trump Taj Mahal admitted to several willful violations, no criminal charges were brought.

Is it any wonder that Donald Trump's dalliance with "higher" education also brought allegations of fraud and racketeering? In 2005, by now nearly in his sixties, he launched Trump University, a seminar series promising to teach students the secrets of successful real estate investment from instructors who were "handpicked" by Trump himself. Gold elite classes cost nearly $35,000.[103] In November 2016, Trump agreed to pay $25 million to settle several associated lawsuits, including those alleging civil fraud and rack-eteering.[104]

This is just a sample. We have not even touched on how Trump allegedly gained at least $413 million (in today's dollars) from his father's real estate empire mostly by using tax schemes that experts later told the *New York Times* appeared to be fraudulent.[105] And all of this was *before* he became president of the United States.

A hallmark of the crooked behavior that was never criminally charged is that in some instances related civil cases were brought by federal or state authorities and by individuals. The decision not to criminally prosecute him or his businesses appears to be the result of business as usual—going light on the wealthy. But could government corruption also be at play?

Donald Trump was not the first privileged American to use apparent unlawful behavior to gain and sustain power and wealth—and then to use that wealth to gain immunity from further offenses. What makes him unique, though, is how high he climbed. During his campaign, transition, inauguration, and while in office, he has surrounded himself with comrades, some of whom reportedly got rich off of shady practices and siphoning government funds. Some have been convicted and are now in prison. Others remain untouchable either for lack of trying or due to legal loopholes. And Trump himself has continued with his own corrupt and possibly criminal behavior as we all read about in Robert Mueller's report on Russian interference in the 2016 presidential election. Yet under current Justice Department policy, he is immune from federal criminal prosecution, at least while he remains in the White House.[106] It's hard to envision a future where justice catches up with him. But for now, let's imagine a world where the government had held Donald John Trump accountable for those many offenses he apparently committed well before he launched his presidential campaign in 2015. As Pulitzer Prize–winning investigative journalist Jesse Eisinger has observed, "That's a world where 'President Trump' is an impossibility."[107] It's within our power to create that world where he and anyone like him is an impossibility. The damage already done by our forty-fifth president demonstrates the dangers we face if we fail to do so.

BIG DIRTY MONEY

II

DEFINING WHITE COLLAR CRIME

P hiladelphia is a city where revolutionary ideas come to life. It was there one cold December evening in 1939 that Professor Edwin H. Sutherland shared a breakthrough theory he'd been developing for over a decade. The soft-spoken sociologist from Indiana University chose the Crystal Ballroom of the eighteen-story Benjamin Franklin Hotel to unveil his transformative criminology framework.[1] The location fit his circumstances. The swank hotel was just three blocks down Chestnut Street from the old Pennsylvania State House, where the founders signed the Declaration of Independence and the framers attended the Constitutional Convention. To be clear, Sutherland's crowd was not a bunch of provocateurs eager to shake up society. This was a stuffy assemblage of sociologists and economists gathered together for the joint annual meeting of the American Sociological Society and the American Economic Association.[2] As the society's outgoing president, Sutherland was scheduled to deliver an address on the first night of the conference. They were not expecting a revolution.

Sutherland's demeanor was genial and his words bland, but the lecture—"The White Collar Criminal"—gave the world a catchphrase and launched an entire discipline. Half a century later, experts acknowledged that it had "altered the study of crime throughout the world in fundamental ways by focusing upon a form of lawbreaking that previously had been ignored by criminological scholars."[3] It was an impressive legacy for a Nebraska-born man who began his career in sociology with a correspondence course offered by the University of Chicago's Home Study Department.

Sutherland crushed the conventional wisdom as to the causes and nature of crime. He asserted that his peers' current "conception and explanations of crime" were both "misleading and incorrect." Crime was not "closely correlated" with poverty or the "psychopathic and sociopathic conditions statistically associated with poverty," he said.[4] To support his fresh perspective, Sutherland attacked the data. He explained that experts drew the wrong conclusions about crime because the data were incomplete. While it was true that "less than two percent of the persons committed to prisons in a year belong to the upper class," this did not mean that the elite were saintly. The way that crime was "popularly conceived and officially measured" was wrong.[5] The standard measurement tools were lacking. Where did the bad numbers come from? He explained that criminologists narrowly studied "criminals handled by the police, the criminal and juvenile courts, and the prisons."

They myopically focused on "such crimes as murder, assault, burglary, robbery, larceny, sex offenses [and] drunkenness." Excluded from what should be the accurate count, he said, were "vast areas of criminal behavior of persons not in the lower classes."[6]

Sutherland's core thesis in his address that evening came down to this. The experts were not looking at all crime. By ignoring the criminal behavior of professionals, businessmen, and even tycoons, they had a wildly inaccurate picture of who was in the criminal "class." Based on his own detailed research into fraud and conflicts of interest in business and politics, he surmised that crime was not concentrated among the poor. Pulling no punches, Sutherland named names. First, he spoke of the nineteenth-century "robber barons," deeming them "white collar criminals, as almost everyone now agrees." He quoted American industrialist Colonel Cornelius Vanderbilt as admitting his own criminal tendencies when he once quipped, "You don't suppose you can run a railroad in accordance with the statutes, do you?" Sutherland went on to shame various contemporary "merchant princes and captains of finance and industry." Crime was rampant in all occupations, he informed his audience. In particular, "criminality has been demonstrated again and again in the investigations of land offices, railways, insurance, munitions, banking, public utilities, stock exchanges, the oil industry, real estate, reorganizations committees, receiverships, bankruptcies, and politics." White collar criminals were everywhere, he said. It didn't take academic training to discover this. Just ask around. He suggested striking up a conversation with a businessman "by asking him, 'What crooked practices are found in your occupation?'"[7]

IN SEARCH OF A WIDER WEB

Accurately measuring criminal behavior in the upper class was more than just an academic exercise, Sutherland made sure to explain. There were concrete costs and individual victims, and the general public paid a price for these crimes. He contended that the financial cost of white collar crime was likely "several times as great as the financial cost of all crimes which are customarily included in the 'crime problem.'" By way of example, he noted that an "officer of a chain grocery store embezzled" in one year "six times as much as the annual losses from five hundred burglaries and robberies of the stores in that chain." Those costs are passed along to customers via higher prices. He was also concerned with the social impact of white collar criminality. He believed that, more so than street crime, white collar crime creates distrust and "produces social disorganization on a large scale."[8]

Sutherland's most controversial point was that, when studying the crimes of the upper class, scholars should cast a net wider so as to capture more than just actual convictions by *criminal courts*. Toward this goal, he also wished to include in his definition of criminal behavior those unlawful actions by big-business leaders that led to *civil* enforcement by government agencies. By way of example, he pointed to antitrust enforcement actions brought by the Federal Trade Commission.

Using Sutherland's framework, I would label former Countrywide Financial CEO Angelo Mozilo a white collar criminal in light of his $67 million settlement of civil fraud and insider trading charges with the SEC in 2010. The government accused him of

4

relying on insider information when he made $140 million in profits selling stock in 2008. According to the SEC, Mozilo also misled investors by claiming Countrywide was in good shape, falsely claiming that they had focused on making high-quality mortgage loans. In reality, as one SEC enforcement attorney explained, Mozilo "knew that Countrywide was gambling with increasingly risky mortgages and he kept those details from investors while he was actively taking his own chips off the table."[9] The settlement was small change for Mozilo, who reportedly earned more than $500 million in the decade leading up to the crisis. Plus, Bank of America (which had purchased Countrywide) chipped in $45 million of the settlement as required under the indemnification provision in Countrywide's employment agreement with Mozilo.[10] As part of the deal, the SEC barred him from ever again serving as an officer or director of a public company.[11] Mozilo was by then seventy-two. A few months later the Justice Department decided to drop the criminal case against him.[12]

Similarly, Sutherland believed that "convictability"—not an actual conviction—should be the defining factor. He also suggested we count as "criminal" any potential conviction that was "avoided merely because of pressure which is brought to bear on the court or substitute agency." While this might seem like a stretch, he reminded his listeners that night that addressing these unprosecuted acts was conventional practice when it came to studying mob activity. "Gangsters and racketeers have been relatively immune in many cities because of their pressure on prospective witnesses and public officials." Yet "conventional criminologists do not hesitate to include the life histories of such criminals as data." The same approach should be used for high-status offenders.[13]

Sutherland also innovatively suggested that accessories to white collar crimes who are not prosecuted should still be included when measuring the extent of criminality. Once again, he used precedent from street crime studies to support his argument. When the FBI investigates a kidnapping, he explained, "it is not content with catching the offenders who carried away the victim; they may catch and the court may convict twenty-five other persons who assisted by secreting the victim, negotiating ransom, or putting the ransom money into circulation." In contrast, "the prosecution of white collar criminals frequently stops with one offender." To further illustrate how a double standard skewed the data, he recounted the story of T. J. Pendergast, "the late boss of Kansas City," who was convicted in connection with failing to report as taxable income bribes he received from fire insurance companies; yet, Sutherland noted, "the insurance companies which paid the bribes have not been prosecuted."[14] Pendergast, who on the eve of trial pleaded guilty for income tax evasion, was sentenced to fifteen months in Leavenworth.[15]

The influence of money, Sutherland warned, shaped everything from legislation that defines crime to sentencing of criminals. The elite class had the power to define what was criminal and could more readily change laws that either disfavored them or interfered with their predatory business practices. Due to access to power, unlike low-level offenders, white collar criminals "have a loud voice in determining what goes into the statutes," as well as how existing law "is implemented and administered." They can lobby to make laws too weak to deter the relatively large and powerful. Sutherland cited Daniel Drew, a legendary stock manipulator, who once opined, "Law is like a cobweb; it's made for flies and the smaller kinds of insects, so to speak, but lets the big bumble-bees break through."[16]

His critique of sentencing disparities resonates today, eighty years after he spoke. "The crimes of the lower class are handled by policemen, prosecutors, and judges, with penal sanctions in the form of fines, imprisonment, and death." Yet he noted, "The crimes of the upper class result in no official action at all, or result in suits for damages in civil courts, or are handled by inspectors, and by administrative boards or commissions, with penal sanctions in the form of warnings, orders to cease and desist, occasional rescind-ing of a license, and in extreme cases with fines or prison sen-tences."[17]

This was more than just an arcane debate about nomenclature and measurement, he concluded. How we describe crime impacts how we both pinpoint the causes and come up with solutions to stem it. Poverty did not cause criminality. But what did? He sought an alternative theory that might explain the crimes of both the upper and lower classes. The hypothesis he settled on was that crime is learned. Through relationships with others, future of-fenders learn motives, values, techniques, and rationalizations. He set it out starkly: "Those who become white collar criminals gen-erally start their careers in good neighborhoods and good homes, graduate from colleges with some idealism, and, with little selec-tion on their part, get into a particular business situation in which criminality is practically a folkway, and are inducted into that system of behavior." Similarly, the "lower class criminals generally start their careers in deteriorated neighborhoods and families, find delinquents at hand from whom they acquire their attitudes toward, and techniques of, crime."[18]

In a pithy aside, Sutherland found an interesting distinction between the two classes. "The inventive geniuses for the lower class criminals are generally professional criminals, while the inventive geniuses for many kinds of white collar crime are generally lawyers."[19] Reader, this lawyer agrees.

STEALING CANDY FROM A BABY

The following morning, news of Sutherland's groundbreaking speech splashed across national and local newspapers. *The New York Times* carried the story at the top of page twelve, with the all-caps headline "HITS CRIMINALITY IN WHITE COLLARS," followed by a series of subheads, including, "Dr. Sutherland Says the Cost of Duplicity in High Places Exceeds Burglary Losses." Reporters quoted Sutherland as saying that the day's white collar criminals "are more suave and deceptive" than the nineteenth-century robber barons. He also asserted "in many periods more important crime news can be found on the financial pages of newspapers than on the front pages." Likening their actions to "stealing candy from a baby," he said crime blossomed "where powerful business and professional men come in contact with persons who are weak." These offenders included financiers who betrayed the public's trust with "misrepresentation of asset values and duplicity in the manipulation of money."[20] Nearby, the *Philadelphia Inquirer* featured Sutherland's findings above the fold on the Public Ledger page with its largest headline: "Poverty Belittled as Crime Factor: Sociologist Cites Frauds in Business." The lead paragraph dramatically described his "withering denouncement of 'white collar criminality'" and his "revolutionary approach to the previously accepted theories of criminal behavior."[21]

As expected, his public challenge of powerful business leaders as criminals was not received well in that community. But Sutherland was just getting started.

CORPORATE CRIME FOCUS

After his presidential address was published under a slightly different title in February 1940 in the *American Sociological Review*,[22] Sutherland spent another decade engaged in further research to expand it into a book. The 1949 book, unlike the speech, went far beyond individual misconduct. It focused instead on corporate crime. Sutherland zeroed in on what he deemed to be criminal behavior by the seventy largest U.S. manufacturing, mining, and mercantile corporations. He suggested that the majority of them could be classified as habitual criminals. As one contemporary reviewer aptly noted, "The picture which emerges is not a pretty one."[23] Bundled together on his list of infractions were those offenses that lawyers would consider actual criminal matters as well as civil cases. His publisher, Dryden Press, fearing a defamation case, insisted that the names of the corporations be removed from the manuscript before publication. Even his employer, Indiana University, pressured him to remove the corporate names.[24] The pressure was so strong that Sutherland ultimately caved, excising the names of all of the corporations and excluding an entire twenty-page chapter titled "Three Case Histories." Many decades later, in 1983, his groundbreaking book was republished in full by Yale University Press as *White Collar Crime: The Uncut Version*.

Sadly, Sutherland would never know the tremendous impact he had. Months after publication, in October 1950, he slipped and fell while walking from home to campus. Whether he fell victim to a stroke or seizure is unclear. One hopes that, at the very least, he was privy to the many glowing law journal reviews of his book. One write-up said the book presented a "deadly exposé of a way of life which society complacently accepts" and merited "excited promotion rather than mere reviewing."[25] Another offered a mixture of praise, skepticism, and solid advice. It described *White Collar Crime* as a "contribution of first-rate importance" and commended Sutherland for continuing his exploration of "that rich, but largely unexplored field—violation of law in the American business community." The author noted that Sutherland's "data on the prevalence of white collar crime shake the very foundations of our whole system of reformed and regulated capitalism." However, he also criticized him for failing to distinguish among petty regulatory missteps that a corporation might make and bad actions that victimize many. Reservations notwithstanding, the punchline remained: "Professor Sutherland's survey poses a critical problem for American democracy."[26]

GUTLESS GENTLEMEN

While he took some risks, one thing Sutherland left unspoken was how criminology and the criminal justice system itself reflected and perpetuated racism. He used the word "white" to reference the color of the shirt a male professional would wear under his suitcoat in a business setting. In contrast, factory workers wore blue-collared shirts. However, implicit in this naming is the notion of whiteness. Those who had "respectability and high social status" in that era were almost entirely white men.

Sutherland also failed to acknowledge a debt he owed to perhaps the true father of his theory, Edward Alsworth Ross, a founder of the field of sociology. Sutherland does not mention Ross at all in *White Collar Crime*. It's possible he erased Ross because he was an outspoken racist and eugenicist—the pretext used by Stanford University to fire him in 1900.[27] In his 1907 book *Sin and Society*, Ross asserted, "The real weakness in the moral position of Americans is not their attitude toward the plain criminal, but their attitude toward the quasi-criminal." He coined the ungainly term "criminaloid" to describe such a person. A criminaloid was someone "guilty in the eyes of the law; but since they are not culpable in the eyes of the public and their own eyes, their spiritual attitude is not that of the criminal," he explained. Their wealth gave them a sense of impunity. They could do no wrong. Ross wrote, "Unlike their low-browed cousins, they occupy the cabin, rather than the steerage of society."[28] In this work, Ross was concerned with the most powerful members of society. His examples of criminaloids included the "director who speculates in the securities of his corporation, the banker who lends his depositors' money to himself under divers corporate aliases [and] the railroad official who grants a secret rebate for his private graft."[29] Ross saw these quasi-criminals as propelled by basic, hardly evil motives. "They are not degenerates tormented by monstrous cravings. They want nothing more than we all want,—money, power, consideration,—in a word, success; but they are in a hurry, and they are not particular as to the means."[30]

Shining his blistering light on the top tier, Ross depicted the elite cheaters as cowards at heart "who prey upon the anonymous public" but who "is touchy about the individual victim." Such a thin-skinned man was "too squeamish and too prudent to practice treachery, violence, and brutality himself" so "he takes care to work through middlemen." In short, "he places out his dirty work." In addition to being a useful tactic for gutless, gilded-edge gentlemen, using middlemen also helped criminaloids dodge accountability. Ross described this phenomenon of plausible deniability poetically: "With a string of intermediaries between himself and the toughs who slug voters at the polls, or the gang of navvies who break other navvies' heads with shovels on behalf of his electric lines, he is able to keep his hands sweet and his boots clean."[31]

||||||||||||||||||||||||||||||||||||||||||||||

CHAPTER 2

HARM BEYOND MEASURE

N o one measures white collar crime in all its forms, phases, and impacts.[1] Even the FBI admits that "the true extent and expense of white collar crime are unknown."[2] Yet those who are tracking some slices share a common conclusion. White collar crime is on the rise, yet criminal enforcement has cratered.[3] Life has never been easier for gilded grifters. This is obvious to us now. You don't need a seismograph to feel the tremors. We have been hit hard. Our trust in the rule of law is shaken. Journalist Michael Hobbes recently lamented, "An entrenched, unfettered class of superpredators is wreaking havoc on American society. And in the process, they've broken the only systems capable of stopping them."[4] His outrage is admirable. Given how normalized white collar crime has become, righteous reactions may be in the minority.

The theme now for corporate and elite delinquents seems to be: More harm. Less stigma. Even with blood on their hands, there is no shame. In December 2019, the Boeing board of directors fired CEO Dennis Muilenburg after two crashes of the 737 Max killed 346 people. Muilenburg walked away from the disasters un- scathed with his more than $62 million golden parachute.[5] Years before the 2018 and 2019 crashes, employees at Boeing had tried to sound the alarm. Internal Boeing communications submitted to Congress in 2019 revealed efforts by employees there to keep plane production on schedule despite safety concerns.[6] In 2017, a Boeing employee wrote in an internal message: "This airplane is designed by clowns, who in turn are supervised by monkeys." A year later, another messaged: "I still haven't been forgiven by god for the covering up I did last year."[7] Federal prosecutors are report- edly investigating whether Boeing knowingly misled the Federal Aviation Administration about the flight control software when seeking approval for the 737 Max.[8] Neither Boeing nor any cur- rent or former employees, including Muilenburg, have been charged with any crimes.

Another case in point. The 2017 Fyre Festival fraud scheme, which cost investors $26 million and landed ringleader Billy Mc- Farland in prison after pleading guilty in 2018 to wire fraud,[9] created more acclaim than shame for the participants. The scan- dal left hundreds of ticket holders stranded in the Bahamas with- out adequate food and shelter and workers there shorted of pay. Yet it also yielded competing, successful documentaries on Net- flix and Hulu in 2019. Instead of opprobrium for the once ob- scure enablers, the Fyre fraud helped launch some celebrity careers. Consider Andy King, the event producer who worked closely with

McFarland to try to save the doomed music festival by offering to provide sexual favors to a customs agent in order to get bottled water to the island. While he never had to "take one for the team," as he put it, King became a popular internet meme. In January 2020, Evian launched an advertising campaign with him. The company even produced limited-edition customized water bottles with the tagline "So good you'd do anything for it."[10]

Are stories like these that grab our attention anecdotal anomalies or evidence of a growing trend? We simply don't know for sure. Still we must act. If home after home in your neighborhood is on fire, it's time to get the fire department on the scene. When a crime epidemic victimizes millions of people, preventing the spread and healing those hurt must be a top priority. White collar crime, like cancer or influenza, comes in many forms. The most virulent strains require government intervention right now.

Even as we take action, though, we must find a way to measure and prevent the types of crime that cause the greatest injury to the public. In this process, we should be careful to measure harm not only in economic terms. Deciding whether to impose criminal sanctions based on cost was a suggestion economist Gary Becker made in a 1968 paper titled "Crime and Punishment: An Economic Approach."[11] Becker believed that criminal law should focus only on assessing the amount of harm done by the defendant in dollars and cents.[12] He argued that society should only punish offenders if the financial losses they cause exceeded the cost to apprehend, prosecute, and sanction them. He included in his definition of crime "tax evasion and the so-called white collar crimes"[13] and specifically noted that in his world, "there would be no point to cease and desist orders, imprisonment, ridicule, or dissolution of companies."[14] In Becker's view, society is better off if "fines are used *whenever feasible*."[15] He dismissed views that it was immoral to put a price on a crime like one would on a loaf of bread. He insisted that imprisonment was the same as a monetary penalty, just measured in units of time, not in dollars.[16] Such a method condones and perpetuates a system of injustice where only the most wealthy are seen as deserving of protection. And the rest of us are disposable. Under such a caste system, there is no real deterrence as well-to-do predators can just pay a fee for the privilege of defrauding or causing injury and even death.

A notable critique of Becker's views on white collar crime comes from professor of law and economics William K. Black. One central problem with Becker's model, Black explains, is that it requires us to know the amount and cost of each type of crime, yet Becker admitted in his paper that such information was not actually being gathered. Black rightly concludes, "His model, by definition, must fail when it comes to fraud because the incidence and cost of fraud is unknown."[17] Furthermore, a recent academic study by law professors Dorothy Lund and Natasha Sarin found that a Becker-styled approach of overreliance on fines coupled with deferred prosecution agreements leads to corporate criminal recidivism.[18]

ASSAULT WITH A FISCAL WEAPON

The reason we have trouble measuring white collar crime is multifaceted. The first problem is the absence of a shared definition. Despite the ubiquity of Edwin Sutherland's term, we use it to mean different things. There is a difference between how the general public conceives of white collar crime and how those who study—or prosecute—it do. And there is divergence within the academy, from state to state, and from prosecutor to prosecutor. Criminologists Michael Benson and Sally Simpson note that if the proverbial person on the street were asked to define the expression, "most people would probably say something about men in suits who steal money and don't go to prison and let it go at that."[19]

Ask an expert and they would likely say that *fraud* is at the heart of most white collar offenses. In plain language, fraud means using deception to obtain another person's money or property. Criminal fraud comes in many flavors. When a con artist tricks a victim into making a worthless investment, that's securities fraud. When a CEO helps cook the corporate books, that's accounting fraud. When a swindler uses the U.S. mail or a private courier like FedEx in connection with their deceptive scheme, that's mail fraud. The internet or telephone, wire fraud. When an employee arranges by phone to take a hidden kickback from a supplier, that's honest services wire fraud. When a borrower deliberately exaggerates the value of their assets to obtain a bank loan, that's bank fraud. Because fraud depends on nonviolent means to steal, it is sometimes called "assault with a fiscal weapon."[20]

Instead of looking mainly at the nature of the offense, some advocates prefer to focus on the status of the offender, zeroing in on corporate actors. They would define white collar crime to mean the most dangerous or reckless business activities that harm the public health and welfare. Think environmental damage, occupational safety violations, hazardous waste disasters, campaign finance fraud, bribery of public officials, tax evasion, monopolization.[21]

Some scholars have largely given up on arriving at a single definition. As retired sociology, criminal justice, and criminology professor David O. Friedrichs recently concluded, the goal of formulating "a single, coherent, and universally accepted and invoked definition of white collar crime is an exercise in futility."[22] Such resignation does not sit well with criminologists like Brian Payne, who worry that no consensus means we cannot detect white collar crime, measure its pervasiveness, or determine with confidence its causes or how best to respond.[23]

BLUE COLLAR WHITE COLLAR CRIMINALS

Over the years, Edwin Sutherland's words have lost their sting. Instead of describing criminal behavior of powerful corporations and wealthy white people, "white collar crime" is now a go-to descriptor for even low-level occupational crime, such as a clerk sneaking money from the megastore cash register or a desperate parent committing welfare fraud. A worker with a blue collar job could be charged with a white collar offense. In a study of convictions over two years in seven federal districts, Payne explained, "most offenses described as white-collar were actually 'committed by those who fall in the middle class of our society.'"[24] This finding is borne out by FBI data. In a 2000 report on measuring white collar crime, the FBI revealed that in 1997 and 1999, the median value of property lost through any given white collar crime offense was just $210. In contrast, the mean (mathematical average) was

$9.3 million. What this shows us is that while there are tremendous white collar heists, the most commonly charged defendants were involved in small-dollar crimes.[25]

This is unfortunate. Sutherland deliberately led with status. He emphasized that white collar crime was committed by "a person of respectability and high social status in the course of his occupation."[26] The norm now is to focus exclusively on the end of that sentence, so as to view white collar crimes as class neutral. As law professors Ellen Podgor and Lucian Dervan recently observed, "Over the years, the term has come to mean more than what it encompassed in its roots, that being criminality in the corporate sphere. Today, 'white collar crime' is loosely associated with what would be considered non-violent economic crime."[27] Following this trend, some scholars define white collar crime quite broadly as including economically motivated crimes committed on the job. A popular college textbook on white collar crime frames the field in its opening sentence: "Rule breaking in the workplace is common."[28]

Of course, petty workplace offenses need addressing, but they should not be priorities at the federal level. Occupational crime, such as when an hourly employee steals from the cash register, hurts the business and can drive up prices.[29] It also violates states' laws, is fairly simple to investigate and prove (as compared to complex corporate fraud), and can better be dealt with that way. Further, an uptick in this sort of offense by a relatively powerless person would better be addressed through private prevention, especially when big business is the victim. In such cases, investing in better hiring practices and employee supervision is preferable to using up government resources after the fact.

DIGGING THROUGH THE DATA

The data we have now, just as in Sutherland's era, are in a sense "wrong." They are incomplete. Professors Podgor and Dervan wryly note that the absence of a precise meaning of the term "has not inhibited the Department of Justice from its continual press releases announcing prosecutions of white collar criminality."[30]

We all want to know whether white collar enforcement has gone down. Or gone up. For example, one *Washington Post* article from 2019 said that white collar crime prosecutions were "on track to reach their lowest level since records began."[31] This sounds disturbing, but the truth is that it's nearly impossible to know if it is accurate. This is not the author's fault, though. The article referenced a credible report by the very respectable Transactional Records Access Clearinghouse. The TRAC data are gathered, analyzed, and reported by an impressive team at Syracuse University led by statistician and professor Susan Long and investigative journalist David Burnham. They build on information they obtain from ongoing Freedom of Information Act requests made to the Department of Justice. Since 1996, TRAC has operated a public website featuring reports on federal government enforcement, staffing, and spending. As part of this work they create charts and reports on white collar crime trends.[32]

A key source of information they draw on is the U.S. Attorneys' Annual Statistical Report, which covers criminal and civil cases brought by the ninety-three U.S. Attorneys' offices nationwide. We can all access that online. The DOJ published the most recent report in October 2019 for the previous fiscal year.[33] Dipping into that, we see that in 2018, federal prosecutors charged 81,888 defendants in 64,222 federal criminal cases total. Of those, 6,547 defendants and 4,592 cases were categorized as white collar crime. That's about 8 percent of all defendants.[34] But without knowing how many people were credibly accused or investigated for such crimes, it's hard to know if that's a little or a lot.

Also, it's difficult to tell if there's a trend. The DOJ report has been around since 1959. However, the white collar crime category appeared only a few decades ago in 1992. That year, the U.S. Attorneys' offices charged 59,198 defendants in 35,263 cases.[35] But how many were white collar crimes? The 1992 report listed in a detailed narrative section white collar crime cases as including financial institution fraud; official corruption; environmental, health, and safety crimes; money laundering; insurance fraud, health care fraud, and other frauds. Defendants charged with these white collar offenses comprised 5 percent of the total that year. But looking from 1992 to 2018 is like comparing apples to oranges.

Under the white collar crime section of the 2018 report, we see a long alphabetical list of both familiar and obscure felonies. They are: advance fee schemes, fraud against business institutions, antitrust violations, bank fraud and embezzlement, bankruptcy fraud, commodities fraud, computer fraud, consumer fraud, corporate fraud, federal procurement fraud, federal program fraud, health care fraud, insurance fraud, other investment fraud, securities fraud, tax fraud, intellectual property violations, identity theft, aggravated identity theft, mortgage fraud, and a catchall category of "other fraud."[36] Taken together, this is very broad. It sweeps into the definition of white collar crime "blue collar" occupational crime like "fraud against business institutions" and "embezzlement," for example. Also, other categories like "insurance fraud" capture too much. There's faking an accident and trying to collect insurance, which I would not deem white collar crime. Then there's insurance fraud like bilking Medicare out of $205 million, as Judith Negron had done. She was pardoned by President Trump in February 2020—now *that* I would deem white collar crime.[37]

The 2018 report's definition is also too narrow in other respects. Excluded from the white collar section and placed elsewhere in the report are crimes experts would (and indeed the DOJ report once did) consider to be white collar, such as money laundering, bribery of public officials, and bribery of labor union leaders. Instead, those offenses are now listed respectively under "government regulatory offenses," "official corruption," and "labor management offenses." Health and safety violations, including cases brought against corporations that sell dangerous food and drugs to the public, once included under white collar crime back in 1992, had also been moved elsewhere.

Despite some shortcomings, the report for 2018 provides very interesting information. It reveals the reasons why federal prosecutors decided not to file a criminal case or to later drop it. That year, prosecutors declined to pursue or dropped 21,290 criminal matters. Of those, 4,349 were white collar. That's almost the same number of white collar cases actually filed that year. Think about it. Federal prosecutors pass on pursuing white collar cases half of the time. But, remember, that leaves out things like money laundering and bribery, which is not in that category, so the number could be higher. What about other federal crimes? Of 59,630 non–white collar cases filed that year, 16,941 were immediately or eventually dropped—roughly 30 percent. In short, the odds of getting away with a crime are much higher for those accused of white collar offenses whose cases make it to the U.S. Attorneys' offices.

One reason the report identified for declining a criminal matter was lack of evidence. That year, prosecutors *declined* to pursue 13,388 criminal matters due to "insufficient evidence." Almost a quarter of the federal criminal cases that were abandoned due to insufficient evidence were white collar matters. Another rather broad reason for such declinations was "prioritization of federal resources and interests." Notably, prosecutors were far more likely to decline white collar cases than others due to this amorphous "prioritization" reason. Of the 2,573 criminal matters let go for not being a priority, 623 were white collar. Are these markers of innocence or just failure to prosecute because there wasn't enough money in the budget? Or something worse?

ARRESTING FIGURES

To really get a handle on how much white collar criminal behavior gets ignored, we would want to trace all white collar cases from arrest all the way to prosecution and sentencing, documenting all the matters that disappear along the way. And to appreciate the harm to victims, we'd actually begin the tracking process from a victim's complaint onward to see what percent of reported offenses even result in arrests as well as how victims are included and compensated throughout the process.

But no one seems to do that. On the arrest end of things, the FBI collects general crime data on a monthly basis from nearly

18,000 city, county, state, college, university, tribal, and federal law enforcement agencies through its Uniform Crime Reporting system.[38] This is an entirely voluntary effort. The FBI each year collects from participants a month-by-month tally of various categories of criminal offenses. It's up to each agency to decide how to characterize an arrest, something that gets complicated if there are multiple charges. Currently the FBI is hoping to transition from gathering statistics through its Summary Reporting System (SRS) that dates back to 1929 to a more detailed National Incident-Based Reporting System. For now, with SRS data, if you wanted to see how many white collar crime arrests there were in your state or nationwide, you are limited to seeing data on four classes of crimes: fraud, forgery/counterfeiting, embezzlement, and "all other offenses." That last category is not very helpful as it includes any other crime a law enforcement agency reports that didn't fit somewhere else.

And if you want to learn something about the offenders' status, there's not much there. The only information you can see if you were looking at fraud or embezzlement, for example, would be the age, sex, and race of the arrestee. There is no information about the wealth or income of the accused. No mention if they are an individual or a corporation. Even so, what the limited information shows, according to a 2003 FBI report, is that, other than embezzlers, most white collar criminal offenders are white males.[39]

The new reporting system promises more detailed data on a larger group of white collar offenses, but the devil is in the details. Even under the new approach, there's still nothing collected on the employment or socioeconomic status of the offender.

The UCR data could be incredibly helpful for researchers if it were more complete and consistent with what federal prosecutors charge and report. We need the ability to compare actual criminal convictions with the known investigations or prosecutions of corporations and individuals for white collar offenses. But that's not coming soon. In our Big Data era, the absence of numbers that we can plug into an algorithm should not distract us. There are real crimes happening—whether we can count and size up each and every one of them or not—with real victims like us.

The unfortunate shift by academics and law enforcement to an offense-based definition of white collar crime has real-world implications. Most notably, by ignoring an offender's social or corporate status (or what some deem an agnostic view), we are catching a lot of small fish in the net while letting giant individual and corporate predators swim free. This approach can pump up the enforcement statistics without actually making a significant dent on preventing, punishing, and redressing the most damaging criminal activity by the most capable and recidivist offenders.

MEASURE BY MEASURE

What can we do better when it comes to white collar criminal enforcement? I asked several former federal prosecutors this question. They shared the sense that white collar offenses are on the rise, particularly cybercrime. Most believed that we do not have sufficient data on the career-related crimes committed by high-status individuals, or white collar offenses generally. They also agreed that some business enterprises remain too big to fail—and some high-status offenders too powerful to jail.[40]

WHAT CAN BE DONE?

The next president of the United States should establish a new division within the Department of Justice to measure and prioritize for enforcement those white collar crimes committed by the most powerful entities and individuals and those who cause the most harm. This special focus would address the epidemic of the wealthy using white collar crime as a tool for social advancement, predation, and to gain and maintain wealth and political power. This enforcement group would focus on the following four types of crimes. First, offenses committed by business entities or industries, generally referred to as "corporate crime." Second, those committed by the most wealthy and powerful in the private sector, or "elite crime." Third, cybercrime and other forms of predation that take advantage of the speed and anonymity of technology platforms to victimize many. Fourth, crime involving government officials and political campaigns. Finally, the division should put out a regular, comprehensive report that properly groups together all white collar criminal activity, either from arrest or from reporting to a federal agency, all the way through to its ending disposition, whether that means a case was never referred for prosecution, was accepted and denied, or was prosecuted with a conviction and prison sentence secured. A tall order for an immeasurable problem.

||||||||||||||||||||||||||||||||||||||||||||||||||||

CHAPTER 3

CORPORATE CRIME WAVES AND CRACKDOWNS

C orporate crime is up and punishment is down, especially in the Trump era. We cannot just blame him, though. The cynical sense that corporations and senior executives are above the law did not suddenly resonate for millions of people the moment he took the oath of office. That said, there is clear evidence that the Trump administration has made the problem much, much worse. Steven Stafford, spokesperson for the Justice Department, explained in 2018 that the attorney general had set "clear goals" for the DOJ. These were "reducing violent crime, homicides, opioid prescriptions and drug overdose deaths."[1] In other words, corporate crime is not a priority. And it shows.

When corporations are held to account these days, they face much lower fines and their executives rarely face prison time.[2] This is no secret. Business leaders know it—they literally got the memo. In July 2019, top-tier corporate law firm Wachtell, Lipton,

Rosen & Katz shared with clients and the broader public the state of white collar and regulatory enforcement since Donald Trump took office.[3] Bottom line: There has been "a significant drop over the past two years in both the number of white collar prosecutions and the scale of corporate fines and penalties." Even civil penalties leveled by federal agencies were down by as much as 94 percent since the last year of President Obama's term.[4]

Take Walmart, for example. After a seven-year investigation into the retail giant's shady business practices in Brazil, China, India, and Mexico, the DOJ neared a criminal settlement in the final months of the Obama presidency.[5] Under the deal, Walmart would have been required to plead guilty to bribing foreign government officials in violation of the Foreign Corrupt Practices Act and pay nearly $1 billion.[6] Instead, in June 2019, Walmart agreed to pay a $137 million penalty to settle with the DOJ and to disgorge $144 million to the SEC.[7] Instead of an admission of guilt by the parent corporation itself, only its Brazilian subsidiary entered a guilty plea.[8] Why was there no guilty plea for Walmart? Because the corporation entered into a three-year non-prosecution agreement with the DOJ. A non-prosecution agreement is like a DPA, except that instead of filing criminal charges, with an NPA, the government does not file them at all, but could if the agreement is breached. Under the NPA, Walmart will have to enhance its global anti-corruption compliance program and obey the law. If the company behaves, in 2022 the criminal case will just disappear.[9]

It was not just Walmart, though. As the *New York Times* reported, Barclays and Royal Bank of Scotland (RBS) also complained to the DOJ that the Obama administration had been treating them unfairly. With Trump in the White House, "they looked to his administration for a more sympathetic ear—and got one." Under Obama, the DOJ sought $7 billion from Barclays to settle civil claims in connection with the bank's peddling toxic mortgage-backed securities. Under Trump, Barclays paid just $2 billion in that settlement. And RBS, which had been under criminal investigation by the Obama DOJ, entirely dodged criminal charges.[10]

These were not anomalies. Law professor Brandon Garrett and research librarian Jon Ashley track DPAs, NPAs, and prosecutions of business organizations through their Corporate Prosecution Registry project.[11] Consulting with the *Times*, Garrett analyzed corporate enforcement actions by the SEC and DOJ during the Obama and Trump administrations. Comparing the last twenty months of the Obama presidency with the first twenty months of the Trump presidency, he found a huge decline in penalties imposed and a "lighter touch" on the banking industry. In the final twenty months of Obama's term, the SEC imposed $5 billion in penalties and disgorgements of ill-gotten gains. In contrast, it was just $1.9 billion under Trump in his first twenty months. That's a 62 percent drop. The difference is more stark when it comes to criminal cases brought by the DOJ. The Obama Justice Department imposed $14.15 billion in penalties, and Trump's DOJ just $3.93 billion—a decline of 72 percent.[12] This is remarkable considering that the Obama administration was thought to be easy on corporate and white collar crime.

Has there ever been a time in American history when corporate wrongdoing led to criminal accountability and legal reform? There was—very recently, in fact.

We can see this in a handful of sentences from the accounting fraud era of the late 1990s and early 2000s. During this period, one corporate leader after another was caught cooking the books and thereby misleading investors, often motivated to make a company look healthier than it was in order to keep its stock price soaring, along with their own compensation. When the truth came out, stock prices went tumbling—sometimes a company's valuation fell by billions of dollars in a single day. And, unlike today, CEOs and other high-ranking executives were prosecuted, convicted, and sent to prison. In the four years between July 2002 and March 2006, the DOJ convicted more than eighty-two CEOs, eighty-five corporate presidents, thirty-six chief financial officers, and fourteen chief operating officers in corporate fraud cases.[13]

Most memorable were the executives at Enron. An accounting fraud scandal surfaced in October 2001 at Enron, the once high-flying energy conglomerate with a $70 billion market value.[14] Ultimately, several senior executives were successfully prosecuted. At the top was chairman and CEO Ken Lay, who was convicted by a federal jury for charges including conspiracy to commit securities fraud and wire fraud and president Jeff Skilling for these offenses plus insider trading.[15] Chief financial officer Andy Fastow pleaded guilty to two counts of conspiracy to commit securities and wire fraud, top energy trader Tim Belden pleaded to one count of conspiracy to commit wire fraud, and there were many, many more. Some offenders were convicted at trial, others pleaded guilty, and almost all served time in federal prison (except Lay, who died of a heart attack before sentencing).[16] These were long stints behind bars. Skilling served twelve years and Fastow five.[17]

In 2005, Bernard Ebbers, the former CEO of WorldCom, was sentenced to twenty-five years in prison in connection with the

$11 billion accounting fraud that sank his company. In handing down the sentence, Judge Barbara Jones said, "Mr. Ebbers' statements deprived investors of their money. They might have made different decisions had they known the truth."[18] Due to serious health problems, seventy-eight-year-old Ebbers was released in 2019 after serving thirteen years of his sentence. He died at home in February 2020.[19] Rite Aid CEO Martin Grass spent five years in prison after pleading guilty in 2004 to conspiracy to defraud investors and conspiracy to obstruct the government's investigation into accounting fraud at the drugstore chain.[20] After a 2005 indictment, Joseph Nacchio, CEO of Qwest, was sentenced to six years in prison for numerous counts of insider trading of $52 million in shares of Qwest stock as the corporation crashed.[21] In 2007, a federal judge sentenced Cendant Corporation chairman Walter Forbes to twelve years in federal prison for conspiracy to commit securities fraud and making false statements to the government in connection with the largest pre-Enron accounting fraud that cost the company and investors nearly $3 billion. Even after two deadlocked juries, the government tried him a third time to secure a conviction.[22]

This tough enforcement following a flood of corporate mischief was part of a familiar pattern. But right around the financial crisis of 2008, that pattern broke down.

THE FAMILIAR PATTERN

Until quite recently, corporate crime waves and crackdowns followed a predictable pattern in modern America. *First, the dangerous practices of a specific business or industry would cause death or serious economic destruction.* Think of the unsanitary conditions in the early-twentieth-century meatpacking industry, which spread deadly foodborne diseases. Remember the locked doors at the Triangle Shirtwaist Factory that trapped and killed 146 garment workers during the infamous 1911 fire.[23] Or consider the rampant stock market speculation enabled by banks making unwise margin loans that brought the Crash of 1929 and the Great Depression. And remember when the *Exxon Valdez* oil tanker ran aground in Prince William Sound in 1989, dumping 11 million gallons of crude oil into the water, killing birds and sea creatures and destroying the livelihoods of more than 32,000 people who supported themselves fishing in or near the sound.[24]

Next, after the disaster, concern for the victims and contempt for the "villains" would grow, with a focus on the root causes of the crisis, often thanks to attention brought by journalists. Upton Sinclair's blistering 1905 serial and subsequent 1906 novel *The Jungle* exposed the public to the grotesque practices within the Chicago meatpacking industry. Joseph Pulitzer's *New York World* published graphic front-page photos the morning after the Triangle Shirtwaist fire. The National Museum of American History notes that "vivid reports of women hurling themselves from the building to certain death were widely reported."[25] The market crash spread, and subsequent bread lines and bank lines were ubiquitous in the press. News coverage of the *Exxon Valdez*'s gigantic oil slick off the Alaska coast, the suffering wildlife, and the devastated fishermen made the public very aware of what was then one of the largest human-caused environmental disasters in U.S. history.

Then an outraged but organized public would pressure authori-

ties to do several things: make sure this does not happen again, hold those responsible accountable, and help the victims. If the crisis stemmed from clear violations of existing criminal laws, the government might prosecute the responsible individuals and sometimes the business entity itself. If successful, such civil and criminal cases against the wrongdoers could also bring compensation for the victims or their families. For example, in response to the persistence of union organizing and civic leaders like Frances Perkins, New York set up the Factory Investigating Commission to help prevent future tragedies like the Triangle Shirtwaist fire.[26] The owners of the clothing factory were prosecuted, though acquitted. However, there was a civil settlement that provided some compensation.[27] In the case of the *Exxon Valdez* spill, the Department of Justice prosecuted both Exxon and the ship's captain. The corporation pleaded guilty to misdemeanor environmental crimes, and a jury found the captain guilty, though he successfully had his conviction overturned on appeal. But it took twenty years for the victims to receive compensation.[28] And after the Great Crash of 1929, Richard Whitney, the former president of the New York Stock Exchange, was convicted of embezzlement and spent three years in Sing Sing.[29] The fact that Whitney was a classmate of Franklin Roosevelt's at both Groton and Harvard had no currency. The president did him no favors.[30]

Sometimes, with enough sustained pressure, the states or Congress would propose new laws designed to ban or restrict the business practices that led to the tragedy in the first place. However, sometimes it would take repeated incidents for Congress to act. After years of pressure, and on the heels of news reporting, including Upton Sinclair's magazine serial and subsequent popular book, Congress passed and Teddy Roosevelt signed into law both the Pure Food and Drug Act and the Meat Inspection Act in 1906. Following the Triangle fire, "the outpouring of interest helped propel new laws and regulations," the American History museum notes. In response to the Factory Investigating Commission's work, New York enacted numerous new workplace safety laws. And a few decades after the fire, Perkins would make a nationwide impact in her role as secretary of labor in President Franklin D. Roosevelt's cabinet. The Crash of 1929 and the Great Depression led FDR to enact a slew of market and banking reform laws aimed at preventing stock market manipulation and misleading investors while protecting the public from downturns caused by bank runs. And in partial response to the *Exxon Valdez* spill, in 1990, Congress enacted the Oil Pollution Act.

Often, such reform legislation would establish (or strengthen the existing power of) a federal agency to enforce the law and set rules to prevent a repeat catastrophe. The Meat Inspection Act required the existing U.S. Department of Agriculture (created under Lincoln) to inspect livestock before and after slaughter and processing for human consumption. The Pure Food and Drug Act created the Food and Drug Administration. The 1933 Banking Act created the Federal Deposit Insurance Corporation, while a year later legislation created the Securities and Exchange Commission. And the Oil Pollution Act of 1990, which amended the Clean Water Act of 1972, gave the EPA better tools to prevent and respond to oil spills.

Regulating private enterprise to protect people is very popular with the public, but not as welcome by the business community. Rule following can be inconvenient, expensive, and annoying. With tragedy in the rearview mirror, or at someone else's factory or bank, business leaders grow resentful. Risk is everywhere, they argued then and they argue now. Do regulations really do anything but slow innovation and kill jobs? they ask. So the next phase, after reforms are put in place, is for businesses to work hard through lobbying efforts to remove the safeguards. Industry often starts by trying to lift the restrictions on small businesses, or by poking holes in the ones that seem excessive or less sensible than others. Then they go for the kill, right to the heart of the most effective safety measures. If they gain enough money and power, impacted industries will work to "capture" the regulatory agencies and also ideally members of Congress. When this deregulation results in danger and damage again, then the pattern would repeat. Even when there was backsliding, reformers could take advantage of the next crisis to push the law ahead further than it had slid back during a deregulatory period.

SEA CHANGE

After the 2008 financial crisis, this pattern broke down. In the wake of the meltdown, it seemed like certain corporations and executives were above the law. The Justice Department led by Attorney General Eric Holder from 2009 to 2015 let every bank executive engaged in accounting or securities fraud get away without prosecution. For example, as mentioned in the preface, in 2010, Angelo Mozilo, former CEO of Countrywide Financial, agreed to pay $22.5 million to the SEC to settle claims that he had deliberately misled investors. He also agreed to disgorge $45 million of his unlawfully earned profits.[31] When the SEC charged him with both fraud and insider trading, enforcement attorneys claimed Mozilo sold his own stock while he "had access to detailed and alarming information about Countrywide's operations" and "privately described one Countrywide product as 'toxic,' and said another's performance was so uncertain that Countrywide was 'flying blind.'"[32] But the DOJ did not pursue a criminal case against him even though both insider trading and misleading investors, if done with a guilty mind or "willfully," are also felonies.

And we continue to see this today, when the DOJ pursues smaller-time freelance business crooks and lets the most massive swindlers at giant firms go free. And when it allows the firms themselves to enter into DPAs or NPAs, whereby they can be free of criminal sanctions and a felony conviction if they simply follow the law going forward—something they should have done at the outset.[33] Even when corporations are repeat offenders in violation of both the law and an existing DPA or NPA, there are minor consequences. Not only does the DOJ fail to prosecute the people at the top who are responsible, but those very people often keep their jobs or retire with golden parachutes. Boards of directors and officers are typically legally immune (or are at least fully indemnified), thanks to the very protective measures embedded in corporation law over the years that allow them and their firms to take the biggest slice of the gains but socialize the losses. Shareholders take some of the hit if the stock price declines. But under our law, limited personal liability for shareholders means they are not responsible beyond losing their own investment. And unless they were directly involved, the shareholders even of a giant family-owned enterprise will not be held responsible in any way for criminal actions taken by their companies. In the end, our system ensures that most of the externalized costs fall on the victims, their families, and communities.

Let's remember HSBC. Under a DPA from 2012, the bank was supposed to be on its best behavior for five years in order to get the charges that it helped launder hundreds of millions of dollars for Mexican and Colombian drug cartels tossed out. Otherwise, the criminal case could move forward. Yet, after the clock ran out, in January 2018, the DOJ entered into a new DPA with HSBC. True story. This time for defrauding bank clients in a "front-running" scheme. Before this DPA, the head trader involved had been found guilty, yet somehow this did not violate the earlier agreement.[34] Then, in 2019, HSBC Private Bank, a Swiss subsidiary, entered into a DPA with the Justice Department for helping U.S. account holders evade taxes.[35] So much for three strikes and you're out. In this game, strike out and you win the exoneration championship.[36]

How did we get here? How did we move from a legal system that established safeguards to restrain corporate criminality and harm to one that has largely abandoned the tools to deter and punish the worst, most powerful offenders? There are many answers to these questions, but the roots lie in the history of business crime and punishment in the United States, as well as in the way that criminal law involving business transgressions has been used to maintain the social order. Only in those eras when "the people" gained more influence and control over the levers of power in the private sector (including through unionization) and in the public sector (through reform-minded or "tough on crime" ad-

ministrations) have our leaders and our laws worked to hold corporations and their top executives accountable.

COLONIAL BUSINESS AND PROPERTY CRIME

So long as there has been business on this continent, there has
been business crime. In the colonial era, the governing bodies
used fines and public shaming to punish cheats, forgers, coun-
terfeiters, and even merchants who produced poor-quality bread
and beer.[37] Public shaming for such occupational offenses included restraining malefactors in the village stocks (locking metal
or wooden frames with holes to restrain hands and feet), submerg-
ing them in water using dunking chairs, and imposing other similar corporal humiliations. The hope was to discourage the specific
offender from transgressing again and also to set a highly notice-
able example to deter others. For instance, in 1638, Edward Palmer,
a carpenter from Massachusetts, was "fyned £5 & censured to bee
sett an houre in the stocks." His crime? Extortion. The village accused him of overcharging for wood and labor when building the
new wooden stocks for them.[38]

Economic regulation focused on public health, safety, and pres-
ervation of shared resources. A 1725 Pennsylvania law forbade the
exportation of flour prior to its inspection. A 1699 Virginia law
regulated deer hunting season, making it unlawful to kill deer from
February through July. A 1715 New York law prohibited harvesting
or selling oysters between May and September,[39] backed up by a
twenty-shilling penalty per violation. This law contained a *qui tam*
provision, meaning an ordinary person could report the crime to

authorities. Half of this penalty went to the informer and the other half "to benefit the poor of the town where the offense occurred."[40]

There was very little actual *corporate* crime in the colonial period, in part, of course, because there were very few corporations chartered then. Economic historian Joseph Stancliffe Davis found that, other than various colleges organized as nonprofits, only a dozen for-profit enterprises had corporate charters just prior to the Constitutional Convention. Six were canal companies, two toll bridge operators, and the remainder banks or insurance companies.[41]

As with nearly all societies, as legal historian Lawrence Friedman notes, "colonial law punished theft in all of its manifestations."[42] For example, the authorities considered Alexander Graham of colonial Connecticut a "transient person," branding a "B" on his forehead after he was caught breaking into a shop and stealing goods.[43] While harsh, branding was better than the equivalent punishment in England in that era: there, death by public hanging was common for robbery, burglary, and theft. Death was rare for theft and economic offenses committed by white people in the colonies, though a repeat offender in some areas might face capital punishment.[44]

PETTY THIEVES AND SMALL BUSINESSES

By the early nineteenth century, property crimes like larceny, robbery, and burglary were the most frequently punished offenses. Larceny accounted for nearly 60 percent of the cases in Boston's

Municipal Court and around 70 percent in the Philadelphia Court of Quarter Sessions in 1830.[45]

Carrying over from the colonial era, there were also many laws designed to regulate specific businesses. For example, in the 1850s in Mississippi, it was a crime to "fraudulently pack or bale" any cotton. In Maryland, it was illegal to destroy tobacco plants or counterfeit "any manifest or note of any inspector of tobacco."[46] States also empowered local authorities to license a wide range of professions, such as pawnbrokers, taverns, and sidewalk vendors. Municipalities had the authority to impose fines and even jail sentences on those who violated the codes. Yet there is little evidence that many were sent to prison for violating city and town ordinances.

Wars have always provided hustlers and scoundrels with opportunity. During the Civil War, Congress grew concerned about businesses using wartime shortages to provide low-quality goods while overcharging the federal government. According to author Tom Mueller, "When Brooks Brothers ran out of wool, the company began pressing rags together with glue to make 'shoddy' uniforms." He cites an 1861 article in the *Sacramento Daily Union* reporting that the uniforms "resolved themselves into their original elements within a week after being put on by the soldier."[47] In response, U.S. senator Jacob W. Howard from Michigan sponsored the False Claims Act of 1863, later known as Lincoln's Law. The law relied on ordinary citizens to detect fraud and granted them standing to bring lawsuits on behalf of the government.

In describing the *qui tam* provision, Senator Howard wrote, "The bill offers, in short, a reward to the informer who comes into court and betrays his co-conspirator, if he be such; but it is not confined to that class . . . [It is based on] the old-fashion idea of hold out a temptation, and 'setting a rogue to catch a rogue,' which is the safest and most expeditious way I have ever discovered of bringing rogues to justice."[48] Under Lincoln's Law, in addition to paying a fine for each misrepresentation made, the government contractor had to return double what they had earned. The whistleblower, known as a "relator," was entitled to half of the money recovered.

While fraud and related crimes were on the books, the bulk of people who landed in prison by the late nineteenth century were not there for violations of this type. The 1880 census showed nearly 58,000 inmates imprisoned nationwide. Of them, only 1,500 were there for counterfeiting or forgery allegations, a little over 250 for embezzlement, and only a small number for con games, fraud, and tax fraud.[49]

PROGRESSIVE ERA REFORM

The progressive era was a golden age of taking on big businesses and robber barons. The excesses of industrial corporations in the late nineteenth century led to reforms that carried into the early twentieth. The challenge to corporations came from the organized labor movement. In 1886, Samuel Gompers founded the American Federation of Labor (AFL) and along with member unions fought for higher wages, an eight-hour workday, better working conditions for skilled labor, and an end to child labor. The Law, in the form of police officers, sided with industry in its battles against organized labor. During an 1877 strike at the

Michigan Central Railroad in Detroit, three hundred special police officers were sent in to help break the strike; at an 1896 strike at a streetcar company in Milwaukee, the police chief, under the mayor's direction, dispatched the police force to protect scab labor and to arrest striking workers.[50] A laudatory 1896 account of the New York City police described them as harboring "a great antipathy to labor strikes and the disorder that accompanies them." As Friedman concludes, the police "were the servant of power and wealth."[51]

At the congressional level, laws passed from the 1890s to the 1920s countered the increasing power and abuses of growing industries. In 1890, there was the Sherman Antitrust Act. This law prohibited price-fixing, bid-rigging, and monopolization. It was one of the first statutes to include criminal penalties for corporations. A very popular law, it passed the Senate by a vote of 51–1 and the House by 242–0. The 1904 muckraking of journalist Ida Tarbell would lead to the 1911 breakup of Standard Oil by the U.S. Supreme Court.[52]

In 1909, the Supreme Court in *New York Central v. United States* first recognized that criminally convicting a corporation did not violate the U.S. Constitution.[53] The government prosecuted the New York Central and Hudson River Railroad Company under a 1903 law that prohibited carriers from providing discounts off their published transportation rates. The railroad's assistant traffic manager, Fred Pomeroy, was paying rebates from corporate funds to sugar refiners in order to attract their business to transport sugar from New York to Detroit. The Supreme Court rejected the railroad's contention that this penalty was unconstitutional as it deprived the "innocent stockholders" of the company "of their property without opportunity to be heard, consequently due process of law." Instead, the court asserted corporations can be criminally responsible "for an act done while an authorized agent of the company is exercising the authority conferred upon him." This case clearly established that corporate entities could be vicariously liable for crimes committed by their employees.

More economic power for the people came in 1913 with ratification of the Sixteenth Amendment, which granted Congress the power to collect income tax, and the Seventeenth Amendment, which provided for the direct election of U.S. senators by popular vote. Prior to that, U.S. senators were elected by state legislatures. This change would make the Senate more accountable to the people. And in 1914, Congress passed two companion laws to the Sherman Act: the Federal Trade Commission Act (which prohibited unfair and deceptive practices, including misleading advertising, and created the FTC) and the Clayton Antitrust Act (which clarified some of the Sherman Act, and also prohibited anticompetitive mergers).

Not surprisingly, it was right in this era of reform that the corporate lobbying organization, the U.S. Chamber of Commerce, was founded, in 1912, as the battle for workers' rights, for consumers' rights, and for citizens' rights heated up.

As corporations gained more power and wealth, legal and philosophical questions arose about corporate responsibility. Specifically, who beyond the corporation itself should and could be held accountable for crimes committed by employees on behalf of the enterprise itself. With a family-owned small business, such a question would not usually arise. Because the owners and day-to-day managers were one and the same, when businesses were small and local, finding the responsible person was not difficult as a practical matter. Yet in the early twentieth century, with giant business's need for capital from the public, came what Adolf Berle and Gardiner Means called the separation of ownership from control.[54] Shareholders were numerous, distant, and uncoordinated. Directors oversaw but did not run the day-to-day affairs. Professional managers were growing in power.

Would or could the law hold any or all of the following accountable? The low-level corporate employee who performs the unlawful act if he does not personally benefit. The distant high-level manager who makes demands, who possesses both control and the ability to prevent illegal activity, but deliberately keeps himself in the dark about the details. The board of directors. The distant shareholders. So, of course, it followed that corporations (which are chartered by states) began to incorporate in those states where corporation laws were more favorable to executives and boards—the people who controlled the corporations. There was a "race to the bottom" in that era by states—first New Jersey, beginning in 1897; then Delaware, after 1913, when New Jersey tried to roll back its liberal corporation law[55]—to attract new business revenue by insulating stockholders, executives, and board members from responsibility for corporate harm. Over time, the law would even evolve to the point where businesses incorporated in Delaware could include "exculpatory" language in their charter so that directors and officers, even if grossly negligent in their oversight or who made ill-informed decisions that led to large shareholder losses, could not be made to pay money damages for the harm they caused.[56]

The complexity and scope of business crime flourished as the stakes and opportunities grew. As businesses became more power-ful through the use of the corporate organizational form, greater distinctions emerged between how law enforcement would treat crimes by big business enterprises as compared to crimes commit-ted *against* big businesses. The absence of bank and investment firm regulation, as those enterprises flourished, would also help lead to the Great Crash of 1929.

THE ROOSEVELT REFORMS

After he took office in March 1933, President Roosevelt took im-mediate action to help the victims after the Crash and the Great Depression. But he also focused on the corporate villains who op-erated outside regulation. In 1933, with his leadership, Congress created the Home Owners' Loan Corporation, an agency with almost 20,000 employees. HOLC purchased underwater mort-gage loans at full value and then helped the affected homeowners refinance in order to avoid foreclosure. By 1936, HOLC had refi-nanced more than one million home mortgages, or 20 percent of all mortgages at the time.[57] Further, FDR built on the ongoing Senate investigation led by chief counsel Ferdinand Pecora that allowed the Justice Department to prosecute some bankers and speculators. He led Congress to pass a series of laws designed to protect investors and the public to avoid another crash. These in-cluded the Banking Act of 1933 (also known as Glass-Steagall), which separated commercial banking from investment banking; the Securities Act of 1933, which promoted full, truthful disclo-sure in the offering of investments to the public; and the Securities

Exchange Act of 1934, which regulated stock exchanges, brokers, and trading.

It was in this era that Edwin Sutherland embarked on his research of white collar crime. He focused on firms who were violating Progressive Era laws and New Deal regulations.

INVISIBLE INDUSTRIAL VIOLENCE ERA: 1940s TO 1960s

The efforts to criminalize acts of corporate violence arose out of the sale of dangerous products and the release of toxic chemicals into the air and water.[58] Some of this hazardous behavior had gone on for decades without detection. One example is the Hooker Chemical Company, owned by Occidental Petroleum Corporation. From 1942 to 1953, Hooker dumped 21,800 tons of chemical waste into a trench in Niagara Falls, New York.[59] The trench was called Love Canal, after the developer William T. Love, who years earlier had envisioned a model city would be built there. In 1953, Hooker covered over the sixteen-acre landfill with dirt and sold it to the city's school board for one dollar, transferring liability for industrial wastes to them. More than a hundred homes and a school were built on that landfill, but no one told the families about the hazardous substances underground. In the 1970s, after a record rainfall, the chemicals began leaching out, causing a rash of health problems, including birth defects, miscarriages, and high white blood cell counts. A former EPA administrator called it "one of the most appalling environmental tragedies in American history."[60] A follow-up health study of Love Canal published in 2008 confirmed earlier findings of low birth weight and increased congenital malformation of babies born to mothers who'd lived there during their pregnancies.[61]

Another disaster was the sale of thalidomide, prescribed to pregnant woman between 1957 and 1961 for morning sickness. Thousands of women miscarried, and more than 10,000 children, mostly in Europe, were born with phocomelia, a rare condition in which a baby is born without fully developed limbs. Many did not survive beyond their first birthday. While the drug was never approved for use in the United States, doctors did prescribe it here and at least forty children were born with phocomelia.[62] In 2012, more than fifty years after the drug was recalled, the CEO of the German corporation that manufactured it apologized.[63]

In the 1960s, just a decade after Sutherland's book was released, there was little attention paid to prosecuting businesses. As Professor John Poulos explained, in that time "punishments were modest and reflected a cultural belief that the kind of injury inflicted was moderate." No one thought of stockholders as victims. "In a sense, stockholders were thought of as being remiss if they invested in a corporation that engaged in questionable conduct. It was a whole culture that supported the kind of robber baron view of the corporate entity."[64]

1970s REFORM WAVE AND CRACKDOWN

Beginning in the 1970s, during and after the Nixon administration, a wave of new laws were enacted to punish bribery overseas, pollution, and other bad but profitable practices of large corporations. In 1970, Congress enacted the Organized Crime Control Act, which included the Racketeer Influenced and Corrupt Organizations Act (RICO). While RICO initially targeted classic mobsters, the language is such that prosecutors and private parties have successfully used this law against other ordinary business entities. That same year, the Bank Secrecy Act, which aimed to help the U.S. government detect money laundering, was also signed into law. Also in 1970, President Nixon created the Environmental Protection Agency, and later Congress amended existing environmental law to give the newly created EPA regulatory authority. In 1972, the Consumer Product Safety Act was passed; in 1974, the Safe Drinking Water Act and the Hazardous Materials Transportation Act.

In response to the Watergate scandal, new laws addressed government corruption and the influence of money in politics. In 1974, Congress passed and President Gerald Ford signed a law amending the Federal Election Campaign Act to create the Federal Election Commission, set stronger limits on campaign contributions, and improve disclosure requirements for political spending. In 1977, Congress passed and President Carter signed into law the Foreign Corrupt Practices Act. This statute made it a felony for a U.S. corporation (including its employees) to bribe foreign government officials, such as by paying kickbacks to officials abroad in order to get business for a foreign branch of a U.S. firm.

Along with these new regulatory tools, in the late seventies we saw a period of strong enforcement coupled with individual accountability. As Professor Kenneth Mann described in his 1985 book *Defending White-Collar Crime*, when Stanley Sporkin led the SEC from 1974 through 1981, the agency "conducted an aggressive campaign against fraud by corporations and corporate managers." And over at the DOJ in the post-Watergate era, there was a "heightened awareness of the cost to society of white-collar crime."[65] In 1976, Robert B. Fiske Jr., the U.S. Attorney for the Southern District of New York, wrote that the SDNY had "devoted a major portion of its resources to combat business crime."[66]

BUSINESS BACKLASH

Efforts to restrain business took on a political cast, with conservatives espousing probusiness sentiments and liberals advocating for prosafety, anticorruption regulations. In 1971, responding in part to this wave of business regulatory legislation, respected corporate lawyer and former president of the American Bar Association Lewis Powell sent a confidential thirty-four-page typed memorandum titled "Attack on American Free Enterprise System" to a leader at the U.S. Chamber of Commerce.[67] The memo might have languished in the files had Nixon not nominated Powell weeks later for a position on the U.S. Supreme Court. While it's not entirely clear what immediate influence his recommendations had, we can see that the chamber did eventually implement much of what he suggested. Powell was alarmed by the "varied and diffused" sources of attack on the "American economic system." He was not so concerned about "Communists, New Leftists, and other revolutionaries who would destroy the entire system." Instead, he was much more disturbed by "perfectly respectable" people who were loudly and clearly voicing criticism of the business community. Dissent came "from the college campus, the pulpit, the media, the intellectual and literary journals, the arts and sciences, and from politicians." He also fretted that the media, especially television, "plays such a predominant role in shaping the thinking, attitudes and emotions of our people."[68] He was perplexed that "the enterprise system" fueled by American corporations, which funded private universities and media companies (and indirectly public universities through the payment of taxes), "tolerates, if not participates in, its own destruction."[69]

Powell expressed special concern about criminal accountability in his attack on consumer advocate Ralph Nader. Quoting a passage from a *Fortune* magazine feature on Nader, Powell wrote: "He thinks, and says quite bluntly, that a great many corporate executives belong in prison—for defrauding the consumer with shoddy merchandise, poisoning the food supply with chemical additives, and willfully manufacturing unsafe products that will maim or kill the buyer. . . . He emphasizes that he is not talking just about 'fly-by-night hucksters' but the top management of blue chip business."[70] Nader was then, and is not today, alone in this view.

What Powell seemed to overlook was that the very integrity of "the system" he hoped to preserve was undermined, not strengthened, by allowing business leaders to defraud, poison, and injure. Instead of suggesting that corporate America's leaders clean up their acts and become law-abiding citizens, Powell outlined a multipronged counterattack that focused on asserting influence on college campuses, in secondary schools, on television, in scholarly journals and books, and, most important, in the "neglected" political arena, courts, and with corporate stockholders.

As a starting point, Powell called on "businessmen to confront this problem as a primary responsibility of corporate management." He recognized, however, that if corporations served on the front lines, they could draw negative attention. This was where the Chamber of Commerce could step up. He saw the chamber's role as that of labor unions. He wanted to organize the business community to strengthen its power against consumer advocates, against labor, against academia, and against the press. He believed this offensive would take "careful long-range planning and implementation, in consistency of action over an indefinite period of years, in the scale of financing available only through joint effort, and in the political power available only through united action and national organizations."[71] Powell denied that America was controlled by big business. If only. Sadly, he asserted, "the American business executive is truly the 'forgotten man.'"[72]

SHORT-LIVED PERIOD OF CORPORATE CRIMINAL ACCOUNTABILITY

By the late 1980s, Congress started to strengthen the tools to punish and prevent fraud in government contracting. And the DOJ responded to a huge upsurge in corporate fraud. In that period, during the savings and loan (S&L) crisis, 1,500 thrifts and savings banks failed, costing at least $153 billion, of which taxpayers bore 80 percent of the losses.[73] Given the widespread fraud that led to the demise of many of these institutions, regulators made thousands of referrals of the most serious S&L offenders to the DOJ.[74]

After he took office in 1989, George H. W. Bush made it a priority for the DOJ to investigate and bring these cases to prosecution. No one was above the law, not even bankers. Federal prosecutors convicted more than a thousand bankers in connection with the S&L debacle.

As noted at the start of the chapter, this accountability trend continued in response to the corporate accounting scandals of the late nineties and early aughts, from Cendant to Enron to World-Com and beyond. But then, around that period, a shift occurred. While it looked like the bad guys were getting caught, this crackdown was short-lived. Even as law enforcement was willing to prosecute, we have to remember why the S&L crisis and Enron happened in the first place. Years of deregulation and lax supervision had made these frauds harder to prevent and CEOs less afraid of the consequences. This would include a number of laws enacted by Presidents Carter and Reagan that gave the S&Ls too much freedom and created the conditions for fraud. It would also include legislation enacted under President Clinton—namely, the Private Securities Litigation Reform Act of 1995, which made it more difficult for shareholders to hold corporations and executives accountable for securities fraud. Furthermore, in the Carter and Clinton administrations, legislation was enacted that allowed the credit default swap and private mortgage securities markets to flourish, enabling the toxic mortgage-backed securities that eventually blew up the banking system in 2008.

In response to the accounting fraud epidemic epitomized by the Enron fiasco, there was the Sarbanes-Oxley Act of 2002. This law was supposed to remove the "dumb CEO" defense, whereby executives could plausibly deny knowing that the numbers reported to shareholders were too rosy. Another promising provision was Section 308, the Federal Account for Investor Restitution (FAIR) Fund Act.[75] This allows the SEC to use civil penalties and disgorgement from wrongdoers to fill a fund to benefit harmed investors. In the first ten years of its existence, the SEC returned more than $14 billion to investors through FAIR funds.

THE GREAT ESCAPE

Sometime after Enron, the old patterns started to crack. There used to be a crisis followed by public awareness, then prosecution of the villains, help for the victims, and reform legislation that endured for at least a few decades. But we didn't even make it ten years after the accounting scandals to arrive at the global financial crisis of 2008. And we barely caught our breath after that before the current white collar crime epidemic really took hold.

Because no high-level bankers were held personally account-able, and because money was poured into the banks to rescue them, to provide giant bonuses to the bankers, and to keep fueling the coffers of bank lobbyists, the banks went into the reform period stronger than ever. They got the legislation they wanted. After all, the banking conglomerates had some of their very own law firms helping to draft portions of the Dodd-Frank Wall Street Reform and Consumer Protection Act. According to *The American Lawyer*, the U.S. Treasury Department relied on one top-tier law firm in particular, Davis Polk, to help craft an early version of the bill.[76] There were, however, a few exceptions, portions of the law not wel-come by the banks, and they kept fighting to weaken and remove them. On the hit list were the provisions creating "bounty fees" for whistleblowers, the Consumer Financial Protection Bureau, and the Volcker Rule (designed to forbid speculative short-term trading by federally insured banking firms using customer funds).

And unlike the prosecutions that followed the Great Crash of 1929, the S&L debacle, and the Enron era, the DOJ after the 2008 meltdown prosecuted nobody. Or rather, the DOJ prosecuted someone almost nobody had heard of. The only Wall Street executive prosecuted for his role in the mortgage crisis was Kareem Serageldin. This was so notable that in May 2014 the *New York Times* devoted a full feature in its Sunday magazine to his story. Serageldin was a forty-one-year-old Egyptian-born banker who grew up in Michigan and worked for Credit Suisse in London.[77] Serageldin helped cover up more than $100 million in losses in the bank's mortgage-backed securities trading book. A federal judge sentenced him to thirty months in prison for conspiracy to falsify books and records and commit wire fraud. Think about it for a moment. Worldwide there were forty-seven executives convicted and sent to prison by 2018 for their roles in the 2008 meltdown. Iceland jailed Icelanders. Spain jailed bankers from Spanish banks. In Ireland, it was bankers from the Anglo Irish Bank, and so on.[78] But the only bank executive who was sentenced to prison in the United States was born in Egypt and had committed his crimes in London.

Similarly, at the local level, Manhattan district attorney Cyrus Vance Jr. had all of Wall Street in his jurisdiction for enforcing New York state law, but the sole bank his office chose to prosecute was Abacus Federal Savings Bank, a small institution owned and operated by a family who'd come from China to the United States and that largely served the immigrant community. In May 2012, Vance brought a 184-count indictment against the tiny community bank, including nineteen employees for residential mortgage fraud. They were handcuffed together and marched into court.[79] Several employees pleaded guilty to inflating borrowers' income information on mortgage loan documents, but the bank and its officers took the case to trial. In June 2015, a jury acquitted Abacus and its officers on all charges.[80] No wonder the 2017 *Frontline* documentary about the family was called "Abacus: Small Enough to Jail."[81]

PROOF ENOUGH

The public claims the Justice Department made at the time were not always credible. Lanny Breuer, former assistant attorney general for the Criminal Division of the DOJ, faced a lot of heat. When asked on *Frontline* to provide a reason criminal cases were not pursued against Wall Street bankers, he said, "We looked at those as hard as we looked at any others," but explained, "when we cannot prove beyond a reasonable doubt that there was criminal intent, then we have a constitutional duty not to bring those cases." That's the old standby excuse in any white collar case. Intent is always the most difficult element to prove. Plus, his reasoning is backward. He seems to imply that somehow if prosecutors after the fact, in any case, fail to secure a guilty verdict, they have violated the Constitution. Nonsense. There's no way to predict how a jury will deliberate.

Even more troubling, Breuer also said that to convict for fraud,

"I have to prove that you had the specific intent to commit a crime and that the other side relied on it."[82] This is false. The government does not need to prove reliance. Reliance is a necessary element in a civil fraud case brought by a private party. It is absolutely not an element for a securities fraud or wire fraud case brought by the federal government. Breuer, of all people, should have known that. Federal judge Jed Rakoff drew attention to this error in an essay castigating the Justice Department.[83]

Why was the Justice Department so unwilling to even try to prosecute executives? Some say they lost their courage after a jury acquitted two Bear Stearns hedge fund managers in 2009. But why didn't they try with a different, less complicated case against a CEO like Angelo Mozilo of Countrywide Financial? It seems rather suspicious that the SEC was able to get him to settle charges of securities fraud and insider trading, but the DOJ chose not to use the same law to bring a criminal case. And if the DOJ had been really committed, then it could have created a task force, as was done in the S&L crisis, to prioritize criminal prosecution.

Even former Fed chairman Ben Bernanke questioned the lack of post-crisis prosecutions. Bernanke told a reporter in 2015 that "it would have been my preference to have more investigation of individual action, since obviously, everything that went wrong or was illegal was done by some individual, not by an abstract firm." He also said, "Now a financial firm is of course a legal fiction; it's not a person. You can't put a financial firm in jail," but "obviously illegal acts ultimately are done by individuals, not by legal fictions."[84]

When the banks collapsed in the fall of 2008, trillions of dollars were committed to rescue the entire banking system. Republican president George W. Bush admitted, "I've abandoned free market principles to save the free market system." And yet, no one saved American families. They had advocates, but public interest groups were not as well funded or staffed as corporate and bank lobbyists. The millions of families who lost their homes to foreclosure were not spared the rough justice of the free market. And the executives responsible for peddling high-risk mortgages and deceiving their own investors? Somehow the Justice Department lost the will to prosecute. They will say they did not have the facts, they did not have the law. But the truth is that they did not have the courage.

CHAMBER OF TACTICS

Lewis Powell's plan to arm the U.S. Chamber of Commerce for a counterattack on any challenge to the free enterprise system was working. In 2009, the chamber wrote an amicus brief to the U.S. Supreme Court in support of convicted Enron CEO Jeff Skilling. Skilling contended that an entire white collar crime statute, the honest services fraud offense, was unconstitutional.[85] While that bold argument did not prevail, the court did limit the offense so it applied more narrowly to only kickback-type schemes. Skilling won his appeal and ultimately was able to negotiate a reduction in his prison sentence. In 2010, 2014, and 2017, the chamber filed amicus briefs to limit protection of corporate whistleblowers under the Dodd-Frank Act, including for cases before the U.S. Supreme Court. Staying on message, in 2019, the chamber also argued in a court brief that people who commit commodities fraud should not be subject to criminal charges under the wire fraud statute.[86]

And for years the chamber has tried to weaken the Foreign Corrupt Practices Act, which is thought of as a "jewel in the crown of America's fight against international business bribes and corporate favors."[87] Prosecutors successfully use this law to help "other countries crack down on bribery, and [extract] billions of dollars in fines." Yet this is a law that Donald Trump has been lambasting for years, both as a candidate and as president. In 2012, he complained that he was restricted from bribing foreign officials: "Every other country in the world is doing it—we're not allowed to."[88]

THE PATTERN BREAKERS

The moment the pattern broke is not caught on camera, though it's pretty close. In March 2013, Attorney General Eric Holder appeared before the Senate Judiciary Committee for a routine oversight hearing. Senator Charles Grassley, the committee's ranking Republican member, grilled the AG. "On the issue of bank prosecution, I'm concerned we have a mentality of 'too big to jail' in the financial sector, spreading from fraud cases to terrorist financing to money laundering cases," he said. "I think we are on a slippery slope." The senator went on, "I don't have a recollection of DOJ prosecuting any high-profile financial criminal convictions in either companies or individuals." The senator wanted to know from Holder whether failure to prosecute stemmed from what Assistant Attorney General Breuer raised with him about the effect such prosecutions would have on the financial markets.[89]

Holder addressed this question head-on. He told Grassley that he was "concerned that the size of some of these institutions becomes so large that it does become difficult for us to prosecute them." He was concerned that "if we do prosecute [them], if we do bring a criminal charge, it will have a negative impact on the national economy, perhaps even the world economy." Attorney General Holder went on to suggest that this problem of size might be better addressed by Congress. By then, Congress had chosen not to break up the banks by size. But people are not corporations. No person is too big to fail. No board of directors is indispensable. He did not offer a reason for not investing resources to investigate and bring credible cases against bank executives in the United States. Prosecuting only a single bank executive—one with a Middle Eastern–sounding name and based in London—and calling it a day is disgraceful.

Many were angry, but to be fair, Holder was being truthful about the persistence of the Too Big to Fail reality and the related Too Big to Jail problem. But there was backlash. In response, the DOJ released a video in which Holder clarified the government's view and asserted that "there is no such thing as 'too big to jail.'" He said that "some have used that phrase to describe the theory that certain financial institutions, even if they engage in criminal misconduct, should be considered immune to prosecution due to their sheer size and their influence on the economy. That view is mistaken." Walking back the importance of collateral consequences, Holder said that "a company's size will never be a shield to prosecution or penalty" if there is evidence of a crime.

He sounded quite reasonable when he also said that the appearance of criminal wrongdoing is not enough to bring a case. But there's the rub. Smoke rising off in the distance gives the appearance of fire. And no, we should not prosecute someone for arson on that basis alone. We need to send the fire truck over to investigate. Especially when the line between a mere civil infraction and a crime is often one of intent, resources are needed to gather the necessary evidence, to flip the right witnesses. We also need prosecutors who have the skill to simplify complex ideas in front of a jury. There was a way, but was there a will? In the video, Attorney General Holder also addressed the question, What about the bankers? "To be clear," he said, "no individual or company—no matter how large or how profitable—is above the law." By that time, though, it was almost too late to consider whether any banker was above the law. By then, the statutes of limitations had run out. They were now beyond the law for sure.

ROT FROM THE HEAD DOWN

As a follow-up action, in September 2015, the new deputy attorney general, Sally Yates, issued new guidance on prosecuting business organizations in a document informally referred to as the "Yates Memo." Her guidance was used to update the official prosecution principles in the U.S. Attorneys' manual (now called the Justice Manual). Yates emphasized the importance of individual accountability. The bottom line was that, if corporations engaging in wrongdoing wanted to get leniency and reduced fines in exchange for their cooperation with the government, they would need to turn over evidence on all of the employees involved in the misconduct. A day after issuing the memo, Yates delivered a speech at New York University Law School. She stated that corporate misconduct should not be treated differently from any other matter. "Crime is crime." She saw it as the obligation of the DOJ to hold lawbreakers accountable "regardless of whether they commit their crimes on the street corner or in the boardroom. In the white-collar context, that means pursuing not just corporate entities, but also the individuals through which these corporations act." In a gracious move, she praised Eric Holder for his words supporting individual accountability. She said, "He made clear that, as a matter of basic fairness, we cannot allow the flesh-and-blood people responsible for misconduct to walk away, while leaving only the company's employees and shareholders to pay the price." She added, "As he pointed out, nothing discourages corporate criminal activity like the prospect of people going to prison."

But they had already walked away by then. All of the high-level bankers. Nothing encourages corporate criminal activity like the prospect of never going to prison.

Yates might have done more had she lasted. When Trump was elected, she was elevated to the role of acting attorney general. After she warned the president not to hire Michael Flynn as his national security advisor, and when she refused to enforce the first Muslim travel ban, on January 30, 2017, just ten days into his presidency, Trump fired her.

IMMUNITY AT THE TIPPY TOP

With Yates gone, the Justice Department set out to roll back the new policy of individual accountability. Deputy Attorney General Rod Rosenstein had made an announcement to that effect in November 2018. While addressing an international conference in

Maryland on the Foreign Corrupt Practices Act, he said that the United States would now go even lighter on individual corporate criminals.[90] As journalist Dylan Tokar reflected, "Rosenstein's announcement that day in November washed away the final vestiges of any real acknowledgment by the Justice Department that it had failed to adequately respond to the financial crisis."[91]

First, Rosenstein introduced a commendable project, the new Task Force on Market Integrity and Consumer Fraud. This DOJ task force, by teaming with other federal agencies, is meant to focus on rooting out financial fraud, health care fraud, consumer fraud, and fraud against the government. It is a good model. But it should be expanded to become part of a larger division with dedicated resources to combat elite crime. After that, Rosenstein said the department was "announcing changes" to its policy concerning "individual accountability in corporate cases." On the surface, what came next seemed sensible: that the DOJ "should focus on the individuals who play significant roles in setting a company on a course of criminal conduct." The DOJ wanted to know "who authorized the misconduct, and what they knew about it." All good.

However, what followed was troubling. Rosenstein said the DOJ would not require "companies to identify every employee involved regardless of relative culpability." This is concerning for a number of reasons. First, who at the corporation gets to decide who is culpable? Senior management would likely be the ones authorizing what information is handed over to the Justice Department. So they would be in a position to try to avoid revealing the names of people who may have communicated with them or implicated them. The employee who conveyed information between levels of a business firm's hierarchy or between divisions is critical. They might cooperate. Ordinary people with little involvement but some information have a lot to gain from telling the truth and blowing the whistle, especially if they run no risk of punishment due to their minimal involvement. This is human nature. Experienced prosecutors know that the ideal way to actually get the necessary evidence to catch the higher-level individuals in a larger criminal conspiracy is to flip the lower-level people.

Rosenstein leaned on high cost to justify this change. "Our policies need to work in the real world of limited investigative resources." Priorities are important, of course, but so is logic. Why not demand full cooperation and in every case a complete list of names, titles, and roles, and then make the decision at that point about whom to interview based upon the findings as they develop?

In light of this revised, watered-down approach, is it any surprise that with the recent wave of corporate wrongdoing, we are seeing further DPAs and NPAs and few to no high-level executives prosecuted?

Rosenstein ended his remarks in a way that must have given comfort to the criminal defense lawyers in the room. "In summary, our corporate enforcement policies should encourage companies to implement improved compliance programs, to cooperate in our investigations, to resolve cases expeditiously, and to assist in identifying culpable individuals so that they also can be held accountable when appropriate. It is not always possible to achieve all of those goals, but the new policies strike a reasonable balance." No one would have the fear of God put in them (if they were still awake).

At the time of this address, Rosenstein had been tangled up for two years in overseeing the Trump-Russia investigation led by Robert Mueller. While speaking at that November 2018 conference, he championed individual accountability. Months later, in March 2019, he stood silently while his own boss, Attorney General William Barr, misled the public into believing that the soon-to-be-released Mueller Report had cleared President Trump of wrongdoing. Far from it. The report came out on April 18, 2019, along with the truth. Even with major sections redacted, we could see clearly the individual who was responsible. Mueller's team presented substantial evidence that the president had obstructed justice, but any prosecution would have to wait until he left office. Mueller would later explain, "If we had confidence that the president clearly did not commit a crime, we would have said so."[92] Ten days after Barr released the Mueller Report, Rosenstein tendered his resignation.

||||||||||||||||||||||||||||||||||||||||||||||||||

CHAPTER 4

VICTIMS IN THE SHADOWS

I t went viral. A two-year-old girl in footie pajamas is crying in the toy aisle of a Family Dollar store. Her mother is lying on the floor, motionless. The toddler pulls her mother's arm. She cries out, "Mommy." No response. She sits down beside Mom on the linoleum, patting her face, trying to rouse her. Mom does not move. A friend appears in the aisle and shouts, "Mandy, Mandy!" He pulls on her arms and tries to wake her. When that fails, he reaches into her purse, retrieving a phone, saying he'll call her boyfriend. A voice off camera says an ambulance is on the way. An EMT with a yellow vest pulls a crash cart in front of the frame. The video ends.[1]

Millions who watched this footage from smartphones, laptops, or televisions screens shared a moment of deep distress with that frightened toddler. Before we even knew her mom's name was Mandy McGowan, we strongly reacted to this fentanyl overdose.

We had access to this intimate tragedy in September 2016 because the moving images of a desperate child beside her mom's motionless body rapidly migrated from YouTube onto cable news. Some viewers responded to this publicly broadcast private moment of shame with empathy, but many more expressed contempt. It is easy to see McGowan's daughter as the sole victim—at emotional and physical risk due to Mom's neglect. Most viewers didn't know her personal story or the full context. McGowan was not just brought low by her own addiction and poor choices. She was also an indirect victim of white collar crime. She was easy prey in a rapacious scheme to get rich by flooding the United States with highly addictive pain pills. The friend who'd crushed a line of fentanyl that McGowan snorted before going shopping had directly contributed to her overdose. But the original enablers were big businesses, their owners, and the distributors and pill-mill doctors along the distribution chain who profited off opioid addiction and misery.

INVISIBLE VICTIMS

The widespread belief that white collar offenses are mainly victimless crimes is an obstacle to justice. If we continue to perpetuate this myth, law enforcement has little incentive to invest needed resources to detect and punish perpetrators. Correspondingly, without strong deterrence, business leaders in particular will choose profit over people and we will all be less safe. We cannot simply rely on the good conscience of executives to do the right thing. For them, victims are invisible at best. In a society that celebrates wealth and success, lawmakers and prosecutors revere and excuse the misdeeds of the powerful and instead erase or blame the victims.

It's easy to fall into this trap. White collar crime differs from violent crime; for example, with violent crime it's easy to see who the perps and the victims are in real-time, face-to-face encounters. When the crooked schemes are more complex, involving numerous players inside of a large business organization and taking place over a long period of time in many locations, finding the crime and the victims is fuzzier. The more elaborate a scam is on the inside, the more unclear it is from the outside who the villains and the victims are.[2]

Even when victims are known and vocal, we sometimes get distracted by the money and audacity of elite offenders. Journalists and scholars feed our fascination with the mechanical details and motives of criminal risk taking by these seemingly successful executives. The desire to get inside the minds of elite cheaters supports the nonfiction financial crime thriller genre, as well as academic research.[3] Stories about victims, not so much. Even the field of victimology, which studies individuals and communities harmed by crime, neglects white collar crime victims, according to a recent article by criminology professor Hazel Croall.[4] Also, we don't always recognize our own victimhood because, as Croall notes, we "cannot detect some offenses such as the excess of harmful chemicals in the air, in household products, or in food." This lack of awareness limits the utility of victim surveys and similar tools. While we may remember being scammed by a telemarketer or cheated at the used-car dealership, we are unlikely to even know about corporate crimes and regulatory offenses that impact our health, safety, or the environment.[5]

As for prosecutors, the importance of presenting real victims to the jury cannot be overstated. The ability for the wealthy to buy off victims who could be crucial witnesses becomes a barrier that some prosecutors, who also depend for reelection upon the largesse of wealthy donors, will not work hard enough to get past. Even before deciding whether to bring a case, prosecutors consider community impact, so crimes and victims that are less visible may not be pursued at all.[6]

PORTRAIT OF THE VICTIMS

White collar crime victims come in all shapes and sizes. The elderly couple who loses their life savings to a trusted big-shot money manager running a Ponzi scheme. The honest local storefront business that cannot stay afloat in the face of competitors who peddle shoddy goods online and are nowhere to be found for refunds. The trustworthy employees who refuse to follow unlawful orders and are fired by their boss and cannot get a good letter of reference for a new job. The retired workers whose pension fund is raided by corporate management. The families who purchase a home in a city where prices are inflated due to lots of cash sales made by money launderers. The cities drained of resources after being gouged by corrupt contractors. The hurricane victims who suffer twice when housed in toxic-gas-emitting trailers. The hardworking high school senior rejected from college because a classmate's family paid off a coach to gain admission.

We can also paint a portrait by the numbers. Counting up money lost—such as to taxpayers during the S&L debacle or to

communities because of tax evasion today. Customers tricked—
the millions defrauded with fake Wells Fargo accounts. Deaths
caused—by the PG&E natural gas pipeline explosion and the
Massey Energy Upper Big Branch coal mine collapse and the
737 Max crashes and the faulty GM ignition switch. Injuries
sustained—by babies in unsafe car seats. Homes lost—in the 2008
mortgage crisis and the PG&E wildfires. Diseases spread—by
hazardous waste dumped in Love Canal and salmonella-tainted
eggs and asbestos in talcum powder.

Others count behavior that is perfectly legal but harmful—the
so-called lawful but awful practices. Harm caused by food poisoning, air pollution, unsafe working conditions. Each year around
48 million people in the United States get ill from food poisoning, according to the CDC.[7] Thousands die from unsafe working
conditions in the United States. Millions die worldwide from air
pollution, according to the World Health Organization.[8] And correspondingly, lives are saved with appropriate regulations. For example, according to the EPA's estimates, around 180,000 adult
deaths were prevented in 2010 due to the reduction in particulate
matter stemming from the 1990 Clean Air Act amendments. That
same year there were 86,000 fewer hospital admissions and 1.7
million fewer asthma attacks.[9]

Also measuring victims is the National White Collar Crime Center (NW3C), which conducted a phone survey of around 2,500
adults and released the results in 2010. The organization reported
that almost one quarter of all households in the United States said
they had been victimized by white collar crime.[10] Around half
were targets more than once, yet they rarely report these crimes to
the police.[11] By comparison, a 2008 survey by the Bureau of Justice

Statistics revealed that around 13.5 percent of households were victims of property crime and 1.9 percent of individuals age twelve or over reported being victims of violent crime.[12]

LASTING IMPACT

But pure numbers, counting economic costs and direct injuries, get us only so far in measuring the impact. The known psychological effects of fraud victimization are quite severe. Feelings of stress and anxiety are common, with greater impact on the elderly, who stand less of a chance of recouping their losses. In some cases, severe depression leads to suicide. With securities fraud, when a victim's spouse learns about the money lost, divorce can follow. People also experience shame when they make an investment, purchase a product from, or interact with a person or business that has cheated them. As with victims of sexual assault and domestic violence, society teaches us to blame ourselves for being a participant, for not preventing the harm. When a parent is injured or dies as a result of fraud victimization, the whole family suffers emotionally and may slide into poverty.[13]

Beyond those directly impacted, white collar crime creates cynicism and mistrust, especially in the business community with respect to the rule of law.[14] We see this in the antivaxxer movement as well as among citizens so disillusioned with politics that they put their hope in populist demagogues who parrot their grievances and who decry everyone as corrupt, but then go on to fleece the public when in office. Or they choose not to vote at all.

PORTRAIT OF A VICTIM

Mandy McGowan said she first got hooked on OxyContin and other prescription opioids after her neck surgery a decade before her overdose. She was a survivor of child sexual abuse and a series of violent relationships with abusive men.[15] Those who watched the Family Dollar video with untempered disdain perhaps expect addicts like McGowan to possess the strength to resist powerful post-traumatic neurological responses to highly addictive chemicals. But how realistic is that? Given the stigma associated with addiction and the limited options for treatment for those who seek help, restraint and recovery are extremely challenging. But beyond brain chemistry, what has made fighting addiction so much more difficult is that McGowan and so many others like her are up against a multibillion-dollar criminal enterprise that successfully—and, until recently, secretly—grew larger and more powerful by knowingly spreading the scourge of opioid addiction to millions of Americans.

What became of McGowan and her daughter? Child welfare officials took immediate custody of the little girl, who later went to live with her uncle. As for mom, relatively speaking, she was lucky. She survived her overdose in September 2016. By comparison, more than 42,000 people in America died that same year of opioid overdoses. Of those, about 40 percent were tied to prescription drugs.[16] Yet the path to long-term sobriety has been rocky, even for someone with the good fortune that, paradoxically, came from the bad publicity. After learning about her overdose, a local center offered her six months' residential treatment for free. Around two months later, she pleaded guilty to child neglect and endangerment in connection with the incident. She was lucky to initially receive probation.[17] But shortly after McGowan finished the drug treatment, her daughter's father suffered a fatal overdose. So did his adult son. Overwhelmed, she relapsed with alcohol. She spent some time homeless, and then in jail. Two years after the video, she was living in a halfway house, clean and sober, accepting that she might never regain custody of her daughter.[18] We can only hope the best for both of them going forward.

DRUG PUSHING, NOT ADDICTION, IS THE CRIME

Though her trauma was hugely public, McGowan is set up as a villain in that video. The bad mother. This blinds too many of us to her and her daughter's victimhood. She is not alone, performing the sad spectacle of opioid addiction. We have seen all too many of these raw public overdose videos. Parents passed out in parked cars. Collapsed on public roads. Barely breathing at the bus stop. As the scope and depth of the opioid epidemic becomes more widely known, and as it touches so many families up close and very personally, we can see that expressions of sympathetic concern are overtaking those of pure contempt. Yet, to cure this epidemic, we need more than empathy. To end the multigenerational cycles of abuse, addiction, and abandonment, we need free substance abuse treatment available to the millions who are regularly turned away or incapable of paying. We also need a more accessible health care system that promotes good mental health and affordably and comprehensively treats the millions of Americans in need.

And most of all, we need to expose and punish the businesses and real people who have knowingly profited off—and continue to profit off—addiction. They are as bad as the drug pusher on the street corner or the kingpins behind the cartel. Like sociologist Edward Ross said, they are criminaloids. They keep their hands sweet and their boots clean, but they are as culpable as a street thug. This includes companies like Purdue Pharma and many members of the prominent Sackler family. By shining a light on this family business and others, with hindsight we can see Mandy and her daughter as victims of longtime unprosecuted and underprosecuted white collar criminality. Further, we can see the limitations in a system that punishes a handful of perpetrators after the fact, instead of one that funds regulators and law enforcement sufficiently so as to prevent deadly harm in the first place.

There is an important connection between white collar criminals and this personal tragedy and the larger opioid epidemic. Significant personal and financial losses for the American poor and middle class are caused by failure to detect, punish, and prevent white collar crime. By looking the other way for too long, the legal system allows the uber-wealthy to prey upon the rest of us. Then, when millions of people fall victim to their schemes, the victims are blamed and shamed. True accountability never comes if the government does too little to help. The victims of white collar crime are not empowered by our legal system in the same way that victims of violent crime are, and we need to do something about it fast.

CREATING A MARKET OF ADDICTS

By 2006, when Mandy McGowan's neurologist first prescribed OxyContin to her, the manufacturer, Purdue Pharma, had already earned more than a billion dollars on this one drug. While the company had profited in the past, this was next-level riches. Because it was a private firm, owned by members of the Sackler family, its specific trajectory over the years is not entirely clear. What we do know is this. In 1952, brothers Mortimer and Raymond Sackler bought Purdue Frederick, a business founded in 1892 by two physicians. Their older brother, Arthur, helped them finance the acquisition and retained an option to purchase one third of the company. The two brothers restructured it and earned a good living selling commonplace pharmaceutical products like earwax remover, antiseptics, and laxatives.[19]

The three brothers were prosperous and philanthropic. In 1974, they contributed $3.5 million to the Metropolitan Museum of Art in New York City to fund construction of a new wing. The Sackler Wing would house the Temple of Dendur, a 1965 gift to the United States from Egypt, then awarded to the Met. Completed in 10 BC after the Romans conquered Egypt, the temple features, on its outer walls, carvings of Caesar Augustus of Rome attired as a pharaoh. This twenty-one-foot-tall sandstone structure once sat on the west bank of the Nile River.[20] It now rests on a large stone platform, alongside a reflecting pool into which children cast pennies as they make secret wishes for the future.

When Arthur died in the late 1980s, his brothers bought out his option in Purdue. After that, the firm has for decades been controlled by the two remaining Sackler brothers and some of their descendants.[21] Neither Arthur nor his heirs appeared to bear any responsibility for the business thereafter.[22]

After operating as a successful pharmaceutical firm for years, Purdue developed and gained government approval for a standout product, a new pain reliever called OxyContin, a morphine derivative. In its first year, sales reached $48 million.[23] Designed for cancer treatment and palliative care, the drug was supposed to be offered to those in extreme cancer-induced pain or for whom death was likely near. As a result, in theory, the risk of long-term addiction would not be a troubling side effect as these patients were not expected to live much longer. The Sacklers should have insisted that OxyContin be limited to cancer patients and for end-of-life pain relief, but Purdue's owners had a bigger market in mind.[24] Why not expand sales to all types of relatively healthy people who came to their doctors with noncancer pain complaints? Providers were encouraged to offer the drug—a controlled substance—for a whole spectrum of pain. Around 20 percent of American adults suffer from chronic pain—defined by some as constant pain that lasts for at least six months—so the market was vast.[25] Back pain. Neck pain. But Purdue wanted providers to also push OxyContin for acute pain, such as after dental surgery. There would be resistance from medical professionals, as, even in the mid-1990s, evidence showed that prescription opioids were highly addictive and often diverted from patients to others for sale and recreational use.

So, to overcome the resistance, Purdue claimed it had found the holy grail. It basically said that this product was different because the way it operated was different. Unlike other morphine derivatives, which provide instant effectiveness, Purdue claimed that, when taken as a pill, OxyContin would release the active ingredient over a twelve-hour period. For the right patient, this meant ongoing pain relief without as much risk of abuse. The company decided to launch a marketing and promotional campaign based on the claims that this sustained release made it both more effective and less prone to abuse, addiction, and diversion. The only problem was that these claims were not true. The company knew it, and so did the Food and Drug Administration. The assigned FDA medical review officer who evaluated the 1995 new drug application that Purdue submitted was not impressed. He concluded that this twelve-hour release was not significantly better than the usual immediate-release oxycodone. The only advantage was the ability to take a pill less frequently.[26]

Yet the company still pitched its fantastic story to a large and very receptive audience. Over nearly six years, beginning in 1996, Purdue funded more than 20,000 educational programs related to pain management. This type of forum attracts health care providers who are there to learn, but who are also subject to marketing pitches.[27] Many proselytizers, including doctors and nonprofit groups, were paid for promoting the drug as a safe and effective way to treat pain. But that was not true. The drug was extremely addictive. Chewing it, crushing and snorting it, or injecting it gave a high as powerful as heroin. *Washington Post* reporters explained, "As more and more people were hooked, more and more companies entered the market, manufacturing, distributing, and dispensing massive quantities of pain pills."[28] The more popular it became as a prescribed drug, the more popular it became diverted as a street drug.

In 2000, OxyContin sales surpassed $1 billion. The Sackler

business offered big incentives for top sellers. In 2001, the average salary for a sales rep was $55,000. In comparison, the bonus potential at Purdue was immense. That year, the average annual bonus was $71,500, and the highest $240,000. In 2001 alone, Purdue paid out more than $40 million in bonuses to incentivize drug sales.[29] Trips to Hawaii for the salesforce. Coupons and free trials to hook patients. This patient starter coupon program offered a free seven- to thirty-day prescription. In a single year, 34,000 coupons were redeemed nationally. Purdue could afford these incentives as every single new OxyContin patient was worth around $200,000 to the company.[30]

To convert the pain-afflicted into devoted patients, Purdue needed to get doctors and other health care providers into the fold. Specific training was offered to sales reps on how to push this drug and methods for "overcoming objections" from doctors. The company trained sales reps to falsely claim that "it was more difficult to extract the oxycodone from an OxyContin tablet for the purpose of intravenous use."[31] Yet Purdue's own studies showed how easy this was to do. Often, the company pushed the pain reliever on doctors who lacked sufficient experience in either pain management or addiction.[32] Talented sales staff repeated lies that it was "less addictive"[33] due to its twelve-hour release formula. The company also trained staff to falsely claim to health care providers that this pill did not create euphoria or a buzz and that treatment could stop abruptly without side effects.

These fabrications and more by Purdue management and employees were part of what has been described as "the most aggressive marketing campaign ever undertaken by a pharmaceutical company for a narcotic pain killer."[34] The promotion paid off. By

June 2001, the company had earned nearly $3 billion on Oxy-Contin, with this single pill at one point accounting for 90 percent of the firm's sales. There were winners, and there were losers. The overdoses and deaths would accrete in sync with company earnings. So many lives could have been saved with earlier intervention. But, then again, so much profit would have been lost. In 1999, approximately 8,000 deaths were caused by opioid overdoses. Of those, around 40 percent, or 3,442, were from prescription opioids. By 2007, total opioid overdose deaths numbered 18,515, with 12,796 of those from prescriptions. Apparently, greed was more powerful than empathy. And the money kept rolling in.[35]

REGULATORS PROTECT CORPORATE PROFITS

Where were the regulators and lawmakers? Some were struggling with limited budgets and didn't have the money or personnel to monitor and halt new drug advertising and promotions that were misleading. Others may have been complicit in letting prescription opioids sales mushroom. In 1998, Purdue failed to submit a marketing video called "I Got My Life Back: Patients in Pain Tell Their Stories" to the Food and Drug Administration before circulating 15,000 copies to physicians. The FDA managed to review a later version of the video after the Government Accountability Office (or GAO, then called the General Accounting Office) raised concerns.[36] In 2002, after the FDA finally reviewed the video, it concluded that Purdue had overstated the benefits and down-played the risks of its miracle drug. Purdue had already discontinued circulating this video and others by the summer of 2001, but it never retrieved the videos already with physicians.

What took so long? The agency was and is still shockingly understaffed. In 2003, John B. Brown, the acting administrator of the Drug Enforcement Administration, testified before Congress. He told the committee that by 2001 his agency had observed "levels of abuse never before seen. DEA has never witnessed such a rapid increase in the abuse and diversion of a pharmaceutical drug product."[37] But somehow the FDA did not make it a priority to review the Purdue marketing. In 2002, the FDA had only thirty-nine staff members tasked with reviewing more than 34,000 pieces of promotional material from all businesses.[38] By 2004, OxyContin was one of the most abused drugs in the United States.[39]

Some state government officials fanned the flames. As the epidemic spread, with around nine hundred pill mills across the state of Florida, according to columnist Carl Hiaasen, Governor Scott "sought to shut down a new state prescription-monitoring database that was designed to stop people from 'doctor shopping' and to identify outlaw physicians who were overprescribing." The governor thought maintaining the database was an invasion of privacy. Fortunately, he changed his mind. Why might elected officials want to support the spread of highly addictive drugs? Follow the money. The major opioid manufacturers and distributors were past, present, or future campaign donors. Opioid pushers and individuals associated with them "donated $8.4 million to Florida candidates and political committees between 2006 and 2012."[40]

THE FIRST CRIMINAL PLEA FOR PURDUE

Eventually, the law caught up with Purdue. Sort of. On May 10, 2007, in a federal courtroom in Abingdon, Virginia, the company and three top executives—none Sackler family members—entered guilty pleas for illegally misbranding OxyContin from January 1, 1996, to June 30, 2001.[41] They all admitted to violating the Federal Food, Drug, and Cosmetic Act (FD&C Act). Specifically, Purdue Frederick Company, which manufactured and distributed the drug, pleaded guilty to a felony charge of introducing a misbranded drug into interstate commerce as part of an effort to defraud doctors and patients. The CEO, general counsel, and chief medical officer each pleaded guilty to a single misdemeanor charge of misbranding. In a press release, U.S. Attorney John Brownlee showed no rhetorical mercy. It was greed that drove this dangerous product into the market. "With its OxyContin, Purdue unleashed a highly abusable, addictive, and potentially dangerous drug on an unsuspecting and unknowing public. For those misrepresentations and crimes, Purdue and its executives have been brought to justice."[42]

Those bruising descriptors directed at the offenders in 2007 did not match the criminal sentences meted out to them. Violating the misbranding provision of the FD&C Act allows for a prison sentence of up to one year. Three years would be possible if the crime was done with an intent to defraud or mislead. Yet no such sentence was imposed on them.[43]

For the Purdue executives and the corporation, punishment was just a cost of doing business. And the family behind the firm was not directly touched at all. The top executives agreed to pay a total of $34.5 million in fines.[44] The corporation committed to paying $600 million in a combination of forfeitures, penalties, and civil and criminal fines. As part of the settlement, the company agreed to pay for an independent monitor to ensure Purdue would "market and promote its products in an honest and responsible manner" so that the public would be "confident that we will keep close watch on how Purdue sells its most dangerous products."[45]

The only people going to jail were the victims. The addicts paid the price in prison or with their lives. Surrounding communities also suffered from increased crime. One county in Virginia estimated that OxyContin "was behind 80–95% of all crimes that were committed there" in 2000.

Even with the 2007 felony plea, two branches of the Sackler clan kept up appearances as their OxyContin business continued to thrive, with the government expecting the pills to be sold using honest marketing materials. They continued to bask in all their money, luxury, and social status. In 2013, *Vogue* magazine featured a multipage photo spread of Mortimer Junior and Jacqueline Sackler's "unpretentious" summer estate in the Hamptons. Images included two healthy children in pirate costumes happily frolicking on the lawn while Mom lounges on a tasteful chair.[46] A window into modern-day gilded-edged family life that—surprise—made no mention of that felony plea for their pharma business or their financial links to deathly crime. Between 2008 and 2015, Purdue paid the family more than $4 billion. In mid-2019, their worth was pegged at more than $13 billion.[47]

NO SHAME, NO GAIN

The *Vogue* article's emphasis on taste and philanthropy mentioned no victims. But there were many. The heartland was hit the hardest. West Virginia. Kentucky and Ohio. Along with Massachusetts, Maine, Maryland, New Hampshire, and Washington D.C. These places have recently experienced the highest opioid-related death rates in the country.[48] At one point, physicians wrote more opioid prescriptions per year in West Virginia than the total population. Soon this small state had the highest rate of opioid overdoses nationwide. OxyContin and other pain relievers destroyed families in small towns and big cities across America. Hundreds of thousands of Americans have died of opioid-related overdoses since the pill entered the market. To be exact, according to the Centers for Disease Control and Prevention: "From 1999 to 2017, almost 218,000 people died in the United States from overdoses related to prescription opioids."[49] That was more than half of the nearly 400,000 opioid deaths during that time frame. The number of prescription-related deaths initially increased over time.[50] Once hooked on prescriptions, with less availability due to the crackdown on prescribers and without addiction treatment available, addicts then turned to cheaper, more available street drugs.

VICTIMS FIGHT BACK

Suddenly, Purdue was a target of both highly critical reporting and, finally, legal action by families of victims with an onslaught of civil litigation around 2017. There were thousands of cases. By 2019, nearly every U.S. state was suing Purdue. At last, the states were now stepping up to speak for the victims and take on the criminal corporation. Avoiding a televised public trial, Purdue settled with the state of Oklahoma for $270 million in March 2019. Even though they were not named defendants in that case, the Sackler family agreed to contribute $75 million of the settlement.[51]

At last, the family was in the hot seat. In 2019, Massachusetts attorney general Maura Healey brought a civil action against two Purdue companies and seventeen individuals. Among those named were eight Sackler family members.[52] The complaint was brutally direct. "Dangerous opioid drugs are killing people across Massachusetts. Prescription medicines, which are supposed to protect our health, are instead ruining people's lives. Every community in our Commonwealth suffers from the epidemic of addiction and death. Purdue Pharma created the epidemic and profited from it through a web of illegal deceit."

Purdue's best defense in the court of public opinion (and in the many lawsuits it now faced) was that it was not the only opioid maker and seller. Josephine Martin, a spokeswoman for the company said, "The complaint filed by Massachusetts is a misguided and very political effort to try to place blame on a single manufacturer for what is a complex public health crisis that—even by Massachusetts's own Department of Public Health's assessment— is currently being driven by illegal heroin and fentanyl." There were by then bigger players in the prescription drug manufacturing business. OxyContin accounted for just 2.5 billion of the 76 billion oxycodone and hydrocodone pill sales between 2006 and

2012.[53] So why so much blame for the Sacklers' company? It's likely because Purdue started the crisis. The fact that it could not capitalize on it like their competitors is hardly something to boast about from either a moral or material perspective.

By early September 2019, Purdue Pharma and the Sackler family were in talks with the U.S. Department of Justice to resolve the federal criminal and civil investigations into the sale of OxyContin. Separately, they were also negotiating a resolution of thousands of other civil cases for between $10 billion and $12 billion,[54] the largest proposed Big Pharma settlement to date.[55] Under the tentative settlement, Sackler family members were expected to contribute at least $3 billion over a seven-year period.[56] But there would be no admission of wrongdoing. And that money would not come out of their pockets. As part of the proposed deal approved by its board of directors, Purdue would file for bankruptcy, the old firm would be dissolved, and a new one would be established to produce and sell pharmaceuticals, including Oxy-Contin. The profits from these new sales would go to pay the settlement. Plus, the so-called personal contributions from the family would come from the sale of a European company they owned, Mundipharma.

While around twenty-seven states and localities supported Purdue's settlement, at least twenty-five[57] still opposed it. In Massachusetts, Attorney General Healey explained her reasoning in an op-ed published in the *Washington Post* in early September 2019. Healey spoke up for the victims across the Commonwealth—the thousands of families who'd lost loved ones to the epidemic. She praised the work of educators who have developed drug prevention programs for public schools. She acknowledged law enforcement officers who have learned how to administer lifesaving overdose medication like Narcan, and prosecutors who have convicted heroin and fentanyl dealers. She was suing Purdue, which had created and profited off the epidemic. And she had the courage to be the first prosecutor in the country to also sue individual members of the Sackler family. Healey elevated the victims.

This litigation was an exercise in supporting victims, seeking truth, and demanding accountability. Healey explained she would seek all of the evidence of what the Purdue managers knew. She wanted internal emails, board of director minutes, business plans. She hoped to put all of the records online for the public to read. And she wanted Purdue to admit what it did was wrong.[58] As expected, on September 15, the firm filed for bankruptcy protection under Chapter 11. With the states still busy litigating, and the DOJ working out a settlement, news broke in January 2020 that the U.S. Attorney in Vermont might be also investigating Purdue in connection with a criminal kickback scheme.[59]

THE FORTUNATE FAMILIES

The financial consequences will likely be minimal for the Sacklers personally. They seem to have plenty of extra money. New York attorney general Letitia James recently tracked $1 billion in suspicious wire transfers as well as the use of Swiss bank accounts and shell companies to move money secretly around the world.[60] Even so, these defendants and their descendants will walk away with substantial wealth secured.

While actual criminal punishment may never materialize for the Sackler family, public opprobrium has. As details emerge through court reporting about their ruthless practices, an association with the Sackler family has become as poisonous as the drugs they peddle. In July 2019, the Louvre used dark tape to cover over the Sackler name on the walls of the Paris museum.[61] In New York in early 2019, as the negative publicity about the Sacklers spread, the Metropolitan Museum of Art began "rethinking" its "gift acceptance policy." At the time, the response seemed pro forma, with general praise of the family and an attempt to distance the source of the gifts to the museum from OxyContin.[62] But such a position became untenable. In May 2019, the museum announced it would no longer accept gifts from members of the Sackler family linked to OxyContin. A significant news event in the art world, it involved "severing ties between one of the world's most prestigious museums and one of its most prolific philanthropic dynasties." Other major museums had come to the same decision, including the Tate Modern in London and the American Museum of Natural History in New York.[63]

It's all well and good that the public can now visit the Met knowing it will no longer accept blood money, but this symbolic move does nothing at all to help the devastated families from coast to coast who have not picked up the pieces of their shattered lives. They need our charity much more than these museums right now.

PREVENTION, NOT JUST PUNISHMENT

In the case of Purdue Pharma, of course, a payoff to surviving families is only a partial solution. White collar crime preys on the weak, the desperate, and the voiceless, whether it's Big Pharma violating public welfare laws; bankers pushing predatory mortgage loans; telemarketing fraudsters targeting the elderly; Silicon Valley startups offering quick, painless, and useless blood test results; or a guru leader trusted by devoted employees who bankrupts the company while walking away with riches.

Yes, a critical part of prevention is punishment. Punishment that stings can have a deterrent value. But it's not enough. We cannot possibly and do not want to prosecute and imprison every businessperson who is involved in wrongdoing. But we do need to make an example of those who are the worst offenders. Further, without any sort of official blame and punishment, these leaders continue to assert influence and are role models for the next generation of leaders. But we need actual prevention to protect us all.

And this is where the political battles reside. The most libertarian among us believe the government should punish fraudsters and lawbreakers after they offend, and leave the rest of us alone. But there are problems with too little punishment, much too late. To begin, those willing to break the law are at a huge advantage relative to their competition. They can profit where others fear to tread. With their abundant cash, they can afford to lobby to have the laws changed so that what society used to deem unlawful and immoral becomes perfectly legal, or at least punishable only with minor fines. We have a bit of that system right now. Unlikely, uneven, and unremarkable punishment neither deters harm nor encourages people within business organizations to behave well at the outset.

Punishment alone also does nothing to reverse the damage, and it fails to address the structural problems that create victims to begin with. In the case of addiction, economic inequality, job loss, unaffordable health care, and unavailable and ineffective drug treatment all compound the problem, if not cause it. To address these structural problems requires allocating public resources in the form of drug treatment facilities, inpatient hospital beds, and free health care to the many who need it.

There will always be ups and downs in the economy, jobs shifting and changing. There will always be paths for addictions, whether alcohol or legal or illegal drugs. Similarly, businesses will sometimes cut corners and deliberately cheat, leaving their employees suddenly out of work and struggling. Investors will be defrauded of their life savings through no fault of their own. The damage done to victims and their families is more lasting and harder to overcome in a society with few safety nets, where what we all pay to just get by regularly keeps so many of us in debt and on the edges of insolvency. If the basic necessities in life like health care and education were free for all, and if there were job guarantees during the inevitable private sector business cycle reversals, we would be much more resilient. We will need public funding through higher taxes to provide such an equitable system. Who better to provide it than those who have more than enough, who can weather hard times, and who quite possibly got rich off their own predatory business investments.

FORGIVING OURSELVES

Victims of white collar crime in its many forms blame themselves. Unwitting targets of simple scams and complex fraud schemes feel embarrassment and shame. Their friends and neighbors often blame them for their misfortune, instead of the distant strangers who profit greatly from their misery. As criminologist Cassandra Cross describes, "Victims of online fraud are constructed as greedy and gullible and there is an overwhelming sense of blame and responsibility levelled at them for the actions that led to their losses."[64]

We see this self-blame beyond the realm of fraud. Candice Anderson blamed herself for nearly a decade after her boyfriend died in a car crash while she was behind the wheel. But it was the auto company who was to blame and who covered up its responsibility. People who fall prey to miracle weight loss pills and plans often believe they failed or got sick due to their own lack of discipline. In fact, they are up against a $70 billion-a-year diet industry that knows these too-good-to-be-true stories sell widely but do not work, and in some cases raise the risk of heart attacks or strokes.[65] Parents who purchase unsafe car seats blame themselves when tragedy ensues, even when it was the manufacturer who put profits over safety, ignoring the internal advice of its own engineers.[66]

Changing this "victim-blaming discourse" is essential. While of course we want to train the public to be more careful, all too often law enforcement throws its hands up when it comes to fraud and criminality—and says essentially, too bad, buyer beware. Recognizing the pain of victimhood, many U.S. Attorneys' offices across the country provide some reassurance on their websites, drawn from a DOJ handbook written in 1998.[67] This guidance acknowledges the emotional toll of dealing with "family, friends and colleagues blaming you" or "your lack of judgment" when "in reality, calculating, skilled perpetrators are to blame for these criminal acts."[68] The message is: *We see you. You are not alone. It's not your fault.*

The genius of the "best" white collar schemes is to make victims partially complicit in their own victimhood. An organized-crime tactic, the more refined predators also know quite well how to do this. We saw this with the mortgage crisis of 2008. Just like the opioid crisis, it was decades in the making and it impacted millions. Borrowers who were deliberately targeted for high-risk mortgages and refinancing on homes appraised at far more than their true value were later stigmatized when they could not pay. Blaming them allowed Congress to turn its back on the millions of families who lost their homes to foreclosure. When a way to bail out underwater homeowners was being debated, opponents exploited feelings of envy and blame.[69] In contrast, not only did no high-level bankers go to jail, but they all kept their profits and are still calling the shots on Wall Street and in Washington.

||||||||||||||||||||||||||||||||||||||||||||||||||||

CHAPTER 5

MUTUALLY ASSURED IMMUNITY FOR THE UPPER CLASS

W e all laughed about it back then. Even for those outside New York City, the eye-rolling and schadenfreude were swift and pervasive. Someone risked it all on Wall Street to secure his kids' admission to preschool? True story. While big deals with the devil were all over the front pages, the goal here seemed unbelievably small. Or, perhaps for the elite Manhattan set, too believable. Spots in the prestigious 92nd Street Y apparently were so coveted in 1999 that Jack Grubman, Wall Street's top telecom analyst, broke the law and brought enforcement and regulatory hell down on himself and the entire brokerage industry, just to get his twins admitted to preschool. Or that's how we remember it. But in retrospect, the benefits were richer than just that, and their reach spread well beyond Grubman.

FELONS OF FINANCE

Well before the brokerage scandal, big-money crimes in lower Manhattan in the 1980s and 1990s were legion. Back then, the Department of Justice made examples of the most notorious felons. They caught and prosecuted the men who drew attention to themselves and embarrassed law enforcement.

The exploits of crooked corporate takeover artist and inside trader Ivan Boesky were so well known that Hollywood produced the 1987 movie *Wall Street* based on his behavior. Michael Douglas, the actor who played the Boesky-inspired Gordon Gekko, won an Academy Award for his performance and unfortunately glamorized the role. By then, "Ivan the Terrible" had already been featured on the cover of *Time* magazine.[1] He was said to work the phones hard from his Fifth Avenue office, taking insider stock tips all day long with his 300-line telephone console. Boesky was a little rough around the edges. Reportedly expelled from a Michigan prep school, he never graduated from college, but did earn a law degree in Detroit. Perhaps insecure about his status, he joined the Harvard Club so he could wine and dine prospective investors, leading them to falsely conclude he was an Ivy League graduate.[2]

The "Greed is good" speech that Gekko delivers in the film *Wall Street* echoed Boesky's 1986 address to business school graduates. Capturing the ethos of the era, Boesky proclaimed, "Greed is all right, by the way. I want you to know that. I think greed is healthy. You can be greedy and still feel good about yourself."[3] Months later, in November 1986, Boesky settled insider trading charges with the SEC. The $100 million he paid was split evenly. Half went to the U.S. Treasury and the other half was made available for investors who could prove to a federal court that they suffered from his trading.[4] Then, a year later, just a week after the film was released in December 1987, a judge sentenced Boesky to three years in federal prison. He had pleaded guilty to a single criminal count of making a false statement to the SEC. The charge was light because he had cooperated with the Justice Department by flipping on his friends, including junk bond king Michael Milken at Drexel Burnham Lambert.[5] While his attorney requested he serve his sentence at the Community Food Bank in New Jersey, he was sent to Lompoc, a minimum-security prison near Los Angeles that was known as "Club Fed West."[6]

Boesky's cooperation helped bring about the convictions of a half dozen others, including a former Drexel trader on racketeering charges[7] and Milken on securities fraud and conspiracy charges.[8] Also infamous from that era was Jordan Belfort, chairman of brokerage firm Stratton Oakmont, a classic boiler room pump-and-dump operation. Belfort and a colleague pleaded guilty in 1999 to several counts of securities fraud and money laundering. Over a seven-year period they had manipulated the stock price of thirty-four companies and cheated investors out of hundreds of millions of dollars. As part of their plea, they agreed to forfeit $16 million to help establish a fund to partially compensate the people they bilked.[9]

This innovative crime-soaked era prompted the government to get creative as well. Back then, trading on material nonpublic corporate information was so rampant on Wall Street that the U.S. government took a challenging case involving Minneapolis lawyer

James O'Hagan all the way to the U.S. Supreme Court.[10] O'Hagan used confidential client information he heard around the law firm to invest in corporations he knew were takeover targets. Because O'Hagan's law firm represented the acquirers, he could be considered a temporary or constructive insider of the acquirer. But he was absolutely an outsider of the target companies. Under previous case law, defining the classical insider trading offense under Section 10(b) of the Securities Exchange Act and related Rule 10b-5, such an outsider was free and clear to trade the target's securities. The goal of that appeal was to persuade the Supreme Court to expand the scope of the law to also prohibit this type of "outsider" trading. Before that, convictions had been overturned if someone trading the stock of a company was a complete outsider, because they had gotten their material nonpublic information from a different source. After the O'Hagan decision, that type of outsider trading, in which the trader misappropriates information from a source to whom he owes a duty of trust and confidence, was now unlawful.

BABIES AND BANKERS

What happened with the babies and the bankers was really just a sidebar in a huge financial scheme that brought misery to millions of victims. Jack Grubman and his sponsors at Citigroup helped to inflate the dot-com stock bubble in the late 1990s with their outsized optimism about internet stocks, fueled by the prospect of fat investment banking fees. This tale fascinated because it weaves together the special privileges the superwealthy take in their personal and professional spheres. The fuller context of this specific case reveals a broader truth. Sometime after the accounting scandals and before the 2008 meltdown, efforts to prosecute the powerful began to decline. It seems that today we have separate rules for the very wealthy and the rest of us. Breaking the law and paying a fine is just a cost of doing business. The very rare prison stint these days for the elite is served in a Club Fed or home confinement. Those without power cannot take advantage of wealth-enhancing illegal schemes. Worse, they're punished, imprisoned, and even summarily executed on the street—as we saw with Eric Garner—for far less. It's a reinforcement feedback loop for criminal consequences for the upper class—in the absence of any, they commit more crimes.

IMPLICIT IMMUNITY

The concept of implicit immunity for the upper class has now expanded far beyond the territory that Edwin Sutherland staked out in 1939 to 1950. This is more extensive than "white collar criminality" as he conceived of it then, and as it is normally understood today. There are three aspects to this. First, the superwealthy enjoy immunity from unlawful conduct well beyond offenses committed in the workplace, even from violent crimes. Second, this immunity often extends beyond those who actually have tremendous power and connections to those who look similar or to strivers who appear to have a chance to advance into the higher echelon—in other words, young, middle-class, or affluent white males. Third, this implicit immunity is part of a culture and system of mutually assured immunity. From prep school and beyond, the elite cover for each other. If there's trouble with addiction or anti-social behavior, the elite find expert help or manage to resolve these problems privately, outside the public eye, off the "official record." In the best case, the young "rebels" thus have the space to grow up, reform, and become their better selves. In the worst case, those who still land in positions of authority, reformed or not, might be subject to extortion. They may look the other way or go light on those who may "have something" on them. And they may subconsciously or intentionally project their own unsavory youthful (and adult) activities onto those who look like them, and therefore give those pseudo-selves a second or third chance, a light touch. A pass. Forgiveness has an important place in justice, but this isn't forgiveness—and there's certainly no component of rehabilitation. For those who have no ability or intention to start over and stop cheating and victimizing others, it's a dangerous practice.

Implicit immunity spills over into the realm of violent crime as well, including rape and other predatory behavior. Young (and old) white men get off with a "boys will be boys" defense, with no jail or very light sentences, imposed by judges who openly state that they don't wish to destroy the bright futures[11] to which these favored offenders are entitled. Or, at least it seems, many want them to achieve a "respectable" future that is more in their reach than their nonwhite counterparts. One infamous example was Stanford University student Brock Turner, who in 2015 was caught sexually assaulting an unconscious woman but served just three months in jail, even though the prosecution had asked for six years.[12] The young woman he assaulted, Chanel Miller, stepped out of the shadows in 2019 with her powerful memoir, *Know My Name,* in which she recounts her terrifying experience.

A few more examples. Then contrasts. In 2009, after DuPont heir Robert H. Richards IV pleaded guilty to raping his three-year-old daughter, the judge sentenced him to probation and suspended his eight-year sentence. Why? Because the judge said Richards—who was six foot four and weighed over 250 pounds—would "not fare well" in prison.[13] More recently, there was Ethan Couch, the sixteen-year-old who in 2013 was driving while drunk at seventy miles per hour in a forty-miles-per-hour zone. He crashed into a driver whose car had broken down, killing her along with three Good Samaritans who had stopped to help her. A passenger in Couch's car was paralyzed. What precipitated this tragedy? Couch had gone out, stolen beer from Walmart, and achieved a blood alcohol level three times the legal limit. He pleaded guilty to intoxication manslaughter. While the prosecution asked for a twenty-year sentence, the judge gave Couch no jail time at all—just rehab and probation for ten years. Why? The judge had sympathy for his defense. His lawyer claimed he was a victim of his wealthy upbringing. An expert psychologist testified that Couch suffered from "affluenza," a condition brought about by his rich parents who'd never set proper boundaries, he argued. This "affluenza defense" seems preposterous. But it worked.[14] Apparently, the ailment is not easily cured. In 2015, two years after the judge went easy on him, Couch violated the terms of his substance-free probation by attending a party where alcohol was served, and then vanished. He was tracked down at a resort town in Mexico.[15] After the authorities brought him back to the United States, Couch was sentenced to jail and released in 2018.[16] He resurfaced in January 2020 when Texas authorities arrested him on a probation violation for testing positive for THC, the active chemical in marijuana. He was released the following day from jail because prosecutors thought the low level detected through his drug monitoring patch might have resulted from legal CBD oil.[17]

And then there is Harvey Weinstein, accused predatory sexual assaulter and rapist who for decades was allegedly able to destroy the careers of many actresses and employees while remaining untouchable by the law.[18] This invincibility came from the power he wielded in Hollywood and the money he could deploy hiring private detectives to dig up dirt on accusers and threaten journalists.[19] And, of course, because other high-level men in the entertainment industry and media had gotten away with similar predatory behavior for years, if he was going to go down, so would they. And eventually they did. It took tremendous, concerted effort to expose him. It was largely due to women's anger after Donald Trump won the election in November 2016, just weeks after the obscenely offensive *Access Hollywood* tape went public. That recording of Trump saying to host Billy Bush: "I moved on her like a bitch. But I couldn't get there. And she was married." Then: "You know, I'm automatically attracted to beautiful—I just start kissing them. It's like a magnet. Just kiss. I don't even wait. And when you're a star, they let you do it. You can do anything."[20]

And yet, even after the exposure and the criminal and civil charges, Weinstein is likely to keep a good deal of his money. In December 2019, there were reports of a $25 million deal between Weinstein and his more than thirty accusers, where Harvey himself would pay nothing and would not admit to any liability. Any money would be paid by insurance companies representing his former studio, the Weinstein Company. While he awaited a criminal trial in Manhattan involving two accusers, Weinstein saw himself as the victim.[21] "I feel like the forgotten man," he told a journalist in early December 2019.[22] After a jury found Weinstein guilty of rape and a felony sex crime in March 2020, the judge sentenced him to twenty-three years in state prison.[23] A stunning reversal of fortune.

BACK TO JACK

What was on Jack Grubman's mind when he imagined his twins' future? Attendance at the 92nd Street Y preschool was said to ensure admission into one of the city's most selective prep schools. It was a feeder school for four-year-olds. Around 2,000 preschoolers each year competed for just 650 kindergarten seats in those top private K-12 academies.[24] In turn, these prep schools were considered surefire gateways to postsecondary success, leading to easy admittance to an elite college. Or so people said. For "Masters of the Universe," to use Tom Wolfe's memorable phrase, children's school "achievements" are more than ego-boosting trophies. Access to these elite spaces, for those trained to excel (or at least tread water) in them, can have long-term material consequences. Future social connections, marriage partners, business colleagues—and not just for the kids.

This path from private preschool to private prep school was prized for another reason. There was robust competition among the New York middle and upper classes to help their children escape the default neighborhood schools.[25] Even entry into a preferred *public* school was highly competitive,[26] often secured with years of test prep and tears. Parents knew that the public school system needed significant resources to bring more schools up to the standards of the selective ones. But these same parents were not hoping to change the laws and pay higher taxes to improve all schools for everyone. Instead, they applied their (vast) resources to game the system on behalf of their own children. What made the Grubman case entertaining at first was the interlacing of two seemingly incongruous spheres—babies and banking—but in the end it was no laughing matter for the investors who lost $1.7 trillion by November 2000, when the dot-com bubble he was helping to blow up had begun to burst.[27]

RATING GAME

Here's how it went down. Grubman, a managing director and research analyst at Salomon Smith Barney, a Citigroup subsidiary, was admired in the industry and pulled in around $20 million in personal income a year.[28] He was thought to be the highest paid analyst in his day. He was a longtime skeptic of AT&T as a tech company with a solid future. Part of his job was to rate its stock for investment, and he scored the corporation at "neutral" for three years and disparaged the company in his research reports. Then, suddenly, in November 1999, he upgraded his "neutral" rating two notches to the highest classification, "buy." Zoom. Right up to the top, skipping right over the intervening "outperform" notch, which would have been a more customary next step up. The timing was interesting. Grubman announced this upgrade shortly after his boss, Citigroup co-CEO and co-chairman Sanford "Sandy" Weill, asked him to take a "fresh look" at AT&T.[29]

Why did his boss make such a request? It's complicated. His motives appear to be mixed. First, the basics. As co-head of Citigroup, Weill had shareholder profits in mind. Growing earnings meant keeping customers of this newly formed banking supermarket happy. The Fed had loosened restrictions on its predecessor, Citicorp, which then merged with insurance firm Travelers in 1998. Then came the related repeal by Congress of the Glass-Steagall Act. Now the newly formed Citigroup was a giant financial services supermarket, housing commercial banking (offering savings accounts, checking accounts, and loans to both consumers and businesses), investment banking (brokerage accounts and raising capital), and insurance. Grubman's team at Salomon was part of Citi's investment banking business.

Housing so many businesses under one roof created all kinds of conflicts of interest. Sometimes a practice that would help one class of customers could hurt another. Most retail customers (actual human beings) on the investment banking side of the business were looking for reliable information for their securities portfolios held in their brokerage accounts. A strong rating from a top analyst like Grubman would encourage them to buy AT&T stock for their account. A neutral, hold, or worse could motivate them to sell. This was good information of the type retail customers wanted. On the flip side, a low rating by a Citi analyst made some existing or future institutional clients of the investment bank unhappy—including corporations like AT&T, which were highly prized customers. Citigroup could earn fees from a big corporate client like AT&T in many ways. For example, Citi could act as an underwriter, helping the client bring in fresh money from investors for new issues of stocks and bonds. Their neutral rating might make AT&T executives unhappy and deter them from bringing business to the bank.

It is easy to see the conflict between the desires of retail and institutional customers. Say Citi was competing for a good piece (or any) of that lucrative multimillion-dollar underwriting business from AT&T. Why would AT&T want to work with Citi if their star telecom analyst was telling investors he was lukewarm on the company's prospects? This was not a rhetorical question. It actually happened. More on that in a moment. First, we need to see that even more conflicts of interest existed for Citi's Weill himself. Like many other top executives, he wore several hats. In addition to his primary roles at Citigroup, Weill also served as an outside director on other corporate boards, including—wait for it—AT&T. As it happened, so very symmetrically, Michael Armstrong, the CEO of AT&T at that time, also sat on the Citigroup board. Clearly, this was not just a nursery school story.

KID PRO QUO

Grubman was by nature and calling a trader, and ready to trade on his own behalf. Right when he was taking that fresh look at AT&T, he told Weill about the trouble he was having gaining admission for his twins into the prestigious preschool program. Around the time of Grubman's November 1999 upgrade, Weill made a phone call to the school. Then, by early summer, he pledged $1 million of Citigroup funds to be paid in equal installments over five years to the 92nd Street Y—and *voilà*, both of Grubman's twins gained admission.[30] What was in it for Citi? While Dad was fretting about the preschool, AT&T was planning an initial public offering of a tracking stock to mirror the performance of its wireless unit. This was exactly the sort of IPO for which Citi would love to serve as an underwriter. AT&T CEO Mike Armstrong had the power to select a lead underwriter. But as noted above, AT&T might not want to engage Citi's services when Citi's own analyst was "neutral" on the firm.

Getting Grubman to a "buy" rating could be an important sweetener to help Citi land the underwriting deal. Beyond the underwriting contract, that "buy" rating could buy something else: loyalty. Recall that AT&T's Armstrong also served on the Citigroup board. This was important at the time because Weill was in the middle of a power struggle with his cochairman and co-CEO, John Reed. With Armstrong on his side, Weill would have another board ally to guide his ascent to undivided control of Citi. If this scheme played out as planned, everyone (but the investors relying on honest ratings) would win. Grubman would get the twins into preschool. Weill would land the underwriting deal and become the sole leader of Citi. And Armstrong would have willing investors wrangled by Citi for the new stock issuance in light of a treasured "buy" rating.

It worked. In February 2000, just months after Grubman upgraded AT&T, the company announced that the Salomon Smith Barney subsidiary of Citi would serve as one of the lead underwriters for its wireless tracking stock offering. The $63 million in investment banking fees Salomon earned from the deal far exceeded Weill's $1 million donation on Citi's behalf to the 92nd

Street Y.[31] And Weill achieved personal success as well. In late February 2000, John Reed stepped down, and Weill became the sole chairman and CEO.[32]

To be clear, making a donation directly to the Y—even to help secure spots for an employee's children—is not necessarily unlawful. In contrast, agreeing with the admissions director to pay her secret kickbacks in exchange for those spots would be illegal. Such a scheme would be a classic conspiracy to commit honest services wire fraud and honest services mail fraud.

Who finally connected the dots to reveal the kid pro quo here? Papa Jack himself. A few years later, in November 2002, news broke of his written confession. In an email to a friend from earlier that year, Grubman wrote, "I used Sandy to get my kids in the 92nd Street Y preschool (which is harder than Harvard)." But was it at all linked to the rating upgrade? Additional, more contemporaneous evidence emerged to help answer that question—a November 1999 memo from Grubman to Weill. The subject was "AT&T and the 92nd Street Y." The first half of the memo covered meetings with Mike of AT&T. In the second half, Grubman wrote of the strain he was under due to "the ridiculous but necessary process of preschool applications in Manhattan." He confessed, "For someone who grew up in a household with a father making $8,000 a year and for someone who attended public schools, I do find this process a bit strange, but there are no bounds for what you do for your children." He added, "It comes down to 'who you know.'" Even celebrity was no admissions guarantee. That year the preschool reportedly rejected pop star Madonna's three-year-old daughter, Lourdes. Grubman provided his boss with a list of the 92nd Street Y board members and implored, "I would greatly appreciate it if you could ask them to use any influence they feel comfortable in using to help us."[33]

CONFLICT ARTISTS

By the time news of Grubman's confessional email was published in November 2002, Eliot Spitzer, the New York State attorney general, and the self-regulatory body NASD were already investigating Citi's conflicts. They wanted to know whether Citi's desire to gain or maintain investment banking relationships with big corporate clients had corrupted its research recommendations.[34] And Grubman had already resigned from his job at Citi's Salomon subsidiary. This was much, much bigger than a preschool predicament. In the words of corporate governance experts, Jack Grubman was "possibly the poster child for abuses." As for ethical boundaries, he "didn't just cross over the line, he erased it." He was supposed to provide impartial ratings to the investing public but had conflicts. It wasn't just the AT&T fiasco. In 1997, he had provided advice to Bernard Ebbers, the soon-to-be-disgraced and eventually imprisoned CEO of WorldCom. He counseled Ebbers on its successful $37 billion takeover of telecom rival MCI. Grubman was working and socializing with Ebbers while at the same time providing to the public what was supposed to be an unbiased evaluation of the transaction. In fact, Grubman maintained a buy rating for WorldCom even after the stock had lost nearly 90 percent of its value,[35] up until a few months before the company had to restate its earnings in 2002. Before emerging from bankruptcy in 2004, the company would further restate its earnings for 2001 and 2002, reducing its pretax profits for those two years by more than $74 billion.[36]

As for Grubman's conflict with Citi, when asked about the problem that he was playing both sides—earning investment banking fees with Citi while advising retail investors—he denied the problem. Instead, he insisted it was a "synergy." He denounced so-called objectivity as simply "uninformed."[37]

Though he was touted as the preeminent telecom analyst, it turned out that Grubman was very, very bad at his job—that is, if you considered his job to be providing solid, unbiased advice on telecom stocks to potential investors and customers. If, however, you thought of his job as bringing in millions of dollars in fees to his employer and parent company, Citigroup, and secondarily lining his own pockets, he absolutely excelled. Why did so many people trust his judgment? Maybe they should not have. It turns out Grubman may not have been the certified genius he led others to believe he was. For years, he told people he graduated from MIT. That was a lie. He failed the Series 7 exam—the entry-level licensing exam to become a registered representative at a brokerage firm—the first time he took it.[38] His actual educational background was revealed in 2000. It seemed odd he would have lied, since he actually earned his undergraduate degree from Boston University and a master's from Columbia—both highly respected institutions. When a *Businessweek* reporter confronted him with the truth, Grubman dismissed his lie as a "stupid mistake." He never really owned up to the fact that he actively misled others. "At some point, I probably felt insecure, and it perpetuated itself," he remarked.[39]

TAKE THE MONEY AND RUN

Grubman shrugged off legal consequences just as easily. In April 2003, the Securities and Exchange Commission banned him from the securities industry. As part of the settlement, he paid a $15 million fine, but he never admitted liability. He didn't sweat the lifetime ban. "I don't like the stigma, but I was going to leave the industry anyway," he quipped.[40] When it was said and done, he was still worth more than $50 million. By comparison, his peers in the investment banking industry felt much more pain, relatively speaking. The SEC, several states, and market self-regulatory organizations entered into a $1.4 billion "global" settlement with ten brokerage firms and one other broker who was also barred from the industry for life.[41] Of that amount, $375.5 million was allocated as restitution for investors. To distribute this money, the SEC announced that an administrator would manage ten different funds.[42]

The evidence shared with the public as part of the global settlement was designed to be helpful to investors who could then bring their own private lawsuits, but they'd have to do this on their own nickel or participate in a class action lawsuit, with plaintiffs' lawyers taking their own cut. The settlement blasted three firms in particular, accusing them of fraud: Salomon Smith Barney (the Citigroup subsidiary), which paid $400 million; Merrill Lynch, which paid $200 million; and Credit Suisse First Boston, which also paid $200 million. The regulators accused the trio of "spinning," which meant trying to drum up business with corporate executives by letting them in on hot stock and bond offerings.

The motive for all the deception was summed up well by Stephen Labaton in the *New York Times*: "At firm after firm, according to prosecutors, analysts wittingly duped investors to curry favor with corporate clients. Investment houses received secret payments from companies they gave strong recommendations to buy. And for top executives whose companies were clients, stock underwriters offered special access to hot initial public offerings." He continued: "The evidence that regulators made public today painted a picture up and down Wall Street of an industry rife with conflicts of interest during the height of the Internet and telecommunications bubble that burst" in 2000.[43]

Under the settlement, Sandy Weill, CEO of Citigroup, was barred from speaking with analysts at Citi about stock recommendations unless a lawyer was present. All of the settling Wall Street firms had to keep their research and investment banking divisions separate. Even though there was no admission of criminal wrongdoing, under Sutherland's framework the behavior would be "white collar crime." This is because the episode involved breaches of trust by persons of respectability and high social status in the course of their occupations. The then new SEC commissioner William Donaldson also referenced this loyalty breach, saying, "These cases reflect a sad chapter in the history of American business—a chapter in which those who reaped enormous benefits based on the trust of investors profoundly betrayed that trust."[44]

STILL DANCING

One would have thought this settlement and censure would lead to better behavior, or at least tighter scrutiny and regulation of these self-serving ratings and recommendations. As many readers may remember, within a few years after this so-called global settlement, several of the ten firms were back at it. These usual suspects engaged in the predatory, abusive, and unlawful practices that helped inflate the housing bubble, which then brought about the subprime mortgage meltdown, and resulted in a global financial crisis that would require a multitrillion-dollar taxpayer-backed rescue from the United States government. Especially Citigroup. The broken banking behemoth needed two separate bailouts, in 2008 and 2009. The $476 billion in cash and other guarantees Citi received far exceeded any other financial institution. And it was more than the total amount of unemployment benefits paid for all the folks unemployed during the recession the following year.[45] The Citi CEO who replaced Weill when he retired was Charles Prince. In the summer of 2007, with subprime mortgage bonds tanking and markets already in turmoil, Prince famously told a *Financial Times* reporter, "When the music stops, in terms of liquidity, things will be complicated. But as long as the music is playing, you've got to get up and dance. We're still dancing."[46]

In great contrast to the accounting scandals that peaked at the turn of the millennium, no one went to jail as part of that giant brokerage industry scandal in 2003. Not a single person. In fact, Citigroup only agreed to join the global settlement on the condition that New York attorney general Eliot Spitzer would not prosecute.[47] The lesson was clear. Their behavior would get bolder. This implicit immunity for the upper class would help bring us the global financial meltdown inside of five years.

OPERATION VARSITY BLUES

Maybe you've got some sympathy for parents ready to do anything it takes for their kids. Recall that Grubman wrote in his memo to his boss, "There are no bounds for what you do for your children." One would hope that, short of an emergency, legal boundaries would matter to most parents. When desperate, though, who wouldn't steal a loaf of bread or medicine for their child. Couldn't you imagine exceeding the speed limit to get your oldest child to her SAT test on time? (Reader, don't judge. I would have been happy to pay the speeding ticket.) Violating the securities laws and misleading investors apparently to help get one's toddlers admitted to a posh school should not be of the same order. Yet the words "But I did it for my children" is almost never a plea that ordinary people can use to excuse their misbehavior.

Compare Grubman with homeless, jobless Tanya McDowell. In 2011, McDowell, who lived in Bridgeport, Connecticut, enrolled her son in an elementary school in neighboring Norwalk.[48] The Connecticut police arrested her and charged her with first-degree larceny and conspiracy to commit first-degree larceny. What had she allegedly taken? They claimed that by enrolling her son in the wrong town, she'd stolen $15,686 from the Norwalk public schools. She pleaded guilty to the charges in connection with her son's enrollment. She had to post a $25,000 bond to get released from jail. A mother, with a small child.[49]

The disparities in sentencing of white versus black offenders is, of course, a topic for a whole other discussion, but the regularity of these types of heavy-handed, often violent and cruel, interventions in the lives of nonwhite Americans—whether poor or wealthy—contrasts greatly with the ease with which most white Americans navigate their lives, even when the latter are caught up in truly harmful conduct.

It is with this backdrop that we can assess Operation Varsity Blues, a bold federal investigation unveiled in several waves, beginning in March 2019. Criminal charges were eventually leveled against more than fifty celebrities and other wealthy parents who schemed with a corrupt college admissions consultant to secure admission for their children into elite universities, including Georgetown, Stanford, Yale, Wake Forest, the University of Texas at Austin, UCLA, and USC. While the scam was active between 2011 and 2018, parents paid consultant William "Rick" Singer more than $25 million. And they got results. Singer's efforts included bribing coaches to claim that his clients' kids were star athletes, even though many never participated in their high school teams' sports. His criminal web included parents, students, college coaches, and test administrators.

By December 2019, twenty parents had either entered guilty pleas or had plans to do so.[50] Some parents pleaded to conspiracy to commit honest services wire fraud. Others have also been charged with bribery. While we saw a roundup of many parents, what few know is some have so far escaped prosecution. For example, as *The New Yorker* reported in October 2019: "One billionaire family paid Singer $6.5 million for their daughter's admission to Stanford. Her application to Stanford was embellished with false credentials for the sailing team, according to a court filing by prosecutors. The university expelled the student, according to news reports, but she and her parents have not been charged in the case."[51]

The sentences handed down so far have been very light. The Stanford University sailing coach who pleaded guilty to conspiracy to commit racketeering paid a $10,000 fine and was sentenced to one day of incarceration and two years of supervised release, of which six months is home detention. Most prison sentences have ranged from four to six months, with some as low as fourteen days.[52] The longest sentence so far, nine months, was for Douglas Hodge, the former CEO of Pacific Investment Management Company (PIMCO). Judge Nathaniel Gorton called Hodge's behavior "appalling and mind-boggling at the same time." Hodge had paid more than $850,000 to secure admission to elite schools for his four children, including one to Princeton University, as fake athletic recruits.[53]

The Varsity Blues scheme took its toll on the victims, like most white collar crimes. For each applicant whose path into college was rigged, one less advantaged student was denied a place. In the spring of 2017, Adam Langevin, a tennis team captain for his private high school in California, was passed up for admission to Georgetown University, a Division I school, when his classmate Grant Janavs gained admission. Adam was the top tennis player at his school for four years, while Grant, who once played doubles, wasn't even on the tennis team as a senior. It was hard to understand why Georgetown would have chosen Janavs over Langevin for the team. Two years later, everyone found out why. Georgetown tennis coach Gordon Ernst was allegedly on the take.[54] Michelle Janavs—apparently without her son's knowledge—conspired with Singer to pay off Coach Ernst. Singer paid the coach $2.7 million to designate a dozen Georgetown applicants as tennis recruits, including Grant Janavs. Michelle Janavs allegedly wired $400,000 to a nonprofit set up by Singer to secure her son's admission. In October 2019, Janavs pleaded guilty and was sentenced to five months in prison. That month, a grand jury returned a superseding indictment against the coach for numerous criminal offenses related to the alleged bribery scheme, including racketeering and money laundering. Ernst pleaded not guilty.[55]

ACHILLES' HEELS

There is also danger when the powerful elite hide their criminal behavior. Especially when they are in law enforcement. Perps inside the legal system have weapons ordinary civilians might not, but they are also vulnerable in ways that affect how they do their job, which presumably is to protect the rest of us. They can be subject to blackmail or even self-restraint in using their powers against those with knowledge of their dirty past or the means to find out. This is one of those hazy areas where it's hard to measure what *didn't* happen in a particular situation, but there is some disturbing evidence. To see it, let's circle back to the Grubman settlement in 2003.

The crackdown on Wall Street that caught Grubman was

spearheaded by New York attorney general Eliot Spitzer and raised his national profile dramatically. He was particularly proud of the global settlement with the brokerage firms, having been a thorn in Wall Street's side nearly from the moment he took office in 1999. In 2002, he oversaw a $100 million settlement with Merrill Lynch over analyst advice, using a then obscure 1921 New York law called the Martin Act. This investigation of Merrill led him to dig further, discover widespread conflicts, and ultimately work with the SEC and others to conclude the global settlement a year later. Three years after that, he ran for governor of New York and won. There's a saying about state attorneys general. It comes from the National Association of Attorneys General (NAAG). It is already an unfortunate acronym when spoken aloud, pronounced "nag." It is also used derisively by those who believe these state officials wield their power and engage in media grandstanding to advance their personal ambitions. For them, N-A-A-G stands for the National Association of Aspiring Governors.

On the surface, this step up the ladder to the governorship seemed quite ordinary. A natural move for someone who is ego driven and accomplished. Princeton undergrad. Harvard Law School. Attorney general. Governor. Nothing stopping him—it seemed. But there was an obstacle. A big one. And, clearly, Eliot did not get the memo. Not an actual memo. The proverbial one. The unspoken understanding of mutually assured protection. A code of conduct that people who are well aware of their own substantial sins should not cast the first stone. The feds caught him on wiretap in February 2008. He'd paid as much as $80,000 to shell companies that were fronts for an escort service while he was attorney general and later as governor. The investigation first began in the summer of 2007 when his bank reported suspicious activity it thought might be money laundering.[56]

Governor Spitzer announced his resignation on March 10, 2008, days before the fateful collapse and government-backed industry rescue of Bear Stearns. Why then? He had been involved with prostitutes for a long while, and compromising information about it had long been available. The timing was auspicious. Whoever blew the whistle on him took him out of commission right when, as governor, he could have helped his attorney general investigate and perhaps bring criminal charges against Wall Street bankers, a process he enjoyed. Instead, he was sidelined.

But consider this ironic twist: even though Spitzer repeatedly solicited prostitution, an illegal activity, no criminal charges were brought against him. He had busted numerous people in a prostitution ring when he was attorney general, but this time he was given a second chance. After some years, he began to rehabilitate his reputation. He landed a cable news show and seemed to have emerged from the scandal. In 2013, he even had the confidence to run for public office again, but lost. Then he was actually the subject of an extortion scheme by a twenty-seven-year-old sex worker who threatened to tell his family about their encounters.[57]

After observing Spitzer's initial fall from grace, before he became New York attorney general, Eric Schneiderman must have gotten the message. He must have. The humiliating resignation from the office of a governor based in part on his misdeeds as AG should have been enough of a cautionary tale. But just in case it wasn't, there were people out there who knew things about Schneiderman himself. *Kompromat.* Accusations of physical abuse by several women.[58] They would remind him. Here's what we know.

Shortly after he took office in January 2011, Schneiderman began investigating Trump University (by then renamed the Trump Entrepreneur Initiative). In May of that year, he subpoenaed documents. In August 2013, on behalf of the state of New York, he sued. In the complaint, Schneiderman alleged that this fake educational institution had brought in tens of millions of dollars of revenue largely by misleading customers through false promises and outright lies. Trump claimed to have handpicked the instructors. But he had not. Plus, they had little training themselves. Victims spent thousands of dollars of their savings and went into debt to attend these courses.[59]

When there was an opportunity for the attorney general to bring criminal charges against Trump's fake university, he instead orchestrated a civil settlement. In 2013, while he was investigating Trump's enterprise, rumors were circulating that Schneiderman had physically assaulted several women. This information was apparently passed by attorney Peter Gleason to Trump's then personal lawyer, Michael Cohen, who said he discussed it with Trump himself. And we can see evidence on Twitter that Trump let Schneiderman know he had some dirt on him. On September 11, 2013, private citizen Donald Trump tweeted the following: "Weiner is gone, Spitzer is gone—next will be lightweight A.G. Eric Schneiderman. Is he a crook? Wait and see, worse than Spitzer or Weiner."[60] This was an obvious allusion to sexual impropriety; otherwise, there would have been no reason to include Anthony Weiner in the tweet. While Spitzer had held the same office that Schneiderman did—that of AG—Weiner was a member of Congress. We don't know if Schneiderman read this tweet, but if he message received.

Is it possible this pressure led Schneiderman to go lighter, to agree to a relatively small $40 million civil RICO settlement in 2016, just weeks after Trump was elected president? We will never know. But when the full story came out in May 2018 of the physical assault allegations, Schneiderman did resign from office, under pressure. There is some further support that this damaging information on Schneiderman may have influenced his actions in the Trump University matter. In May 2018, Peter Gleason sent a letter to federal judge Kimba Wood informing her that two women, one in 2012 and one in 2013, had informed him that Schneiderman had been "sexually inappropriate with them." Gleason also told Judge Wood that he'd passed this information on to journalist Stephen Dunleavy, and that Dunleavy offered to speak with Trump about the matter. Gleason said he believed Trump had been informed based on a phone conversation he'd had with Trump's personal lawyer at the time, Michael Cohen. Gleason later explained in an interview that he thought the information was relevant to Trump, given his battle with the New York attorney general.[61]

UNJUST IMMUNITY

From cradle—or at least from arrival in the 1 percent—to grave and beyond, the wealthy and white often get to cut the line, cut legal corners, and gather riches and status while leaving victims in their wake and avoiding the consequences and setbacks that others would face if they similarly offended. Even when the exception proves the rule and the law does go after an elite white offender, it often takes an extraordinary pattern of wrongdoing, and even repeat criminal or abusive behavior, before prison is considered. From preschool through adolescence to college, career, and beyond, the wealthiest get a special pass. Unless they do something really, really out of bounds in a very public fashion, people will look the other way.

Many of those named here—including Sandy Weill—were never accused or charged with a crime. At their tier of wealth and status, it is never entirely clear whether that was due to good behavior or good fortune. Weill's fingerprints were not just on the brokerage scandal. He was also the architect behind the deregulation that contributed to the global financial crisis of 2008. In 2010, the former Citi co-CEO expressed regret for his role in repealing Glass-Steagall, thus allowing the merger of his firm, Travelers, with Citibank to make Citigroup. Then, in 2012, Weill recommended restoring the law and breaking up the banks, including his old bank supermarket, Citigroup.[62] A generous admission? More like an empty mea culpa. It did not come with any forfeiting of the wealth he accumulated as a result of his regretful role. He is poised to live out his years in comfort and with the respect of his peers. Such is the fate of so many who are adjacent to what Sutherland would deem white collar criminality, but which is undercharged and underpunished.

In the words of onetime New York County district attorney De Lancey Nicoll, "The rich can go practically unpunished, unless their crime is so glaring." However, he observed, "the poor have to receive the penalty of their offense in every instance."[63]

|||||||||||||||||||||||||||||||||||||||||||||||||||

CHAPTER 6

FORGIVENESS FOR
THE FORTUNATE

Forgiveness is a gift with tremendous value, both to the grantor and the recipient. We like to think we can offer fresh starts to those who have made mistakes but who could move on with their lives and contribute to their family, friends, and community. In reality, though, forgiveness is often reserved for the fortunate, or for those who look like the very people who hold the power to forgive. There may be a touch of "There but for the grace of God go I" at work here.

In her recent book *When Should Law Forgive?*, law professor Martha Minow asks two central questions: "When can and should legal officials and institutions promote forgiveness between individuals?" and "When can law itself be forgiving?"[1] She observes that forgiveness could be a useful tool to dismantle our system of mass incarceration, but in practice, it's not. "The United States is particularly punitive in defining, prosecuting, and punishing crimes, especially if the accused is a racial minority. As of 2018, the United States is the most incarcerating nation in the history of humanity."[2] Further, we too often expect that those with the least power forgive the transgressions of those who have so much more. Recognizing this double standard, Minow is clear that victims themselves should never be pressured or expected to grant forgiveness. She also emphasizes that personal forgiveness, if granted by a victim, does not mean the offender should go without prosecution or punishment.[3]

There are many entry points for forgiveness in our criminal justice system. At all of them, being white and wealthy more likely delivers this treatment. A simple police interaction. The decision to arrest or file charges. Declining or deferring prosecution. Plea bargaining. Taking a case to trial. Jury deliberation. Sentencing. Acceptance back into society. At each of these steps in the criminal justice process, someone's inclination to forgive can make all of the difference. The notion of forgiveness even affects what we deem "a crime" to begin with.

FORGIVE AND REMEMBER

Let's begin toward the end of the process: at sentencing. Baked into federal sentencing statutes and related sentencing guidelines are invitations for judges to forgive those with privilege, wealth, and connections to power. Judges have greater discretion in sentencing in white collar crime cases, compared to the harsh mandatory terms elsewhere in the federal criminal code. We see this play out in the justifications judges offer when they ignore recommended sentences. The reasoning sometimes shocks the public, but is perfectly in line with the law. That needs to change.

It was not supposed to be this way. With the Sentencing Reform Act of 1984, Congress hoped to create a system to make federal sentencing more uniform and more fair. This law established the United States Sentencing Commission, an independent agency in the judicial branch that creates and updates the Federal Sentencing Guidelines. It was the commission's job to create rules that would reduce unwarranted disparities in sentences meted out from case to case.

Clearly, the way federal judges reasoned before the Sentencing Commission's guidelines was troubling. Here's one example. In 1976, Marvin Frankel, a federal district court judge, issued a sentencing memorandum for defendant Bernard Bergman. Bergman had been caught engaging in a $2.5 million Medicare and tax fraud involving nursing homes he operated. Though he pleaded guilty to two related charges, he never admitted to any wrongdoing as part of the plea. Together, the two laws he violated allowed for a punishment of up to eight years in prison. Yet judge Frankel issued just a four-month sentence. The prosecutor, Charles Hynes, said that this light sentence would make the public believe that there was "special justice for the privileged." Worse than that, he believed it insulted and demoralized the victims, the elderly people Bergman had exploited. Despite these objections, Judge Frankel described the sentence as "stern." Bergman, though, showed no gratitude or remorse. After the sentencing, he promptly issued a statement claiming to have been cleared of the "wild and vicious allegations that were made against me in the press." Bergman also blamed his accountant.[4] In the sentencing decision, the judge wrote,

"The fact that he has been pilloried by journalists is essentially a consequence of the prestige and privileges he enjoyed before he was exposed as a wrongdoer." Judge Frankel rationalized the short sentence because Bergman, an Orthodox rabbi, "appeared until the last couple of years to be a man of unimpeachably high character, attainments, and distinction."[5]

JUSTICE FOR SCALE

Then came the Federal Sentencing Guidelines. At this point, they are a complicated law unto themselves. Here's how it works. You consult what appears to be a simple table that fits on a single page in order to figure out the recommended sentence for a convicted felon. There are two basic variables: criminal history, if any, and the severity of the offense. The severity of the offense (referred to as the offense level) is rated on a scale of 1 to 43, and the criminal history from a category 1 to 6. The chart itself appears simple enough. But things get much more complicated when you try to figure out how to translate from the criminal statutes the defendant violated and the offense level. You need to consult a large tome to come up with the inputs you need to then arrive at the correct offense level number. Fraud, for example, has nineteen different inputs to use in order to determine the offense level. It's a similar story with criminal history.

To illustrate, consider a white collar crime that came up in the Operation Varsity Blues cheating scandal. Honest services wire fraud. Some of the coaches are accused of this felony. The fraud part and dishonest part involve allegedly taking secret bribes from parents to lock in admission for their children, thereby defrauding the university that employed them. The wire part is using the telephone or email to do so. Correspondingly, parents were accused of conspiring with the coaches to do the same. The honest services wire fraud offense is detailed in Title 18 of the United States Code, sections 1343 and 1346. The statute calls for imprisonment of up to twenty years. But that's not going to happen for these defendants because of the guidelines. This is why the longest sentence we've seen so far is nine months. Bottom line: it would be very, very difficult for a first-time offender engaged in basic honest services wire fraud to get a recommended prison sentence of twenty years. Factors that would increase the sentence would be millions of dollars at stake and special attributes like use of a firearm or a cargo shipment.

While the goal was to remove judicial discretion and reduce bias, keep in mind that the guidelines are advisory; they are not mandates. The Supreme Court made that clear in *United States v. Booker* in 2005. After that decision, research by the U.S. Sentencing Commission shows increasing disparities across the ninety-four federal districts, including for defendants convicted on fraud charges.[6]

SAME OLD, SAME OLD

More than forty years after the guidelines were instituted, we see justifications similar to the Bergman case where judges issue lighter sentences than recommended by the prosecution. In March 2019, Judge T. S. Ellis III sentenced former Trump campaign chairman Paul Manafort after a federal jury in Virginia convicted him in 2018 on charges including filing a false tax return, failing to report a foreign bank account, and bank fraud. Manafort tried to hide in bank accounts overseas the proceeds from lobbying for Russia's favored Ukrainian politicians, and he falsified his financial records to get loans.[7] Separately, in a case in D.C. federal district court, he pleaded guilty to conspiracy charges involving money laundering, tax fraud, failing to register as a foreign agent, false statements, witness tampering, and more.[8] Sentencing guidelines called for between nineteen and twenty-four years just for the Virginia federal court case alone.[9] Yet, since judges have discretion after *Booker*, Judge Ellis imposed just under a four-year federal prison sentence for Manafort. He deemed the guidelines' range to be "totally out of whack" in comparison to light sentences for other white collar criminals. He said, "The government cannot sweep away the history of all these previous cases."[10] Echoing Judge Frankel's praise of Bergman, Judge Ellis said Manafort had "lived an otherwise blameless life" and that he had "earned the admiration of a number of people."[11]

This assessment of Manafort's "otherwise blameless life" drew gasps and derision. Columnist Virginia Heffernan noted that "Manafort has been known for more than 40 years as a member of the torturers' lobby." She added that "Manafort amassed millions by essentially deflecting criticism of his brutal clients and opulently enabling them."[12] In early May 2020, the Federal Bureau of Prisons released Manafort from custody, permitting him to serve out the remainder of his seven-and-a-half-year sentence (for both cases) in home confinement. He took advantage of Attorney General Barr's order to ease overcrowding in the prison system because of the coronavirus. However, Manafort did not meet any of the early-release criteria. He neither had served half of his term nor did he have just eighteen months left.[13]

THE INJUSTICE OF FORGIVENESS

Now, let's look at the beginning of the process: arrest. When he was a younger man, Eric Garner was a horticulturist at the New York Department of Parks and Recreation. Due to health problems, including asthma, he left that job and found himself trying to piece together a living for his family. When he was forty-three years old, one day in mid-July 2014, he was doing just that: trying to earn some money. Standing on the sidewalk in front of a beauty supply store in Staten Island, he pulled Newport cigarettes out of several packs and sold them for fifty cents apiece to passersby.[14] That day, a fight started nearby on the sidewalk, Garner helped break it up, then the plainclothes police arrived. They spotted Garner and circled him. A white officer, Daniel Pantaleo, placed him in a choke hold that lasted a full seven seconds while he wrestled him to the ground. Struggling for air on the sidewalk, Garner repeated "I can't breathe" eleven times before he lost consciousness. The New York City medical examiner determined Garner's death to be a homicide. For more than twenty years before his killing, the New York Police Department had banned the use of choke holds.[15] The prohibited maneuver along with chest compression during the arrest "set into motion a lethal sequence" that included internal bleeding in his neck.[16]

While riding in an ambulance to the hospital beside Garner, Officer Justin Damico filled out an inaccurate police report. He cited Garner for a felony tax crime that requires proof that he'd sold more than 10,000 untaxed cigarettes. Later the officer "acknowledged that the felony charge was incorrect because Garner actually had with him five packs of Newports that contained a total of less than 100 cigarettes."[17] What was the actual offense? It was a mere misdemeanor. Small-time cigarette tax evasion.[18] The state of New York imposes a relatively high per-pack tax on cigarettes, on top of the New York City tax. A pack of cigarettes purchased there could have set a smoker back $12.85 at that time. That's around 64 cents per cigarette. But smokers could buy packs in nearby states for less money.

Given the lower excise tax on cigarettes in New Jersey, a pack there was just around $8.20. For the more industrious, this created an arbitrage opportunity. Arbitrage, a term familiar in the investment realm, simply means the nearly simultaneous buying and selling of an asset to take advantage of the price discrepancy. Garner was carrying around five packs stamped from Virginia, where cigarettes sell for about $5.25 a pack, or just around 26 cents each.[19] It was a win-win for him and his customers. By offering Virginia-bought cigarettes for 50 cents each, instead of over 64 cents, they saved money, and he could in theory make $4.75 per pack. If he sold two cartons a day, that would bring in around $100. But he likely had to give a cut up front to the cigarette smugglers who'd transported the cartons north from Virginia. This small-time hustle, though unlawful, was quite common in New York when a successive series of tax increases were imposed by then mayor Michael Bloomberg.[20] Through July 5, 2014, the year Officer Pantaleo killed Garner, the NYPD had made 439 arrests for selling loosies.[21] Some repeat sellers have earned jail time or were sentenced to community service. For Eric, the penalty was death.

Garner was the person who deserved forgiveness, not his attackers. Yet they were the ones who benefitted from leniency, forgiveness, and institutional immunity. In 2015, New York City settled claims with Garner's estate with a $5.9 million payment. While the Civil Rights Division of the U.S. Department of Justice recommended an indictment, on the eve of the five-year deadline to bring federal charges against Officer Pantaleo, Attorney General William Barr aligned himself with the federal prosecutors in Brooklyn and declined.[22] Defending this decision, the prosecutors said there was insufficient evidence.[23] It largely came down to proving intent. At a press conference and in a related press release, U.S. Attorney Richard Donoghue explained that in order to bring federal criminal civil rights charges against Pantaleo, the prosecutors had four elements to prove beyond a reasonable doubt. First, that he acted under color of law. This means in his official capacity. Next, "that the officer used objectively unreasonable force under the circumstances." In addition, they had to prove that "the officer violated the law willfully." Finally, they had to prove that the officer's "wrongful conduct caused bodily injury to the victim." Donoghue also explained that the primary focus of the investigation was on intent. Specifically, "whether the force used was objectively unreasonable" and "whether the officer acted willfully in violation of the law."[24]

But what is "unreasonable"? Under the law, reasonableness is contextual and subjective. U.S. Attorney Donoghue said reasonableness of a particular use of force "must be judged from the perspective of a reasonable officer on the scene, rather than with the 20/20 vision of hindsight." In plain English, here's what that means: federal prosecutors believe that a jury would consider the violent arrest of a nonviolent black man violating the tax laws to be reasonable. Right there is the problem. Any police force and jury is embedded in a society besieged by implicit and often overt bias. So built into the law around reasonableness is the already racist status quo.

Eric Garner was running a small-time street hustle, cheating New York State and City out of a negligible amount of tax revenue. For that, he was strangled on the street and his killers went free. In comparison, let's take a look at how the law treated Deborah Kelley, a middle-class white woman who that same summer of 2014 was running her own street hustle. A Wall Street hustle, that is.

WALL STREET STREET HUSTLE

Deborah Kelley was in the investment business, a managing director of a small brokerage firm in New York City. She earned commissions buying and selling bonds for her wealthy clients. The more trades Kelley made, the more money she earned. The best clients had the biggest investment portfolios. In her line of sight was the New York State Common Retirement Fund, with more than $184 billion in assets—the third largest pension fund in the country. This giant pool of money was managed for more than one million beneficiaries throughout the state. Teachers. Police officers. Firefighters. Earning modest salaries in public service, these workers counted on the pension fund being there for them when they retired. With the more than $10 billion flowing out annually in payments to existing retirees, keeping investment returns up and costs down was critical. If the investments in the fund did not perform well, New York taxpayers would suffer.

Taxpayers already paid for the regular contributions made by the state and local governments into the fund. Any shortfalls to cover future pension payments would be on the taxpayers too. So the fund needed to grow. The government in Albany employed internal managers to watch over this golden nest egg. These employees in turn outsourced the actual investment mechanics to licensed broker-dealers.

That's where Kelley came in. She could earn sizable commissions by buying and selling bonds for that state pension fund. She had her eye on the gatekeeper for that giant pot of money, Navnoor Kang, a young Columbia graduate.[25] Kang ran the portfolio of fixed-income securities for the fund—an attractive $55 billion in assets. Somehow, he secured this trusted position shortly after he was fired by a reputable financial management firm in California over trouble with his entertainment expense reporting.[26] Many of the bonds in the state pension fund portfolio were paying very low interest, so Kang was tasked with getting them sold and replaced with higher-yielding ones. He was in a position to hire outside brokers to make those trades.[27] In March 2014, Kelley's firm had no bond business at all with the New York retirement fund. Zero. Two years later, she was executing about $180 million a year in trades for the fund, personally earning nearly $200,000 in commissions, thanks to Kang.

The indictment came a few days before Christmas in 2016. The feds exposed Kelley in a "pay-to-play" bribery scheme. It turned out she and another broker, Gregg Schonhorn, had paid Kang more than $100,000 in secret bribes to secure bond orders with the pension fund. The joint indictment described the kickbacks Kang received. Vacations. Lavish meals. Concert tickets. A Panerai wristwatch. Access to strip clubs. Prostitutes. Crack cocaine. The federal charges against Kelley included the white collar crimes of conspiracy, securities fraud, and honest services wire fraud. Also, because she'd participated in a cover-up—lying to the SEC under oath about the bribes—prosecutors also charged her with obstruction of justice.[28] Months later, in May 2017, she pleaded guilty and faced up to five years in prison. But Kelley, an upper-middle-class white woman, was not locked up. Instead of incarceration, the kind judge sentenced her to just six months of home confinement and three years' probation. The judge also required her to give back her ill-gotten gains, pay a $50,000 fine, and perform a thousand hours of community service.[29]

Why not prison? At the sentencing, Kelley told the judge, "As hard as I try, I cannot understand why I did this. It was the worst decision of my life." The judge explained his reasoning, pointing to the numerous letters of support from family and friends: "There is no question in my mind that Ms. Kelley is a good person who has been a hugely positive force in her family and her community."[30] That was it. Really. Forgiveness.

A year after her guilty plea, Deborah Kelley, by then in her late fifties, got a fresh start. She found a new job and moved on with her life.[31] The system worked for her. Forgiveness allowed her to land on her feet and start over, something a repentant crack dealer would surely not have been able to secure.

The way this unfolded is not surprising. Judges favor white collar defendants, considering them "more sensitive to the impact of the prison environment than are non-white collar defendants." Judges interviewed have explained their reasoning, without any sense of irony, that prison will not provide general deterrence and will not rehabilitate white collar offenders. What's more, some claim that an indictment is more damaging even than incarceration for such offenders. The lack of similar concern for poor offenders is astonishing. One judge wrote of a physician who committed Medicare fraud, "I didn't want to send him to jail because I felt that it would deprive him and his family of the livelihood he could make as a doctor and it would deprive the neighborhood of his services."[32] Such empathy rarely extends to the burglar or the small-time drug dealer. Researchers note that many judges discussing their views on white collar crime are driven by empathy less evident in their "common crime sentencing."[33]

FORGIVE AND FORGET

Why should we even spend time thinking about a onetime, non-violent, middle-management offender like Deborah Kelley? Kelley's story, like so many others that move into and out of the news cycle, has an emotional impact. It either gets our blood simmering or provides comfort that redemption is still possible. But after the outrage, or satisfaction, subsides, nothing changes—at least not for the better.

So what should we make of her treatment in the criminal justice system? Let's begin with a charitable framework. With a recent trend toward promoting restorative justice instead of punishment, some reformers might deem her merciful sentence to be a good outcome for all. If Kelley had been truly remorseful and not likely to reoffend, why jail her? Even without being a pure prison abolitionist, one could argue that it's difficult to identify the harm caused or even any specific victims of her admitted crimes. If she was having her brokerage firm charge the standard commission to the pension fund that other brokers did, and if she got the best prices on bonds for the fund, then how can the damage be concretely measured? One could attempt to calculate whether she got market prices. But with bonds, it's complicated. Unlike stocks, which have readily available, published market prices, bond values are much more opaque. Perhaps that was why the government did not claim the fund or pensioners lost any money as a result of the bribery scheme. As for lying to the government, while morally wrong and a violation of law, some might contend that Kelley's obstructive behavior did not actually hinder the investigation and conviction of the most culpable character, Kang, so it did not deserve incarceration.

And yet. Many also would reasonably react with outrage by the judge deciding not to impose a prison sentence. To the general public, the facts here don't seem to support this leniency, even if the federal sentencing guidelines do. Kelley was an experienced professional who should have known better. She was motivated by personal gain. She admitted to engaging in bribery and fraud, and lied to the government in an attempt to hide her crimes. She should have been well aware these gifts were unlawful bribes. Brokerage firms train employees. Plus, there had been a recent scandal involving the very same pension fund.

In 2010, former New York State comptroller Alan Hevesi pleaded guilty in a pay-to-play bribery scheme. Among other felonies, Hevesi admitted pressuring managers of the New York pension fund to invest in Markstone Capital Partners, a limited partnership operated by his friend and generous fundraiser Elliott Broidy.

In exchange for Broidy giving $1 million in gifts, trips, and payouts to state officials, Hevesi approved $250 million of the pension fund assets be invested in the Markstone fund. As part of the scheme, Broidy's company earned $18 million in management fees.[34] Broidy pleaded guilty to a state felony involving rewarding official misconduct.[35] He faced a prison sentence of four years. However, somehow, in 2012, Broidy was permitted to withdraw his felony plea. The judge reduced his charge to a misdemeanor and sentenced him to "conditional release." The comptroller was sentenced to four years in jail, but was released after just nineteen months. Broidy would get a second chance as a top Republican fundraiser on Donald Trump's inaugural committee.[36]

This giant bribery scheme was well publicized. It's almost certain Deborah Kelley would have known about it or been warned not to do the same thing. Even so, Kelley (like Broidy) walked away with no jail time. Plenty of room for discretion was available to her judge. Lots of sympathy provided from a future employer. Second chances galore. For those watching this who expect that punishment would have a deterrent effect, the lesson is somewhat murky. This cheater did not exactly prosper. But she did nearly break even. For the morally flexible, her example is not much of a deterrent at all. Risk-averse rule-followers from her social realm may see her ordeal as off-putting, perhaps as a personal disaster. They would not want to follow her path. However, they would clearly see that there would be few consequences for going down a criminal road, and that it pays to participate in a cover-up once caught red-handed.

The problem for us as a society is the lack of effective punishment besides incarceration. If a judge believes jail will do no good because the admitted criminal has learned her lesson, is this really fair to the rest of us? Don't we deserve something for following the law? Especially when the upside of lawlessness is so lucrative, and the downside risks rare and mild.

INJUSTICE SYSTEM

What makes this outcome galling is the contrast between her special treatment and what the less privileged experience in our criminal justice system. What if Kelley had been poor or black, or Latinx, or any or all of the foregoing? It's hard, perhaps nearly impossible, to square the humane handling of an elite felon linked to a criminal matter involving billions of dollars and affecting millions of people with the frequent harsh and unforgiving treatment of offenders with lower social status caught up in small-time hustles.

Rough injustice for those who are not white is not new in America. We can trace that legacy from slavery through Reconstruction to Jim Crow and beyond. Too many treat this as a relic. Yet even after all the gains of the civil rights movement of the 1950s and 1960s, tacit approval of segregated criminal justice in America is largely unchallenged, even as it's made more visible to all. And today, the approving tone from the top is not tacit; it's explicit. We can see this in President Donald Trump's 2017 advice to law enforcement. When arresting suspected members of a Central America–based gang, he told a gathering of police officers, "Don't be too nice." He added, "Like, when you guys put somebody in the car and you're protecting their head, you know, the way you put your hand over? Like don't hit their head and they've just killed somebody. Don't hit their head. I said you can take the hand away, okay?"[37] The dog whistle is heard loud and clear. In addition to the Trump administration's decision not to charge Daniel Pantaleo in the killing of Eric Garner, the president also pardoned adjudicated civil rights violator Sheriff Joseph Arpaio. In 2017, a federal judge in Arizona found Arpaio guilty of criminal contempt of court for refusing to follow another judge's order. Arpaio was ordered to stop unlawfully racially profiling Latinx drivers and turning those without documentation of U.S. citizenship over to federal immigration officials.[38] Within weeks of the conviction, but before sentencing, the president granted the first pardon of his administration—to Joe Arpaio.[39]

CLUB FED

And what happened to white collar criminal Navnoor Kang, the recipient of the multibillion-dollar pension fund bribes? Prosecutors requested he spend decades in prison. Official sentencing guidelines called for at least seventeen years. Yet the judge gave Kang just twenty-one months. The Federal Bureau of Prisons sent him to a minimum-security facility in West Virginia that residents call "Club Fed." Just a few hours outside of Cleveland, the bucolic Morgantown campus is nestled in a valley surrounded by the Appalachian Mountains.[40] Inmates there can play a variety of sports including volleyball and bocce, participate in crafts including crochet and drawing, and order up specialty items from the commissary including sour gummy worms, clip-on sunglasses, and SPF-30 sunblock.[41] Kang was released in January 2020.

By comparison, dealers of crack cocaine—the very substance used to bribe Kang—face long mandatory minimum sentences and are typically housed in locked cells in medium- or higher-security prisons with yards surrounded by double fences or watchtowers and patrolled by guards. Federal judges have less discretion in their sentencing. Crack cocaine dealers once faced mandatory minimum sentences of five years for as little as five grams—what an addict who also deals might use in a day, but there was no mandatory minimum for the same amount of powder cocaine. While now twenty-eight grams of crack triggers the mandatory five-year minimum sentence, today the median federal prison sentence for crack cocaine offenders is more than twelve years, and for powder ten years.[42] Around the time of Kang's indictment in 2016, more than 44 percent of those convicted for federal drug offenses had mandatory minimum sentences.[43] Around half of the federal prison population today comprises people convicted for drug trafficking offenses, and half of that was for cocaine.

There are *no* mandatory minimum sentences for federal crimes commonly committed by white collar offenders. What more dramatic evidence could there be of elite privilege in the justice system? Just around 9,000 people—less than 6 percent of the total federal prison population—are behind bars for extortion, fraud, and bribery combined.[44] The disparity at the state level is even more stark. Of the more than 1.3 million people in state prisons, only 26,000—just 2 percent—are there for fraud.[45]

||||||||||||||||||||||||||||||||||||||||||||||||||

CHAPTER 7

WHISTLEBLOWERS AND JOURNALISTS

D aniel Ellsberg. Mark Felt. Karen Silkwood. Sherron Watkins. Susan Fowler. Whistleblowers. Heroes. Each was in the room where it happened, and each spoke up. They put themselves at great risk to expose crime and treachery in the highest corridors of power.

In 1971, Daniel Ellsberg leaked a multi-volume top-secret Defense Department report on the history of U.S. political and military involvement in Vietnam, known as the Pentagon Papers, to the *New York Times*, *Washington Post*, and *Boston Globe*, among other newspapers. Publishing the Pentagon Papers helped build public opposition to the Vietnam War.[1] President Richard Nixon saw Ellsberg as a threat and wanted to discredit him. With that goal in mind, the White House sent in two loyalists, E. Howard Hunt and G. Gordon Liddy—his "plumbers"—to break into Ellsberg's psychiatrist's office that September, hoping to find information to damage him.[2] A year later these same plumbers, tasked with hunting down leakers, participated in the break-in of the Democratic National Committee headquarters. FBI Deputy Director Mark Felt was the secret source, first known only as "Deep Throat," who provided invaluable information to reporters Bob Woodward and Carl Bernstein about President Nixon's ties to that very burglary at the Watergate Hotel in the summer of 1972.[3] Without Felt's bravery, Nixon may not have been implicated or have resigned in 1974.

Karen Silkwood was a twenty-eight-year-old lab technician at the Kerr-McGee plutonium plant in Oklahoma, where she made fuel rods for nuclear reactors. While employed there, she witnessed worker safety hazards and in September 1974 testified before the U.S. Atomic Energy Commission (now known as the Nuclear Regulatory Commission) about those concerns. Silkwood also discovered that the company was falsifying safety inspection records by retouching X-rays to hide evidence of faulty seals on spent fuel rods, which could lead to dangerous leaks. In November 1974, she was traveling to meet a *New York Times* reporter to share with him a folder full of evidence of safety violations when she died in an automobile accident. Personnel from Kerr-McGee arrived at the accident scene in minutes. The folder was never found.[4] The medical examiner detected extremely high levels of radioactive plutonium in Silkwood's lungs.[5] Two months after Silkwood's death, the AEC began an investigation after confirming it had found evidence to support her claims, including that X-rays of spent fuel rods had been falsified, that on at least one occasion a worker was sent into a dangerous area without being told they needed to wear a respirator to avoid radiation contamination, and that there was no procedure in place to ensure the respirators were functioning properly.[6] The plant closed in December 1975 and other plants had to enact worker safety measures. At trial, the company tried to blame Silkwood for her own contamination. Ultimately, Kerr-McGee settled with her estate for $1.38 million.[7]

Sherron Watkins was an internal whistleblower at Enron. She sent an anonymous letter to CEO Kenneth Lay in August 2001, warning him of massive accounting fraud at the company. "I am incredibly nervous that we will implode in a wave of accounting scandals," she wrote. After identifying herself, she met with him face-to-face. Though she also spoke with a mentor at accounting firm Arthur Andersen, Watkins did not immediately contact the SEC because she said she "lacked a clear path to make that happen." Today, Watkins believes that if whistleblower protections had been stronger, she would have spoken out in 1996, before things got out of hand, and she might have saved Enron. Watkins wrote a comment letter to the SEC in 2019 urging the agency to stop its plan to gut the "bounty fee" rule created under the Dodd-Frank Act to pay awards to whistleblowers who report fraud at their corporations.[8] Since the Office of the Whistleblower was established in 2011, whistleblowers have provided the SEC with more than 22,000 tips and helped the agency recover more than $1.7 billion from wrongdoers.[9] In addition to Watkins, many others opposed the changes, including Democratic senator Ron Wyden from Oregon and Republican senator Charles Grassley from Iowa. In October 2019, the SEC was poised to vote on final rules that would have weakened whistleblower protections, including capping awards,[10] but the meeting was postponed. Hopefully for good.

Given the initial giant $2 trillion relief bill passed by Congress in late March 2020 in response to the coronavirus pandemic that included $500 billion in loans and other support for large corporations, we will need all eyes right near the boardrooms and conference rooms where decisions happen to encourage corporate leaders to be honest, now more than ever.[11]

Software engineer Susan Fowler exposed the unbelievable sexual harassment and culture of gender discrimination at Uber in an epic 2,900-word blog post. Published on her personal website on February 19, 2017, her piece exposed a sexist corporate culture in which the human resources department ignored complaints of repeated sexual harassment of female employees by the same male manager, and falsely told those who complained that it was a first-time innocent mistake. The company treated employees who spoke up against harassment like *they* were the problem. Blame the victims was the approach there. When she tried to get away from her problematic boss, Fowler's internal transfer requests were rejected because having yet another woman leave his team would make him look bad.[12] Her candid post launched an important discussion about rampant sexism in Silicon Valley. She is using her platform to fight for a ban on what's called forced arbitration. This unfair practice makes getting a job (or purchasing a product or service) conditional on agreeing up front to private arbitration to resolve all future legal disputes. In a workplace context, this means giving up the right to bring legal claims in court, including for sexual harassment and for discrimination on the basis of race, color, age, sex, religion, and disability, for example.[13] In 2018, an estimated 60 million Americans were bound by these types of mandatory arbitration provisions at work.[14]

WE THE WHISTLEBLOWERS

From even before the country's founding, American leaders have respected the power of whistleblowers and have helped to incentivize and protect them. Since the colonial era we have had some laws that encouraged ordinary people to come forward with evidence of business crime and to reward and protect them when they do. We've also developed laws to punish those who tamper with such witnesses. But do these laws go far enough?

The most significant whistleblower regime dates back to the Civil War era, as briefly mentioned earlier. In 1863, Congress passed and President Lincoln signed into law the False Claims Act (FCA). This statute provided the very first federal whistleblower protections since the nation's founding. The law goes by many nicknames, including "The Informer's Law" and "Lincoln's Law." The act targeted businesses that were using wartime shortages to overcharge the federal government. In its initial form, the FCA created a private right of action for citizens to sue any company that was defrauding the U.S. government. As an incentive to alert the government to procurement fraud, the whistleblower was given the opportunity to share a percentage of the recovery. However, it was not until 1986 that the law provided protection for employees from retaliation by their employers.[15] In 2014, the high-water mark for False Claims Act settlements, the Department of Justice recovered $5.69 billion, $3 billion of which were cases initiated by whistleblowers.

At the core of the False Claims Act is a provision based on the concept of *qui tam* (pronounced "kwee tam" or "key tam"), shorthand for the more lengthy Latin phrase *qui tam pro domino rege quam pro se ipso in hac parte sequitur,* or "He who sues in this matter for the king as well as for himself." A typical *qui tam* action is a citizen-driven lawsuit to recover money that a business fraudulently obtained from the government. Under the FCA today, the private party, referred to as the "relator," who initiates the litigation is entitled to a portion of the amount recovered.[16] Once the relator files the lawsuit, the Department of Justice can choose to intervene and take over the matter, using its more plentiful resources to litigate the full case, which could include a settlement or trial or some combination. If the government takes control, penalties can go beyond civil settlements to include criminal consequences, including jail time. If the DOJ declines, then the relator can pursue the case independently.[17] To qualify as a relator you do not need to be a victim of the misconduct, or even an employee of the business in question. This is different from cases where ordinary people hope to enforce laws that target business misconduct such as RICO or antitrust matters. For those, a private party only has standing to bring a civil suit if they have been injured.[18] In contrast, the U.S. Supreme Court has affirmed the use of the FCA's *qui tam* provision even where the individual bringing the case has no injury.[19]

REVIVING THE WHISTLEBLOWER LAW

In 1943, Congress amended the False Claims Act to allow the federal government to intervene in *qui tam* lawsuits to dismiss them, and also eliminated the 50 percent bounty fee for relators. These changes destroyed the incentives for people to bring these cases.

The law slumbered until 1983, when former marine Jack Gravitt decided to blow the whistle on General Electric. Gravitt was a foreman at the GE Aircraft Engine plant in Ohio. His supervisors wanted him to submit doctored time cards to make it look like his work on projects for other clients was performed for the contract GE had with the U.S. government to build B-1 bomber engines. The government contract was a cost-plus deal, so his managers at GE were looking to pump up the costs.[20] In some cases, his bosses simply took a dark pen to write the number associated with the B-1 bomber engine job over the actual commercial jet engine job number he'd written on his time cards. When Gravitt resisted participating in this scheme, he was told to "get with the program." Instead of falling in line, Gravitt typed up an eight-page letter and delivered it to the corporate office in Cincinnati. GE fired him the following day.[21]

Gravitt turned to attorney James B. Helmer Jr. for counsel. At the time, the employment law in Ohio provided Gravitt with no recourse. It was an employment-at-will state with no so-called public policy exemptions to an employer's right to fire employees. In plain language, this meant that GE could fire him for any reason other than one that violated a specific statute, such as the law prohibiting age-based discrimination. There was no law that would protect him just for being honest. Helmer began researching and found something "buried" in the money and finance sections of the U.S. Code. He then brought a False Claims Act *qui tam* suit on behalf of Gravitt in federal court in Ohio against GE. This was such an arcane provision that the attorneys at the Justice Department were confused at first when Helmer served the Office of the Attorney General with a copy of the complaint. When faced with the bad publicity, GE tried to deflect responsibility by complaining to the press that this type of litigation was distastefully akin to "bounty hunting." Nevertheless, the Justice Department was intrigued. Using its rights under the updated 1943 version of the statute, the DOJ stayed Gravitt's claim and took up its own criminal investigation of General Electric.

The government wanted to settle with GE for a paltry $234,000, but no one would provide Gravitt with any information backing up the reasons for this proposed resolution. The lawyers at the DOJ threatened Gravitt that if he opposed the settlement, they would block him from receiving his "bounty." They also warned him that he might be stuck reimbursing the government for its legal expenses.[22]

Despite these threats, the judge required the DOJ to share the proposed settlement information with Gravitt. While the negotiations were under way between Helmer and the DOJ, the court lifted the stay and allowed Gravitt to pursue his own civil case. Helmer was able to take depositions (interviews of witnesses under oath) and send official requests for information for documents to the corporation and its employees. These developments were annoying to GE and the DOJ, as they wanted to settle the matter and keep Gravitt, the "relator," out of it. They jointly sought to dismiss his case, arguing that the False Claims Act gave them the right to handle it without the judge's or the relator's approval. Their position basically was: take it up with Congress if you don't like how the law was written. After a lengthy court battle, in early 1989, just before trial, the DOJ, GE, and four whistleblowers including Gravitt settled the case. Not a slap on the wrist now, GE agreed to pay $3.5 million. The whistleblowers divided up a

$770,000 reward. Thanks to the creativity and persistence of Gravitt's attorney, James Helmer, they secured the first *qui tam* recovery in almost half a century.[23]

The experience fighting both GE and the DOJ taught some valuable lessons, mostly that the 1943 statute needed some changes refreshing. U.S. Senate and House committees called Gravitt and his attorney to testify, along with other experts, including John Phillips, the attorney who founded the Center for Law in the Public Interest. After that, in October 1986, President Reagan signed the amended False Claims Act. Between then and mid-2018, attorneys filed more than 10,000 *qui tam* cases under the FCA. As a result of these legal actions, the federal government has recovered more than $53 billion in funds misappropriated by government contractors. Nearly half the states have also enacted their own versions of *qui tam* statutes.[24] In 2009 and 2010, President Obama signed three separate laws passed by Congress designed to better protect whistleblowers.

WHISTLEBLOWERS AND U.S. CORPORATE CRIME

Whistleblowers play a key role in detecting and reporting corporate crime and public corruption. These brave people risk their careers, their financial well-being, their futures, and in some terrible cases, their lives. New protections aren't just a matter of ethics and fair play—whistleblowers are the keys to saving lives and saving money big-time. Given the success of *qui tam* provisions in the recovery of billions upon billions of dollars in government contracting fraud, it would make sense for Congress to expand the law's reach. Why not give standing to employees (or others with knowledge of serious wrongdoing) at all companies that do business in the United States to sue for fraud and then allow the appropriate regulator with jurisdiction to decide whether to take over the case and share the gains with the whistleblower. This would be better than the patchwork of different and complex whistleblower protections set out in federal law now. These are inconsistent, don't cover all businesses or all criminal wrongdoing, and are difficult to navigate.

Such a change would help nip fraud in the bud and help protect courageous, honest employees who often depart quietly or are even fired when they refuse to follow unlawful orders. Wells Fargo allegedly fired employees who refused to open new customer accounts without authorization. And even years after the fake account scandal broke, in early 2019, employees say they felt pressured to rush through deals.[25] Consider Colleen Graham, the former head of compliance at the U.S. unit of Credit Suisse. She recently filed a lawsuit with the Department of Labor alleging that in 2017 Credit Suisse and the data firm Palantir Technologies urged her to help cover up losses related to a joint venture. They allegedly asked her to persuade the auditing firm KPMG to improperly book revenues. Graham said she refused. At first she was bullied: "I was scared for my safety and the safety of my family," she said. Then she was fired.[26] It's no wonder that they thought she might stay silent. During the financial crisis, senior bank executives were known to have pressured and ultimately fired compliance and risk officials and other honest employees who warned of trouble.[27] And, as we know, none of them were held accountable.

JOURNALISTS ON THE BEAT

Investigative journalists—working on their own or closely with government and corporate insiders—are critical to ferreting out and halting white collar crime in action. Without *Wall Street Journal* reporter John Carreyrou, Theranos would still be in Walgreens offering inaccurate blood tests. Without Woodward and Bernstein, Nixon might never have resigned. The tradition of course goes back much further. Without Ida Tarbell's muckraking serial, published as a book in 1904, the government would not have broken up Standard Oil.

Now more than ever, during this elite crime spree, we need more journalists on the beat. Yet the industry is under economic threat. Print journalism has struggled since the rise and ubiquity of the internet and social media. And investigative journalism requires both time and deep expertise, but it is so easily and quickly reproduced by summarizer and aggregator sites that make money faster and cheaper without having to pay the fact finders who do the digging and original reporting.

Economic threats are not the only ones in town. Physical threats to journalists are all too common across the globe. According to the Committee to Protect Journalists, fifty-six journalists were killed throughout the world in 2018.[28] Many more have been imprisoned in retaliation for their writing. Here in the United States, we have been spared this epidemic, until recently. Freedom of the press is more than words on paper, enforceable in our courts. We are proud of these words in our Constitution and in the Supreme

Court decisions that give them effect. But words alone do not stop fists or bullets.

Physical violence against journalists is becoming alarmingly common here. In May 2017, in the lead-up to a special congressional election, tech millionaire and Republican candidate Gregory Gianforte body-slammed reporter Ben Jacobs at a campaign event. This did not stop voters from electing Gianforte to Congress the very next day. Less than a month later, he pleaded guilty to the misdemeanor assault, but was not sentenced to any jail time.[29] Jacobs agreed not to sue the congressman in exchange for an apology and a $50,000 contribution to the Committee to Protect Journalists. In a statement to the court, Jacobs said, "In recent years, our discourse has grown increasingly rancorous and increasingly vile. This needs to stop."[30]

In late June 2018, Jarrod Ramos shot and killed four journalists and a sales assistant in the *Capital Gazette* newsroom in Maryland. His motive? Seven years earlier, the community newspaper had reported on Ramos's harassment of a former high school classmate. He had already pleaded guilty, but the judge suspended his jail time. For years, Ramos sent threatening tweets to the journalists he would later murder.[31] And in October 2018, Cesar Sayoc, a zealous Donald Trump supporter, sent sixteen packages containing pipe bombs to journalists and politicians whom Trump had repeatedly and publicly deemed his enemies. While the explosives were shoddily constructed, experts said they could have detonated, with potentially devastating effects.[32]

But the leader sets the pace. Donald Trump ran his first presidential campaign vilifying the press, and he has continued to attack the media throughout his presidency and current campaign.

Taking a page out of the authoritarian playbook, he mocks, threatens, and undermines journalists simply for doing their job and upholding our constitutional right to a free press. Knowing all he has to hide, President Trump preemptively attacks journalists, anticipating that when they attempt to expose him later, he will have already eroded their credibility in the public's mind. Or he can complain that reporters are just retaliating against him for his previous attacks on them. The ultimate chutzpah. This is no mystery. In a post-election interview in November 2016, journalist Lesley Stahl said that Trump confessed to her that he had no plans to stop attacking the press. "He said you know why I do it? I do it to discredit you all and demean you all, so when you write negative stories about me no one will believe you."[33]

Trump stepped up verbal attacks on the press even after the 2018 *Capital Gazette* murders. He continued to lambast reporters, deeming them "the enemy of the people" and inviting violence. He refused to condemn Saudi Crown Prince Mohammed bin Salman for ordering the barbaric murder and dismemberment of *Washington Post* columnist Jamal Khashoggi in the Saudi consulate in Istanbul, Turkey. Quite the opposite. He lavished praise on the Crown Prince instead. Khashoggi was a Virginia-based writer who had been critical of the Saudi royal family.[34]

He persists. In June 2019, at a joint press conference, President Trump appeared to joke with Russian president Vladimir Putin about the American press being troublesome. He laughed about undermining the press with Putin, an autocrat known to have ordered the poisoning and other assassinations of journalists. At this event, when asked about journalists, Trump said, "Get rid of them." He added, "Fake news is a great term, isn't it? You don't have this problem in Russia, but we do." Putin smiled and replied, in English, "We also have. It's the same."[35] Russia was ranked 149 out of 180 on the Press Freedom Index. And that was before Putin signed the "fake news" law that criminalizes insulting the government online.

OUR FULL SUPPORT

Intimidation of journalists and whistleblowers began well before Donald Trump. However, Trump has taken it to a new level. His vocal contempt for the press is closer to dictators like Adolf Hitler than it is to Richard Nixon, who also hated reporters. As part of his propaganda, the Nazi leader railed against the *Lügenpresse*, or "lying press." We have simply never before seen this level of disinformation and violent, dehumanizing threats made toward journalists and whistleblowers by a U.S. president. After Trump is gone, we will need to redouble legal efforts to protect them. This includes strengthening and expanding laws as well as prioritizing enforcement and funding. Threats to the press and whistleblowers do not have to be violent or explicit to intimidate and silence journalists who are exposing the truth about power.[36]

This is bad on its own, but the American press is also shrinking in numbers for financial reasons. With the explosion of free online outlets for information, much of the most popular content is of extremely poor quality, when it's not outright propaganda. We therefore need to provide better funding and greater independence to public broadcasting, with a new method for funding on a regional basis so that there can be fully staffed local papers of record that can offer free access and attract readers in every major town and city throughout the nation.

We should celebrate the free press. As we should the whistle-blowers among us who are doing what they can to expose criminality and corruption among the most powerful in the private and public sectors. We need these people now more than ever. Speaking out and exposing corruption is necessary, but not sufficient. We need to enhance and expand laws that encourage whistleblowing and protect them once they come forward.

And we need the government to step up to investigate, prosecute, and hold accountable those whose crimes are exposed by journalists and whistleblowers. There is a danger to society when massive corruption and criminality is exposed but remains unpunished.

HIGHER STAKES

The last thing reporter Daphne Caruana Galizia saw was a flash of light. The explosion was so powerful that her Peugeot flew forward across the Bidnija road,[37] crashing into a field more than 250 feet from the blast site. Caruana Galizia died instantly. She was fifty-three years old. Her adult son Matthew heard the explosion and the car horn blaring. He ran to the scene from their nearby home in the remote rural hamlet in northern Malta. He turned to the world community via social media to describe the horror he encountered that tragic afternoon in October 2017. "I looked down and there were my mother's body parts all around me," he wrote on Facebook.[38] Today he still seeks justice for his mother, who was assassinated at the peak of her career as an investigative journalist. Caruana Galizia spent decades exposing the secrets of the powerful, most recently with a satirical blog. For years, those who felt threatened by her words tried to stop her. But she was not easily intimidated. Ultimately, it took a pound of TNT planted under the front seat of her rental car, detonated remotely, to silence her.[39]

The local officer assigned to investigate Caruana Galizia's death was the same detective who, years earlier, had signed a warrant for her arrest. He had come to her home and taken her to the police station. What was the offense? She'd published a satirical post on her "Running Commentary" blog about a candidate for prime minister of Malta—a country that does not protect the press. All it took was for one of the candidate's supporters to file a criminal complaint against her. Upon release from jail the next morning, she immediately returned to her satirical blogging.[40] She was a strong, determined woman. No doubt she fully understood the grave risk she was taking. When her children were small, some people were angry about her reporting. One after another the family dogs were killed. The home was set afire. So she had a wall built around her property.[41]

Caruana Galizia had many enemies on Malta, especially among the political class, as her work centered on exposing public corruption. A few months before her death, she wrote a blog accusing the country's economy minister of visiting a brothel in Germany. He sued her for defamation and got a court order to freeze her bank accounts. She was on her way to the bank to gain access to her money the day she was murdered.[42] Three men have been arrested in connection with her assassination. Two of them frequented a bar with the minister she'd exposed. At the time of her death, Caruana Galizia was drawing on a trove of documents leaked from a Panamanian law firm to investigate corruption in Malta. These were the "Panama Papers," published in 2016 and whose reach would extend far beyond a small Latin American country and a tiny Mediterranean island.

In November 2019, Malta police arrested Yorgen Fenech, a prominent local businessman who ran hotels and casinos on the small island nation, in connection with her murder.[43] Fenech claimed that the prime minister's chief of staff "was involved in ordering the hit," although it is unclear whether he was being truthful.[44] What we do know, though, is that before her death Caruana Galizia was writing about a company called 17 Black Limited in Dubai, which she said was connected to Maltese politicos. Fenech was the owner of that company.[45]

PANAMA PAPERS

Daphne Caruana Galizia was one of hundreds of journalists who'd dipped into a cache of more than 11 million files from Panamanian law firm Mossack Fonseca. In 2015, an anonymous source who referred to himself as "John Doe" leaked these internal files to two reporters for the German newspaper *Süddeutsche Zeitung*.[46] The newspaper teamed up with the International Consortium of Investigative Journalists (ICIJ). Together, they gave over a hundred media organizations access to the leaked files. Journalists then scoured the files and, in April 2016, began publishing investigative pieces exposing the plumbing behind offshore tax havens where the world's multimillionaires and billionaires hide their riches.

The team chose the name "Panama Papers" as an homage to Daniel Ellsberg and his Pentagon Papers. Their initial release in 2016 exposed many rich people, including Americans. One of the most recognized names on the list was Sandy Weill, the former Citigroup chairman and CEO implicated, but never criminally charged, in the "babies and bankers" scandal. According to McClatchy, Weill "appears as a shareholder in two companies—April Fool Ltd. and Brightao Corp. He's the sole shareholder in April Fool, a shell company in the British Virgin Islands," which apparently was connected to his two-hundred-foot yacht called *April Fool*.[47] Owning businesses outside of the United States is not unlawful. However, Americans must report them on their tax returns. Many use these shell companies and related offshore bank accounts to hide assets and evade taxes. Mossack Fonseca was skilled at creating such vehicles.[48]

The power and importance of ten articles authored by these investigative journalists earned the *Miami Herald,* its parent company McClatchy, and the International Consortium of Investigative Journalists a Pulitzer Prize in 2017 for explanatory reporting. Together, the journalists were able to "expose the offshore holdings of world political leaders, links to global scandals, and details of the hidden financial dealings of fraudsters, drug traffickers, billionaires, celebrities, sports stars and more."[49] Mossack Fonseca at one time had "more than 35 locations around the globe, and [was] one of the world's top creators of shell companies, corporate structures that can be used to hide ownership of assets." The volume of shell companies is astounding. This one law firm was involved with more than 200,000 offshore companies in 200 countries across the globe. Mossack Fonseca dissolved in March 2018. Months later, someone leaked another 1.2 million files, covering the time between the initial release and shortly before the firm's collapse. What is also astounding is how many influential individuals were involved. As journalist Michael Hudson wrote in 2017, "The Panama Papers investigation exposed offshore companies linked to more than 140 politicians in more than 50 countries—including 14 current or former world leaders. It also uncovered offshore hideaways tied to mega-banks, corporate bribery scandals, drug kingpins, Syria's air war on its own citizens and a network of people close to Russian President Vladimir Putin that shuffled as much as $2 billion around the world."[50]

The first American identified in the Panama Papers was indicted in December 2018. Richard Gaffey, an accountant from Massachusetts, pleaded not guilty to federal charges out of the Southern District of New York.[51] Gaffey was accused of participating in what U.S. Attorney Geoffrey Berman called a "decades-long criminal scheme perpetuated" by Panamanian law firm Mossack Fonseca. Gaffey and other fellow foreign defendants "allegedly shuffled millions of dollars through offshore accounts and created shell companies to hide fortunes" using "a playbook to repatriate un-taxed money into the U.S. banking system."[52]

On February 28, 2020, Gaffey pleaded guilty to several charges, including conspiracy to commit tax evasion and to defraud the United States, wire fraud, and money laundering conspiracy. His sentencing was scheduled for after this book went to press.[53] Berman promised that with the end of this unlawful international tax

CHAPTER 8

|||||||||||||||||||||||||||||||||||||||||||||||||||

A CONTAGION OF PUBLIC CORRUPTION

On Friday, January 24, 2020, two U.S. Senate committees hosted a private briefing for U.S. senators where Anthony Fauci, the head of the National Institute of Allergy and Infectious Diseases, educated them about a novel coronavirus outbreak in China. The Chinese government had already reported the first death caused by the virus on January 11. The first person confirmed to be infected in the United States was a man in Washington State, who had just returned from Wuhan, China. His case was reported on January 21. By then, only six people worldwide were thought to have died, but experts were worried.

What prompted this briefing that was announced just one day in advance?[1] On January 23, the Chinese government had closed off all of Wuhan, a city of 11 million residents, where the deadly virus was thought to have first emerged. Experts must have seen the markings of a potential global pandemic. But the rest of us did not know that. That day, the president tweeted that "China has been working hard to contain the Coronavirus," and that "it will all work out well." The World Health Organization did not declare this a "global health emergency" until nearly a week later, on January 30. And it was not until February 11 that the disease caused by the coronavirus was given the name COVID-19.

At the time this book went to print, we did not yet know the information conveyed at that private briefing to the senators by Dr. Fauci or by the others who spoke. But we did know that after attending, instead of informing the public to take precautions to avoid the spread of the virus, instead of challenging the president on his ongoing public assertions minimizing the serious health and economic risks we were all facing,[2] several of those senators decided to protect themselves first. Or more specifically, to protect their own assets. Or that's how it all appears.

CORONA CASH OUT

Senate Intelligence Committee Chair Richard Burr of North Carolina had attended the novel coronavirus briefing. On February 7, he published an op-ed reassuring the public about our preparedness for the virus. Then he sold between $628,000 and $1.7 million worth of stock on February 13. This was a liquidation. He cashed out. He did not make any new purchases. By then he was receiving daily updates about the virus.[3] The stocks he sold included Wyndham Hotels & Resorts and Extended Stay America.[4]

The senator had impeccable timing. As it happens, the S&P 500 reached a record high on February 19, 2020, of 3,393. A month later, on March 23, the S&P 500 was down 33 percent to 2,236, wiping out all the gains since the 2017 inauguration. Given the massive multitrillion-dollar government interventions, the stock market is creeping up a bit, but that is of no use to those without investments. Instead, the worrisome prospect of unemployment because of the nearly nationwide stay-at-home and nonessential business shutdown orders were on most Americans' minds.

We know about Senator Burr's transactions because the Stop Trading on Congressional Knowledge Act (the STOCK Act) requires members of Congress (and other government officials, including the president) to report their securities trades within thirty to forty-five days. The Senate voted 96–3 to pass the STOCK Act, which President Obama signed in 2012. Unsurprisingly, Richard Burr was one of the only three to vote against the law.[5]

Another trader was Senator Kelly Loeffler of Georgia. Loeffler announced from her Twitter account on January 24 that she had attended the meeting that day. She wrote, "Appreciate today's briefing from the President's top health officials on the novel coronavirus outbreak. These men and women are working around the clock to keep our country safe and healthy."[6] Then she began dumping stock the Monday after that meeting. The senator and her husband, Jeffrey Sprecher (the chairman of the New York Stock Exchange), sold between $1.275 million and $3.1 million of stock between January 27 and February 14. The couple also purchased $450,000 to $1 million worth of stock in three corporations, including Citrix, a company that sells telecommuting software. Most notable was their purchase of more than $200,000 of stock in DuPont de Nemours, a company that makes personal protective equipment (PPE) for health care workers.[7]

Responding to news accounts questioning her millions of dollars in stock trades, Loeffler tweeted, "This is a ridiculous and baseless attack. I do not make investment decisions for my portfolio. Investment decisions are made by multiple third-party advisors without my or my husband's knowledge or involvement." She also added, "I was informed of these purchases and sales on February 16, 2020—three weeks after they were made." Yet even if it is true that she did not direct the trades, does that matter from an ethical or legal standpoint if she merely told her broker of the dire news and then he just traded on his own? Senator Burr similarly deflected. "I relied solely on public news reports to guide my decision regarding the sale of stocks on Feb. 13," he wrote in a statement. And for him, if he directed the trades himself but acted while in possession of, but not on the basis of, the information he received at the briefing, does that matter ethically? Legally?

On ethics, *New York Times* columnist David Leonhardt captured it well. "They could have made a difference, but they made a profit."[8] As for the law, the statute to consider is the STOCK Act. In addition to the securities transaction disclosures requirements already mentioned, this law makes clear that members of Congress are not exempt from the insider trading prohibitions of our federal securities laws, including Rule 10b-5. As touched on earlier, the law of insider trading is largely made by federal courts. Let's start from the position that we are only looking at trades of stock in companies of which neither senator is an insider. And let's assume that neither senator was given a tip from an insider at any of the companies whose stock they traded. Given those assumptions, the classical theory does not apply. We'd be looking only at the misappropriation theory. Under the misappropriation theory, as the Supreme Court articulated in the *United States v. O'Hagan* case (involving the lawyer from Minneapolis), an outsider who "misappropriates confidential information for securities trading purposes, in breach of a fiduciary duty owed to the source of the information," can be liable for insider trading. But do senators owe such a duty when they are at work?

Yes. The STOCK Act says that for purposes of the insider trading prohibition, members of Congress owe "a duty arising from a relationship of trust and confidence to the Congress, the United States Government, and the citizens of the United States with respect to material, nonpublic information derived from such person's position as a Member of Congress or employee of Congress or gained from the performance of such person's official responsibilities."

Okay. So pulling that all together to decide whether a senator may have engaged in illegal insider trading, you would need to know a lot more about the information they received during that January 24 private briefing. Was it something they got only from their official responsibilities? Was the information not yet available to the public? Was it "material," meaning, was it of the type that would influence the stock price of a company? If you can answer yes to all of these, you'd still have some more questions to address. Did the senators use that information for trading purposes? Finally, while insider trading is a civil offense, it can also be charged as a felony. To establish the crime, you would need to know if they acted "willfully." And things get even more nuanced if we are looking at a tipper-tippee situation.

The law is complex in this area, and none of these parties or their spouses have been accused of wrongdoing. However, according to news accounts, by March the Justice Department was investigating the trading by several members of Congress ahead of the dramatic market downturn. Then, on May 13, 2020, just before this book went to press, the FBI served a search warrant on Senator Burr to obtain his cell phone in connection with the stock-trading investigation.[9]

If not illegal, is it corrupt? Many would say so. Hiding information about public health gained through a position of public trust in order to seek personal financial gain is a textbook example.

WHAT IS CORRUPTION?

In everyday conversation, when you say something is "corrupt," you usually mean that someone is using a position of trust for personal, selfish gain. Sometimes corrupt acts are also crimes, but not always. Typically, we use the term to describe the acts of a public official, but sometimes we also use it to refer to people in a private position of trust, such as a lawyer acting for a client or a guardian tasked with making decisions for someone incapacitated. In each instance, though, corruption arises when a person who is trusted to serve another betrays that trust to advance their own usually financial desires. But corruption is more than that. Like leaking water, it seeps and spreads and corrodes if not contained. The analogy works, since the word derives from the Latin *corruptus*, a form of the verb *corrumpere*, meaning to damage, ruin, spoil, deface, rot, or contaminate.

The following real-life examples of public corruption also happen to be crimes: A school board member solicits and accepts cash and gifts in exchange for voting to approve a contract with a school bus company. A federal customs agent accepts cash to allow a car to drive through without an inspection. A state narcotics agent skims from the proceeds of an illegal drug ring.

But what about this hypothetical? Once elected, a member of Congress meets only with constituents who have made contributions of more than $10,000 to a super PAC supporting him. Most of us would say this congressman is corrupt—and that the system is as well. Some anticorruption experts, though, exclude any sort of lawful campaign spending or lobbying activity from their definition of corruption.[10] However, like Professor Zephyr Teachout, I believe in a more capacious definition of corruption.[11] The Constitution itself includes rules designed to prevent abuses of trust. In her book *Corruption in America*, Teachout explains the importance of a gift that King Louis XVI gave Benjamin Franklin in 1785 upon his departure from France. It was a tiny portrait of the French king held in a diamond-encrusted gold case known as a snuff box. This gift troubled Americans because it "had negative associations of inappropriate attachments and dependencies." Abiding by the rules in the Articles of Confederation (which predated the Constitution), Franklin gained approval from the Continental Congress so that he could keep the bejeweled snuff box. As Teachout explained, this was "no longer in the realm of private reciprocity and relationships, but was instead a regulated transaction."

Regardless of the definition, this much is clear: the United States has a serious corruption problem, and most of us know it. According to a Rasmussen poll from April 2019, 67 percent of voters believe "big businesses and government regulators often work together to create rules that are harmful and unfair to consumers." Fifty-three percent believe "political corruption is a crisis in the United States." And only 17 percent "now trust the federal government to do the right thing most or all of the time."[12]

As we will soon discuss, the Supreme Court led by Chief Justice John Roberts continues to present obstacles to combating the use by public officials of their office for personal gain. The court has done so by adopting too narrow a definition of corruption and by ruling on the basis of theories without sufficient historical, factual, or practical support for their decisions.

PETTY CORRUPTION

News of corruption by elected U.S. officials in the Trump era is so widespread that sometimes the president's closest supporters believe that the immunity from prosecution that he apparently possesses will protect them even from overt criminality. It's easy to be confused. The petty personal details show us just how immune from accountability some believe they are. Clearly, Congressman Duncan Hunter thought he'd never get caught using campaign funds to pay his personal expenses—including funding his children's school tuition, fancy vacations, and at least five extramarital affairs.[13] Or, if he did, maybe he thought he could throw his wife under the bus. Or if that didn't work, perhaps he believed the whole matter would just go away. That strategy worked for others caught up in similar corruption schemes. But his apparent gamble did not pay off. This *New York Post* headline encapsulates the pettiness of the whole affair: "Duncan Hunter's Wife Admits She Bought Plane Ride for Pet Bunny with Campaign Funds." Congressman Hunter pleaded guilty to conspiracy to steal campaign funds in December 2019. A month later he resigned. In March 2020, a federal judge sentenced him to eleven months in prison.[14]

At the risk of repeating myself, this problem with corruption in America did not start with Trump. He is what got extruded from this rigged system, and he promotes and pardons such behavior from those who pay their respects to him. Let's start with the reasons we developed anticorruption laws in America. Then we can consider the tools in the federal law that Congress created—but the courts have undermined. Democracy depends upon citizens having access and influence over the people who make decisions about our lives. In order for those who represent us to create laws and policies and distribute public funds in a way that serves our needs, they need to actually know what we need. They cannot read our minds. We need to communicate. Our rights under the First Amendment to engage in political speech, including petitioning the government for a redress of grievances, is an essential part of that communication process.

Representative democracy also depends, then, on ensuring that those who occupy offices of public trust act for the common good, not for their own personal financial or political gain. This makes sense. Even if we have the right to speak our mind and articulate for our leaders what our wants and needs are, if officials are being paid off by big benefactors, they won't listen to us or act on our behalf. The law seeks to draw a line between legitimate and illegitimate efforts to influence public officials in their roles as our representatives. As Teachout has noted, historically this has meant taking measures to prevent not just quid pro quo corruption, but also to prevent those in public office from succumbing to human instincts to want to favor those who have been generous. Some would not like to admit it, but we do know that people will, whether consciously or unconsciously, make official decisions in favor of those who can provide or have provided some personal benefit, even if there is no actual agreement or acknowledged explicit link between the personal benefit and the official act. Everyone knows which side their bread is buttered on.

THE DULLING EFFECT OF THE COURTS

Prosecuting public corruption became a top priority in 1976 when the Department of Justice established the Public Corruption Unit. Joining up with "Main Justice" at headquarters to create this unit were four U.S. Attorneys' offices, including the historically independent Southern District of New York. While the desire to root out corruption was there, the tools were soon dulled. In 1999, with *United States v. Sun-Diamond Growers of California*, the Supreme Court began to defang the main federal bribery statute, 18 U.S.C. §201, which defines two distinct offenses: bribery and gratuity. Although both crimes center on giving or receiving something of value in connection with an official act, each is directed at a separate bad act. Bribery is the more serious offense, punished by up to fifteen years in prison. It is defined as corruptly attempting to influence a public official in the performance of official acts by giving or offering them something of value. In this context, "corruptly" means having an improper motive or purpose. Correspondingly, it is also bribery for the public official to demand, request, or receive a thing of value in exchange for an official act. In contrast, the anti-gratuity provision forbids giving something of value because of an official act—like leaving a tip on the table. But instead of a restaurant table, it's a congressman's office table.

Sun-Diamond was a trade association that marketed and lobbied for individual growers and sellers of figs, walnuts, prunes, raisins, and hazelnuts. The association gave agriculture secretary Mike Espy around $5,900 in gratuities, including tickets to the 1993 U.S. Open Tennis Tournament, luggage, meals, a framed print, and a crystal bowl. Although Secretary Espy was acquitted, a jury convicted Sun-Diamond, the D.C. Circuit overturned this verdict, and the Supreme Court agreed to hear the appeal. In the unanimous decision penned by Justice Antonin Scalia, the court affirmed the Circuit Court holding, that in furnishing these expensive gifts to Secretary Espy, Sun-Diamond did not violate the anti-gratuity statute. As Scalia explained, in order to sustain a conviction, the government needed to prove a link between the valuable items and a specific official act performed by the secretary.[15] Here, the indictment failed to even allege such a link. However, the indictment did note that at the time the gifts were bestowed, Sun-Diamond had sought the secretary's assistance with matters of importance to its members. The decision was huge news in D.C. Joan Biskupic wrote in a front-page story in the *Washington Post*, "The court set a higher bar for prosecutors trying to make a case against people lavishing gifts on officials."[16]

The opinion quite clearly told Congress how to solve the problem and prevent this type of behavior if it cared to address corruption. In it Scalia pointed to several other statutes that outlawed outright payments, regardless of the purpose. For example, there's a law that forbids any executive branch employee from receiving any "supplementation" of their salary. There's a law prohibiting bank employees from giving bank examiners loans or gratuities, again regardless of the purpose. He also noted that the Labor Management Relations Act forbids an employer from giving anything of value to a union or union official regardless of intent, subject to minor exceptions (such as for contributing to pension funds). The statute could be fixed by removing the words "for or because of any official act performed or to be performed," thereby making the Sun-Diamond type of gifts illegal. As written, the law required a linkage. Donald Smaltz, the independent counsel who argued the case for the government, made the same point. "For those who believe that no one should be allowed to give gifts to public officials to purchase goodwill or curry favor," he said, "any future refinement of this law must come from Congress, or from the Office of Government Ethics, whose regulations govern the behavior of governmental officials in the Executive Branch."[17]

What does all of that mean? It means that if Congress had truly been concerned about its own corruption, it could have imposed, via statute on itself, the same sorts of gift prohibitions that it had imposed on labor union representatives, bank examiners, and executive officials. But Congress did not. It is a shame, because it could have easily changed both the anti-gratuity provision and the anti-bribery provision. It's not too late, though, and the next decisions show that the need to act is even more urgent.

AN INFLAMMATORY DECISION

That brings us to the June 2016 Supreme Court decision in *McDonnell v. United States*.[18] The opinion was also issued by a unanimous court. (This time, though, it was 8-0 since Scalia had died in February and Republican Senate leader Mitch McConnell had blocked any consideration of President Obama's nominee.) The facts of the case are damning, but the law was very forgiving. In January 2014, Virginia governor Robert McDonnell was indicted on numerous charges alleging conspiracy, honest services fraud, Hobbs Act extortion, and false statements. All of these charges stemmed from the governor's accepting $175,000 in loans, gifts, and other benefits from Virginia businessman Jonnie Williams.

What was in it for Williams? He was the CEO of the Virginia-based company Star Scientific, which developed and sold what he said was a nutritional supplement made from a compound found in tobacco. Through his company, Williams hoped to obtain FDA approval for this supplement, Anatabloc. Williams claimed the tobacco compound anatabine worked as an anti-inflammatory. However, there were no independent scientific studies to support the claim that it had any health benefits. That's why he needed help from the governor. Williams wanted public universities to conduct those studies using grant money from Virginia's tobacco commission. And he hoped Governor McDonnell would assist.

How did Williams grease the wheels? The specific details ripped right from the pages of the Supreme Court decision are better than any summary.

> Governor McDonnell first met Williams in 2009, when Williams offered McDonnell transportation on his private airplane to assist with McDonnell's election campaign. Shortly after the election, Williams had dinner with Governor and Mrs. McDonnell at a restaurant in

New York. The conversation turned to Mrs. McDonnell's search for a dress for the inauguration, which led Williams to offer to purchase a gown for her. Governor McDonnell's counsel later instructed Williams not to buy the dress, and Mrs. McDonnell told Williams that she would take a rain check.

However, that was not the end of the gift-giving story, of course. It continued in 2011:

Governor McDonnell's wife, Maureen McDonnell, offered to seat Williams next to the Governor at a political rally. Shortly before the event, Williams took Mrs. McDonnell on a shopping trip and bought her $20,000 worth of designer clothing. The McDonnells later had Williams over for dinner at the Governor's Mansion, where they discussed research studies on Anatabloc. . . .

Williams returned to the Governor's Mansion for a meeting with Mrs. McDonnell. At the meeting, Mrs. McDonnell described the family's financial problems, including their struggling rental properties in Virginia Beach and their daughter's wedding expenses. Mrs. McDonnell, who had experience selling nutritional supplements, told Williams that she had a background in the area and could help him with Anatabloc. According to Williams, she explained that the "Governor says it's okay for me to help you and—but I need you to help me. I need you to help me with this financial situation." Mrs. McDonnell then asked Williams for a $50,000 loan, in addition to a $15,000 gift to help pay for her daughter's wedding, and Williams agreed.

There were vacations:

In July 2011 the McDonnell family visited Williams's vacation home for the weekend, and Governor McDonnell borrowed Williams's Ferrari while there. Shortly thereafter, Governor McDonnell asked Dr. [William] Hazel [the Virginia secretary of Health and Human Resources] to send an aide to a meeting with Williams and Mrs. McDonnell to discuss research studies on Anatabloc.

And the gifts kept coming:

At a subsequent meeting at the Governor's Mansion, Mrs. McDonnell admired Williams's Rolex and mentioned that she wanted to get one for Governor McDonnell. Williams asked if Mrs. McDonnell wanted him to purchase a Rolex for the Governor, and Mrs. McDonnell responded, "Yes, that would be nice." Williams did so, and Mrs. McDonnell later gave the Rolex to Governor McDonnell as a Christmas present.

This silver Rolex was engraved with her husband's initials. In addition, Williams provided the McDonnells loans to help with the "struggling Virginia properties," rounds of golf for the family, and $10,000 as a wedding gift to one of the McDonnell daughters.

In the indictment, the government claimed that all of these

gifts were in exchange for the governor's "performing official actions on an as-needed basis, as opportunities arose, to legitimize,
promote, and obtain research studies for Star Scientific's products."
Here's what the governor did to help Williams. After the election,
Williams told the governor that he wanted to move his research
forward and asked to be introduced to the people who could help
him. With the governor's introduction, Williams met with Secretary Hazel. McDonnell also sent Hazel more information suggesting protocols for a study of Anatabloc by the Medical College of
Virginia and the University of Virginia School of Medicine.

At trial, the judge instructed the jury that to convict Governor
McDonnell, they had to find that he agreed "to accept a thing
of value in exchange for official action." As noted above, the acts
alleged in the indictment included arranging meetings, hosting
events, and contacting other government officials for Williams.
There was a quid pro quo, it seemed. But that was not enough. The
valuable gifts had to be given in exchange for an official act. The
federal prosecutors contended that the help the governor provided
to Williams were official actions because they related to Virginia
business development, which was a priority of the governor. Their
argument convinced the jury, who convicted McDonnell on the
honest services fraud and Hobbs Act charges. The governor appealed the case all the way up to the U.S. Supreme Court. The
legal issue before the court was whether "setting up a meeting,
talking to another official, or organizing an event (or agreeing to
do so)—without more" qualify as an "official act" under the federal bribery statutes.

The Supreme Court said no. Nothing the governor did for Williams was an "official act." This decision had effects well beyond

just the extortion law under which the state governor had been charged. It also impacted the bribery statute that applies to federal officials only.

Here's why. When prosecuting the governor, instead of limiting their legal analysis to the actual statutes that covered him, the prosecution and defense went broader. They agreed to define honest services wire fraud with reference to the bribery statute, 18 U.S.C. §201—even though that law did not apply to the governor because he was not a federal official. They also agreed that an element of Hobbs Act extortion was obtaining a "thing of value . . . knowing that the thing of value was given in return for official action"—even though the Hobbs Act itself does not contain any of that language. Finally, both sides agreed that for the Hobbs Act extortion allegation, they would use the definition of "official act" found in 18 U.S.C. §201 (again, even though that law that did not apply to him). Because the governor's case turned on that law's meaning, this opinion undermined that law, too. This dulled the main bribery statute—the tool prosecutors use when they go after federal officials who are on the take.

Though Justice Scalia was not involved in the *McDonnell* decision, his words from the *Sun-Diamond* case seventeen years earlier still provided a solution. Congress can just change the law and ban gifts above a set value and be done with it.

In May 2020, the court dealt a further blow to law enforcement's efforts to address public corruption. In *Kelly v. United States*, the court overturned the convictions of two aides to former New Jersey governor Chris Christie who were involved in the Bridgegate scandal. The federal wire fraud and federal program fraud statutes did not apply, because although they acted deceptively, they did not personally obtain money or property when on behalf of the Port Authority of New York and New Jersey they deliberately diverted bridge traffic to retaliate against the mayor of Fort Lee.

BIG DIRTY MONEY IN POLITICAL CAMPAIGNS

Long before the *Citizens United* decision in 2010, the U.S. Supreme Court set the stage for the overwhelming flood of big money, both corporate and personal, in political campaigns. In 1976, in *Buckley v. Valeo,* the Supreme Court first equated money with political speech.[19] The case was brought by a group led by U.S. senator James Buckley from New York against Francis Valeo, who was a member of the newly created Federal Election Commission (FEC). In that decision, the court struck down limits on independent spending by wealthy individuals. However, it upheld limits on direct contributions by individuals to candidates and campaigns. The court justified drawing a line between direct giving to campaigns and "independent" spending by claiming that independent spending would not create the potential for corruption. The court wrote, "We find that the governmental interest in preventing corruption and the appearance of corruption is inadequate to justify [the law's] ceiling on independent expenditures."[20] The court found a First Amendment right in independent spending by individuals, writing, "A restriction on the amount of money a person or group can spend on political communication during a campaign necessarily reduces the quantity of expression by restricting the number of issues discussed, the depth of their exploration, and the size of the audience reached."[21]

In taking this action, the Supreme Court undermined the spending limits set in the 1974 amendments to the Federal Election Campaign Act that Congress had passed after the Watergate scandal. The *Buckley* decision and other actions by the FEC opened the door to what was called "soft money," where political parties spend funds on efforts not linked to individual candidates by collecting unlimited funds from corporations and unions to pay for those soft-money expenditures. To rein this in, in 2002 Congress passed the Bipartisan Campaign Reform Act, also known as McCain-Feingold. This law banned soft money for political parties, created disclaimers and disclosure requirements, and, most important, set limits on corporate and union spending. Under McCain-Feingold, corporations and unions were subject to two major spending prohibitions. The law forbade them both from paying for communications that were considered "express advocacy." It also prohibited corporations and unions from funding "electioneering communications," which meant "any broadcast, cable, or satellite communication" that referred to a candidate for federal office made within thirty days of a primary and sixty days of a general election. The Supreme Court started chipping away at this law in 2007 in *Federal Election Commission v. Wisconsin Right to Life*, when it held that issue ads that do not mention or identify a candidate were permissible even if they ran in those special time frames before elections.[22]

But the Supreme Court took its biggest stride toward permitting corrupt money in politics when it decided *Citizens United v.*

Federal Election Commission in 2010, on a 5–4 vote. Not only had the court by then determined that money was speech in the context of political campaigns, but it had already, in numerous previous decisions, affirmed that corporations had constitutional rights, including under several amendments.

One thing to note. While you may hear folks say that the court declared in *Citizens United* that corporations are people, that is not accurate. The majority decision characterizes the corporation as an aggregation of its owners. Because they saw a corporation as a group of owners, they reasoned these individuals should not relinquish the rights under *Buckley* to spend unlimited amounts to influence elections, simply because they joined together as a corporation. There's a lot wrong with this assessment. To begin, corporations are complex enterprises where all sorts of people interact, including employees, customers, and suppliers. Even if we were to define a corporation as an aggregation of owners, some corporate shareholders are not actual people but are instead big entities such as banks and other types of corporations. In addition, some shareholders are foreign nationals who on their own do not have rights to spend in U.S. elections. And Citizens United, the party that brought the suit, was actually a nonprofit organization with members (called a "social welfare organization"), not a business corporation. The court could have easily found for Citizens, permitting it to run its anti-Hillary movie by declaring that the independent expenditure limit was unconstitutional as applied, as they were a nonprofit promoting a movie, not running a true advertisement. But no, the majority struck down the corporate spending ban altogether without showing much concern for the details. Justice Anthony Kennedy, writing for the majority, asserted that the court "thus rejected the argument that political speech of corporations or other associations should be treated differently under the First Amendment simply because such associations are not 'natural persons.'"

Then came *SpeechNow.org v. Federal Election Commission*.[23] Just two months after the *Citizens United* ruling, the federal appeals court for the District of Columbia made matters worse. The court struck down all limits on contributions to political action committees (PACs) if they made no direct contributions to candidates. Before that, individuals and corporations had strict limits on how much they could give to a PAC, as the PAC would use those funds to contribute directly to candidates. In response, the FEC announced that it would permit unlimited contributions to independent expenditure–only PACs (so-called super PACs) from individuals, corporations, and unions. While super PACs must reveal their donors to the public, thanks to SpeechNow, they can receive donations from so-called dark money conduits that take in money from social welfare organizations (structured like Citizens United) that do not have to reveal their own donors. Super PACs of this type and others can spend unlimited funds to expressly promote the election or defeat of particular candidates. And it's near impossible to figure out where the money that makes it to the advertisements actually originates. If that was not discouraging enough, in 2012, in *American Tradition Partnership, Inc. v. Bullock*, the Supreme Court made clear that *Citizens United* applied to states as well when it struck down a Montana law designed to prohibit corporate spending in Montana elections.[24]

Next, the Supreme Court tackled aggregate spending limits. In 2013, wealthy businessman Shaun McCutcheon joined up with the Republican National Committee. McCutcheon was unhappy that he could only spend $123,000 in total contributions to all federal candidates he supported nationwide during a two-year election cycle. In *McCutcheon v. Federal Election Commission* in April 2014, the court struck down the aggregate limit in a 5–4 decision. As a result, McCutcheon and everyone else with millions of dollars at their disposal has a much louder voice than the rest of us—even in states where they do not reside. Effective immediately, instead of the $123,000 aggregate limit on all contributions to candidates, any individual could then give nearly $2.5 million to individual candidates in aggregate and around $1.2 million to political parties in an election cycle—in other words, nearly $4 million in direct contributions. These numbers have since gone up.[25] And we should not forget that for those itching to flood our elections with more money than even these generous aggregate limits on direct contributions allow, they can still spend unlimited amounts if they do so independently, whether as an individual (thanks to *Buckley*) or a corporation (after *Citizens United*).

What was the justification for erasing the aggregate limit? Chief Justice John Roberts favored a very narrow definition of corruption. Referencing *Citizens United*, Roberts wrote, "Ingratiation and access . . . are not corruption." The court ruled, "Any regulation must instead target what we have called 'quid pro quo' corruption or its appearance." He elaborated, "Spending large sums of money in connection with elections, but not in connection with an effort to control the exercise of an officeholder's official duties, does not give rise to quid pro quo corruption. Nor does the possibility that an individual who spends large sums may garner 'influence over or access to' elected officials or political parties."

It's as bad as it sounds. The only good thing to say about this astonishing decision is that four justices dissented.

CAPITAL VS. LABOR ALL OVER AGAIN

Many probusiness folks who defend *Citizens United* claim it's fine and fair because it puts unions and corporations on equal footing. But it turns out they are not. Some suggest that corporate funding can be balanced out by union funding. There's a lot to say about how this has little to do with individual free speech rights, but it's most important to point out that in all the related cases before and after *Citizens United*, the Supreme Court has put unions at a decided disadvantage relative to corporations.

Prior to the decision, unions were required to allow members to opt out of political spending. In contrast, corporate shareholders are not given that right under the law. Furthermore, after the 2018 Supreme Court decision in *Janus v. AFSCME*,[26] the imbalance is more pronounced. In *Janus*, the court disregarded its own precedent in overturning the 1976 decision in *Abood v. Detroit Board of Education*. Under the *Abood* holding, if a majority of public-sector workers (in that case public schoolteachers) in a bargaining unit voted to unionize, then all employees (the teachers) in the bargaining unit had to pay "fair share fees," even if they did not choose to join the union. Allowing them to skip out on those dues would encourage "free riding," where the nonunion employee would gain from the salaries, benefits, and workplace conditions the union negotiated for them but without contributing to the cost of securing them. The petitioner who dealt a blow to public-sector unions this time was Mark Janus, an employee with the Illinois Department of Healthcare and Family Services. Janus claimed that he did not want higher wages and benefits and disagreed with the union's position seeking them for him in light of a fiscal crisis in the state of Illinois.[27] Justice Samuel Alito, writing for the five-justice majority, said the union "may no longer extract agency fees from nonconsenting employees [because this] procedure violates the First Amendment and cannot continue."[28]

FOREIGN INFLUENCE

Foreign money—from Russia, Ukraine, Saudi Arabia, wherever—making its way into our election process: we read about it all the time and you can be forgiven for just throwing up your hands and thinking it's inevitable and unstoppable. It's not. And, once again, it's not just Donald Trump, though he was the clear benefactor in the 2016 election, in his inaugural campaign funds, and perhaps now in his 2020 campaign. The focus here is just how the Supreme Court decisions, taken together, and for which *Citizens United* is a helpful metonymy, invited dark and dirty foreign funds and influence into our elections.

To be clear, even the Supreme Court has affirmed the constitutionality of the current ban on foreign spending in U.S. elections, including both direct contributions and independent expenditures by foreign nationals. The lawsuit *Bluman v. Federal Election Commission* was initiated in 2011 by Benjamin Bluman (a Canadian citizen) and Dr. Asenath Steiman (who had dual Canadian and Israeli citizenship), both of whom lived lawfully in the United

States. Bluman wanted to make direct contributions to several political candidates, and planned to use his own money to print and circulate flyers in New York's Central Park in support of President Obama's reelection. Steiman wanted to contribute to Republican candidates, to the National Republican Senatorial Committee, and to the Club for Growth (an independent conservative advocacy group). Bluman and Steiman filed their case in the D.C. District Court alleging that the part of McCain-Feingold that banned them from these activities was unconstitutional under the First Amendment. The district court dismissed the complaint.

On appeal, the D.C. Circuit Court ruled in favor of the FEC, confirming that banning foreign nationals from contributing directly to political parties, candidates, and advocacy groups (that use contributions to spend in elections) and from using their own money independently on express advocacy was constitutional. The court wrote in November 2011: "It is fundamental to the definition of our national political community that foreign citizens do not have a constitutional right to participate in, and thus may be excluded from, activities of democratic self-government. It follows, therefore, that the United States has a compelling interest for purposes of First Amendment analysis in limiting the participation of foreign citizens in activities of American democratic self-government, and in thereby preventing foreign influence over the U.S. political process."[29] In January 2012, the Supreme Court summarily affirmed the D.C. Circuit's decision in a four-word ruling: "The judgment is affirmed."[30]

Still, after *Citizens United,* foreign money has flooded our elections. This is due to loopholes as well as the complex networks that reach invisibly across national boundaries—the way the global economy operates today. As the Center for Responsive Politics, the nonprofit that runs the Open Secrets project, explained, "Foreign nationals are barred from contributing to federal committees. However, a foreign corporation's U.S. subsidiary is allowed to contribute to outside spending groups such as super PACs as long as no foreign national directs the contribution."[31] In short, whether lawfully or unlawfully, we welcome foreign funds into our elections (and political system), which are already corrupted. Moreover, we apparently are happy laundering funds that stem from criminal activity abroad. These concepts are not separate.

Ellen Weintraub, the former FEC chair, addressed this very concern in a June 2019 letter to Senate Judiciary Committee chair Lindsey Graham and ranking member Dianne Feinstein in connection with a hearing on "Combating Kleptocracy: Beneficial Ownership, Money Laundering, and Other Reforms." Weintraub did not appear as a live witness but provided her expert views in writing. She wrote, "I am particularly concerned about the risk of illicit funds and foreign support influencing our political system. Foreign dark money represents a significant vulnerability for American democracy. We do not know the extent to which our political campaigns receive foreign dark money, but we do know that political money can be weaponized by well-funded hostile powers." In her letter, Weintraub provided an example from the 2016 election. "In a recent enforcement action, the FEC levied record fines against a super PAC and a number of individuals—including foreign nationals—that orchestrated the donation of $1.3 million from foreign nationals to a super PAC supporting a 2016 presidential candidate." That candidate was Jeb Bush. She noted, "These contributions were funneled into our political system through a foreign-owned subsidiary operating in the United States." But there's nothing Weintraub can do about dark money now.

By early May, just before this book went to press, only three of the six seats on the Federal Election Commission were filled. The FEC has been operating without a policymaking quorum since September 1, 2019.[32] Without a quorum of four, the commission—responsible for enforcing our election laws and regulations—can't make enforcement decisions.[33] Of course, nothing was stopping Donald Trump from appointing new members, with Senate approval, to fill those seats. In an election year, for someone who valued the rule of law and wanted free and fair elections, this would be a priority. But we're dealing with President Trump, who has been caught several times welcoming foreign interference in our elections and who prosecutors say directed his incarcerated former personal attorney Michael Cohen to engage in campaign finance fraud. Remember "Individual 1"?[34] For him, there's no good reason to have a functioning FEC.

In March 2020, the president nominated Trey Trainor to fill a seat on the FEC. What is his background? Trainor, an election lawyer from Texas who publicly supported secret spending in elections,[35] served as counsel for the Trump presidential campaign and in the Trump administration.[36] At his confirmation hearing, Senate Minority Leader Chuck Schumer argued against rushing to fill the seat. "The record of the nominee we have before us—Mr. Trainor—raises significant questions about his fitness to carry out the commission's anti-corruption mandate," Schumer said. Afterward, Senate Majority Leader Mitch McConnell said he was "optimistic we'll be able to move forward with this nominee."[37]

WELCOMING KLEPTOCRACY

The United States is a money laundering mecca. Our legal system, corporate law firms, and accountants are eager to turn blood money into gold. Or pricey, clean real estate. Or shiny cars and yachts. To best illustrate this, we will begin with the revelations from hidden-camera footage from a 2014 undercover operation that nonprofit Global Witness shared on the CBS show *60 Minutes* in January 2016. The many hours of full video footage are available on their website.

Posing as a German citizen named Ralph Kayser, an investigator from Global Witness phoned fifty New York City law firms with practices in private asset protection. His pitch was designed to raise flags as it was based on a real money laundering case. After those phone calls, Kayser was able to secure in-person meetings with sixteen attorneys (at thirteen firms) in their New York offices. He claimed to represent an official from a poor "mineral-rich country in West Africa" who had collected millions of dollars in "special payments." He said these payments to the government official came from foreign companies seeking to secure valuable rights to extract the country's minerals. Kayser used the phrase "facilitation money" to describe what appeared to be bribes. This fictitious African minister wanted to purchase a $10 million brownstone, a $20 million Gulfstream jet, and a $200 million yacht. He explained in each of the meetings that "it would look at least very embarrassing" if the official's name were associated with these purchases. Given that the minister had a salary equivalent to that of an

American schoolteacher, these purchases, if done in his name, would look suspicious.

Fifteen of the sixteen lawyers provided ideas to Kayser as to how to bring these funds into the United States and invest them while keeping the client's name undetected. One of those lawyers was then president of the American Bar Association, James Silkenat. He suggested that some smaller U.S. banks might not be as vigilant about the "know your customer rules"—meaning that Kayser might wish to use banks that violate their obligations and reporting requirements under the Bank Secrecy Act. Silkenat also suggested banking in jurisdictions with more permissive laws than the United States in terms of seeking details "on ownership and source of funds."

Several of the plans involved offshore or domestic entities where the beneficial owners—the real people hiding behind the shell companies—did not need to be disclosed. Some schemes then involved having one of those shell companies buy the townhouse or jet in the United States with the help of the law firm. While the lawyers showed some concern about proceeding, one lawyer, who initially said he did not want to be seen as "laundering money," suggested that the dirty money be wired directly to a bank account he maintained for client funds. Another lawyer suggested the use of a straw man so that when the money moved from the West African country, the minister would no longer be identified. As Global Witness indicated, none of these lawyers violated the law. "A number, including Mr. Silkenat, indicated they would need to carry out more checks before they could take our investigator on as a client. Mr. Silkenat also indicated that he had to make sure that no crimes had been committed and, if so, would have to report them."[38]

Of all the attorneys with whom he met, only one, Jeffrey Herrmann, refused to provide any guidance or assistance in the meeting. Even though Kayser assured him that no American nationals were involved, so the Foreign Corrupt Practices Act might not be triggered, Herrmann refused to continue the conversation. "It's not for me. It's not for me," he said after realizing bribery was involved.[39]

Existing U.S. law does not require the lawyers to report these suspicious activities to the government. Had the lawyers been bankers, though, they would have been obligated to do so. As the investigation made clear, it is quite easy to set up a shell company in a U.S. state without listing an address or the owner's name. More than 2 million such shells had been set up the previous year alone. British anticorruption activist Charmian Gooch, cofounder and board member of Global Witness, explained that, in many states, it's harder to obtain a library card than to set up a shell company. Former UN secretary general Kofi Annan praised the group's work: "By highlighting the importance of transparency, Charmian Gooch and Global Witness have moved global business towards better, fairer, more sustainable practices."[40]

This particular scheme made the TV news and the papers, but in general too little attention has been paid to the way homegrown white collar criminals right here in the United States use a maze of anonymous shell companies to disguise their misdeeds. As Manhattan district attorney Cyrus Vance Jr. wrote in a 2012 op-ed, "My office, time and time again, finds its criminal investigations thwarted by an absurd system of secrecy whereby criminals can hide their money."[41]

COMBATING KLEPTOCRACY

The Senate Judiciary Committee hearing on "Combating Kleptocracy" in June 2019 was refreshingly bipartisan. Democratic senator Sheldon Whitehouse of Rhode Island explained how "America enables global corruption." He said he was sponsoring a bill called the True Incorporation Transparency for Law Enforcement (TITLE) Act, which would obligate states to require corporations and LLCs formed in their jurisdictions to disclose their true owners.[42] Senator Whitehouse laid out the problem starkly. "America too often enables global corruption" by providing leaders, including Russian, who loot their countries, "the shelter of our rule of law for their ill-gotten gains." Referencing the revelations of the Panama Papers, Whitehouse said, "whole industries" in America including law firms, Realtors, title companies, shell companies, and financial services firms "cater to international crooks and kleptocrats." Republican senator Lindsey Graham of South Carolina explained how the use of shell companies to hide beneficial ownership facilitates money laundering, noting that the Russian Internet Research Agency had used money laundering to pay the trolls who interfered in the 2016 election. Senator Graham said that the United States was becoming "second only to Switzerland" for parking illicit money, noting that the U.S. is more desirable for hiding money now than even the Cayman Islands. Whitehouse agreed that American institutions were part of a "kleptocratic racket."[43]

One hearing witness, attorney Adam Szubin, a former Treasury Department official, now with New York–headquartered international law firm Sullivan & Cromwell, said that criminal enterprises can easily set up shell companies in the U.S. and use them "to move dirty money here and abroad with little fear of detection." In fact, the United States is "one of the world's biggest problems" when it comes to shell companies," he said. "We have to make it as hard as possible" for criminals to move money into the United States. He told the Senate committee that he opposed anonymous business structures that allow parties to hide their identities and sources of ill-gotten gains and evade taxes. Szubin explained that wealthy criminal enterprises are drawn to legitimate businesses as they need to invest their illicit funds in real estate, securities, hotel chains, horses, and other high-priced property. "What they really want is opacity. They want the ability to invest in things without having to disclose who they are."[44]

To solve this problem, he said the "single most impactful step" that Congress could take to combat foreign money laundering and terrorist funding would be a law requiring disclosure to the government of true ownership information as companies are formed. Disclosure would help honest businesses and assist law enforcement. If law enforcement can trace the illicit foreign money, then they can identify and freeze the asset. Another witness, Tom Firestone, a former Justice Department prosecutor and a partner at Baker McKenzie who chairs the law firm's North American government enforcement practice, testified that the Foreign Corrupt Practices Act was failing to restrain bribery solicitations or acceptance of bribes by foreign officials. He said it would help corporate employees resist a shakedown if they could tell the foreign official seeking a bribe that not only will I be prosecuted if I pay your bribe, but you will as well.

Sheila Krumholz, the executive director of the Center for Responsive Politics, focused specifically on the need for transparency in the context of U.S. elections. While our campaign finance law bans foreign nationals from directly or indirectly funding our elections, these forbidden funds nevertheless make their way in through the use of shell companies. This unauthorized foreign money goes into campaigns and inaugural committees through a complex network of anonymous LLCs and offshore bank accounts. Krumholz added that, in 2018, more than $539 million in spending was reported to the Federal Election Commission by dark-money groups that do not fully disclose their donors. She urged lawmakers to make the United States "the leader on this issue." She said, "We cannot ignore these weaknesses."

Emphasizing that this is a bipartisan issue, Krumholz added that these evasions have "eroded public trust" in our system. Foreign dark money poses a threat to our sovereignty and national security. She agreed with Senator Whitehouse that when money flows in from "Boris and Natasha LLC," the public does not know who is behind it. However, the beneficiaries of dark-money spending are aware of the original source, which makes the aspiring politician or already elected officials vulnerable to foreign influence.

WINNING THE SHELL GAME

The government is aware that shell companies are used to launder money through all-cash purchases of expensive homes in major city centers. In response, in January 2016, the Financial Crimes

Enforcement Network (FinCEN), a bureau within the U.S. Treasury Department, issued an order seeking information from title insurance companies that would help detect this type of money laundering.[45] The order was part of a pilot program focused on cash sales of high-end homes, ones that sold for at least $1 million in Miami-Dade and $3 million in Manhattan. With cash sales, there's no bank involved, so no Bank Secrecy Act reporting. These transactions are hidden from view. To get a window in, FinCEN ordered title companies to collect and divulge the names of buyers behind shell companies used to pay for homes in cash. This meant the names of individuals who own at least 25 percent of the equity in the LLC or other purchasing entity.

Prior to the pilot, in one of the markets, Miami-Dade, shell companies and other business entities purchased more than $111 million in residences in a typical week there in cash transactions. This was 29 percent of all residential sales. Once the pilot began, Miami-Dade experienced a 95 percent decrease in all-cash purchases of homes by these entities. These cash sales have remained flat since then.[46] The Treasury Department extended the program in July 2016, issuing a new order covering these areas: all boroughs of New York City; Miami-Dade, Broward, and Palm Beach counties in Florida; Los Angeles, San Diego, San Francisco, San Mateo, and Santa Clara counties in California; and Bear County, Texas (which includes San Antonio). Through this more expanded study, FinCEN discovered that 30 percent of these cash transactions involved some questionable buyers. That is to say, they were made by beneficial owners or purchaser representatives that banks had previously flagged in a suspicious activity report."[47] It was renewed again in 2017. Then, in 2018, FinCEN quietly extended and expanded the program to Boston, Chicago, Dallas–Fort Worth, Honolulu, Las Vegas, and Seattle.[48] Along the way, the definition of "all cash" was expanded to include wire transfers, personal and business checks, cryptocurrencies, and virtual payments.

Illicit cash will run to other markets outside the pilot and return to real estate after it ends. To prevent this from happening, Congress should require that all-cash transfers of real estate or personal property over a certain dollar amount (perhaps $100,000) be reported by either the title company (in the case of real estate) or the broker (in the case of artwork or other brokered goods), or if unbrokered by the person who takes the cash as payment.

In October 2019, the Democratic-controlled House voted 249–173 to pass the Corporate Transparency Act, a bill sponsored by Democratic congresswoman Carolyn Maloney from New York. Only twenty-five Republicans supported the bill, and five Democrats opposed.[49] This law would amend the Bank Secrecy Act to require corporations and limited liability companies to disclose, on an ongoing basis, their beneficial owners to FinCEN.[50] There are more than 2 million LLCs in America, and in many states, most notably Delaware, those who establish LLCs do not have to disclose ownership information to the secretary of state. Under the proposed law, reasonable exemptions are provided for businesses that are clearly not shell companies (for example, charities, insurance companies, banks, and businesses that employ more than twenty employees or are large publicly traded corporations). A similar bill is currently languishing in the Republican-controlled Senate. This is a shame, because there's clear evidence that the United

States is becoming a global money laundering haven where the world's oligarchs and criminals send their ill-gotten wealth to be cleaned.

This must be a global effort. Anticorruption advocates recommend disclosure of beneficial owners globally, ideally on a public register. Louise Russell-Prywata, program manager at OpenOwnership, asserts, "If we want to stem the tide of money laundering through corporate vehicles, then public registers of every company's 'ultimate beneficial owners' (UBOs) are an important part of the solution."[51] OpenOwnership, with backing from organizations including the World Bank, is working to develop the technology that would facilitate this transparency by creating a Beneficial Ownership Data Standard.[52] The database now has more than 7 million UBOs registered.

These are just a few ideas on how to stop the United States from acting as a money laundering haven—a crucial step alongside the need to better enforce our existing tax laws, create laws that empower more whistleblowers, and create a special division within the Justice Department to focus on elite crime. However, the people who control the levers of power do not want this change. And it is increasingly difficult to actually vote them out of office. The problem of public corruption and related post–*Citizens United* expansion of money in politics has brought us to this place. It may take a constitutional amendment to turn things around.

||||||||||||||||||||||||||||||||||||||||||||||||||

CHAPTER 9

SUSPICIOUS MINDS

At the end of a fifty-six-day trial, before federal judge Simeon Lake sent the jury off to deliberate the fate of Enron executives Ken Lay and Jeff Skilling, he gave them the following instruction: "You may find that a defendant had knowledge of a fact if you find that the defendant deliberately closed his eyes to what would otherwise have been obvious to him. While knowledge on the part of the defendant cannot be established merely by demonstrating that the defendant was negligent, careless, or foolish, knowledge can be inferred if the defendant deliberately blinded himself to the existence of a fact."[1]

This is known as a "deliberate ignorance" or "deliberate indifference" instruction. Enron prosecutors asked the judge to read these words to the jury. This type of guidance helps prosecutors convince jurors that the defendants acted with a guilty mind even when there is no evidence presented to actually connect all the dots. Given that written confessions rarely exist, jurors in all sorts of criminal cases are often told to draw inferences from the circumstantial evidence to figure out what the accused knew and intended. Even the concept of drawing inferences needs explaining. Lawyers sometimes tell jurors, "If you see the green grass on your lawn before you go to bed and wake up to find it covered in snow, though you did not witness the snowfall, you can reasonably infer from the circumstances that it snowed."[2] Yet things get much more complicated when dealing with complex financial matters.

If the prosecutor shows a video of someone sprinting out of a store clutching a flat-screen television and security guards chasing behind, it's not so hard for a jury to infer what they intended. As white collar crime expert Professor Peter Henning explained, "In murders and cocaine cases, you don't have people saying, 'Hey, nobody told me this was illegal,' but here you do things like set up special purpose entities, and what turns it into a crime is the intent." It takes more work and clarity for a prosecutor to get jurors to the point where they understand enough about accounting fraud or misleading investors to be comfortable determining that an executive knew the books were cooked. Certainly, prosecutors during the accounting fraud era were capable. Why didn't they use the same laws to try the bankers after the 2008 meltdown for accounting fraud?

Why is intent so hard to prove? What counts as proof of a criminal defendant's state of mind? And beyond what a court would allow, what convinces a jury? It's complicated and unpredictable. But to take a jury inside a defendant's thinking requires finesse and experience. This is something, as Jesse Eisinger explains in his book *The Chickenshit Club: Why the Justice Depart-*

ment Fails to Prosecute Executives, prosecutors have lost the skill to perform. Consider the Martha Stewart trial. Jurors found her guilty of conspiracy, obstruction of an agency proceeding, and false statements in connection with her sale of stock in ImClone Systems, a biopharmaceutical company, right before the stock price dropped. She was not actually prosecuted by the DOJ for insider trading, because there was no evidence that she knew of the material nonpublic information about ImClone (that the FDA was poised to reject the company's cancer treatment). Instead, there was only evidence that Stewart had learned from her stockbroker that the ImClone CEO had sold his shares. But when questioned about it, she lied to the FBI and the SEC. In terms of proving her "corrupt" intent for the obstruction charges and that she "knowingly and willfully" made the materially false statements, the jury had to draw inferences of her state of mind from the evidence presented. How did they do that? Henning said, "There is no way of knowing in advance where the tipping point is on intent," but with Martha Stewart, the jurors were influenced by that fact that a friend testified against her and that her assistant had cried.[3]

Yet, of late, concerns about proving intent are often offered up as an excuse for not prosecuting corporate wrongdoers. *There just wasn't enough proof of intent.* As previously noted, that's what the Justice Department said in 2011 when it failed to prosecute any high-level bankers after the 2008 financial crisis.

So why not prosecute? Civil settlements are easier, because if the SEC, for example, took a case to trial, they would only need to convince the jury that the defendant most likely violated the law. But if the DOJ brought the defendant to trial in a criminal case, based on the same wrongful actions, the prosecutors would have to prove each element beyond a reasonable doubt. It's very tough to prove beyond a reasonable doubt that a white collar defendant acted with a guilty mind. Often this means the government must prove they acted knowingly and willfully. Sometimes just willfully. But what does that mean? When it comes to convicting someone for making a false statement to a government agency, for example, the "knowingly" element means the defendant knew the statement was false. The "willfully" element means they made the statement deliberately and with the specific intent to communicate false information. However, there's no requirement that the prosecutor prove the defendant knew about the false statement law itself[4] or knew the false statement would be communicated to a federal agency.[5] For other laws, willfully could mean something different. There are many variations for the "guilty mind" element. And through those cracks in the law slip many a white collar criminal, let off with a negotiated settlement and free to continue their business.

SEE NO EVIL

But there are some crimes in the areas of public health and safety and environmental protection for which the Supreme Court and Congress have made it unnecessary to prove the defendant acted with a guilty mind. Imagine if we could extend this kind of standard to executives in banking and other industries that benefit from a taxpayer-backed safety net yet escape responsibility for their sometimes criminal conduct.

The responsible corporate officer (RCO) doctrine allows the

prosecution of responsible business managers for misdemeanor criminal violations without having to prove they were involved in or knew about the unlawful acts. The RCO doctrine was first recognized by the U.S. Supreme Court in 1943 in *United States v. Dotterweich*. In that case, the court upheld the conviction of a pharmaceutical company president for introducing misbranded and adulterated drugs into interstate commerce in violation of a provision of the Federal Food, Drug, and Cosmetic Act—the same law used to convict Purdue Pharma and its executives when they initially pleaded guilty in 2007. In the *Dotterweich* saga, the Buffalo Pharmacal Company purchased drugs from manufacturers, then placed its own labels on the containers and sent them to others. At times, employees slapped on labels with inaccurate information about the drugs inside, a violation of the FD&C Act. While the jury did not agree to convict the corporation, it did convict Dotterweich, the company's president, on three counts. Afterward, he was fined and sentenced to probation.

The 5–4 Supreme Court majority upheld his conviction, asserting that the government does not even need to show knowledge of the wrongful conduct in order to find that person guilty of a misdemeanor violation of the FD&C Act. Instead, the question was about status, not conduct. Namely, whether the individual had "a responsible share in the furtherance of the transaction."[6]

Justice Felix Frankfurter, who penned the opinion, explained his reasoning in the context of the law's history. Noting that the statute was strengthened through amendments in 1938, Justice Frankfurter wrote that the law was an attempt to "touch phases of the lives and health of people which, in the circumstances of modern industrialism, are largely beyond self-protection."[7] He went on to say, "Such legislation dispenses with the conventional requirement for criminal conduct—awareness of some wrongdoing. In the interest of the larger good, it puts the burden of acting at hazard upon a person otherwise innocent but standing in responsible relation to a public danger."[8]

This opinion was groundbreaking. It was also quite upsetting to justice Frank Murphy, who wrote the dissent and saw it as unjust to "extend liability" to a corporation's "officers who have no consciousness of wrongdoing." He was alarmed that there was "no proof or claim that" Dotterweich "ever knew of the introduction into commerce of the adulterated drugs in question, much less that he actively participated in their introduction. Guilt is imputed to the respondent solely on the basis of his authority and responsibility as president and general manager of the corporation."[9] Yes, it was.

In 1975, this time in a 6–3 decision, in *United States v. Park*, the Supreme Court revisited the RCO doctrine, reaffirming the holding in *Dotterweich*. In this case, Acme Markets and its CEO, John Park, were charged with violating the FD&C Act. The government alleged that food shipped from the Acme warehouse in Baltimore had been contaminated by exposure to rodents. Acme was a giant business with "approximately 36,000 employees, 874 retail outlets, 12 general warehouses, and four special warehouses." Before prosecutors brought the criminal case, the Food and Drug Administration sent a letter to Park in 1970 alerting him to unsanitary conditions in Acme's Philadelphia warehouse. A year later, the FDA conducted a twelve-day inspection of the Baltimore warehouse and found "evidence of rodent infestation and other insanitary conditions." A few months later, there was another inspection in Baltimore, which showed some improvements but also "evidence of rodent activity in the building and in the warehouses" as well as "some rodent-contaminated lots of food items."

While the corporation pleaded guilty, Park did not, and the jury convicted him. He appealed. Park, whose office was located a hundred miles away from the Baltimore warehouse, at company headquarters in Philadelphia, believed he was "not personally concerned in this Food and Drug violation" and thus could not be criminally responsible. The Supreme Court disagreed. In the opinion authored by Chief Justice Warren Burger, the court asserted, "The rule that corporate employees who have 'a responsible share in the furtherance of the transaction which the statute outlaws' are subject to the criminal provisions of the Act was not formulated in a vacuum." It was vital to hold "criminally accountable the persons whose failure to exercise" their "authority and supervisory responsibility." The court reasoned that "the public interest in the purity of its food is so great as to warrant the imposition of the highest standard of care on distributors." The fear of this punishment would inspire vigilance and keep the public safe. Citing an earlier decision, in the case of business regulation, even though the accused does not "will the violation," he usually is in a position to prevent it with no more care than society might reasonably expect and no more exertion than it might reasonably exact from one who assumed his responsibilities."[10]

Importantly, the court once again was willing to impose criminal liability even in the absence of "awareness of some wrongdoing" or "conscious fraud." With status came responsibility, the court asserted. Burger wrote, "The requirements of foresight and vigilance imposed on responsible corporate agents are beyond question demanding, and perhaps onerous, but they are no more stringent than the public has a right to expect of those who voluntarily assume positions of authority in business enterprises whose services and products affect the health and well-being of the public that supports them."[11] Hear! Hear!

So what is necessary, then, to hold a CEO or other officer criminally liable, at least in the case of food or drug adulteration? And why aren't the Sacklers, even as owners, being hauled up under these charges? Here are those requirements. To begin, the government does not have the burden of establishing a "wrongful action." Instead, the court held that "the concept of a 'responsible relationship' to, or a 'responsible share' in, a violation of the Act indeed imports some measure of blameworthiness." What the government does need to show is that "the defendant had, by reason of his position in the corporation, responsibility and authority either to prevent in the first instance, or promptly to correct, the violation complained of, and that he failed to do so." In short: "The failure thus to fulfill the duty imposed by the interaction of the corporate agent's authority and the statute furnishes a sufficient causal link."[12]

When I interviewed several former federal prosecutors who had tried a substantial number of cases in their tenure, not a single one had brought an RCO case. It was just not something they were taught about on the job, and law schools rarely offer courses on corporate crime. That said, some prosecutors have applied RCO principles to criminal violations of the federal securities laws, antitrust laws, and environmental laws, although these cases are rare. As one expert noted, "The common thread amongst these prosecutions is that the statute under which the government seeks to impose liability is public welfare-centered."[13] Notably, some environmental protection laws, such as the Clean Water Act and the Clean Air Act, contain specific language stating that "responsible corporate officers" can be held liable.

BAD EGGS, GOOD LAW

In 2010, an estimated 56,000 Americans contracted salmonellosis after consuming contaminated eggs later traced to facilities operated by Quality Egg, a company run by Austin "Jack" DeCoster and his son Peter. A later criminal investigation revealed Quality Egg had falsified food safety records and lied to auditors for years. In 2014, Jack and Peter DeCoster pleaded guilty in federal court, in their role as "responsible corporate officers" of Quality Egg, to misdemeanor violations of the FD&C Act for introducing the contaminated eggs into interstate commerce. In 2015, the district court judge sentenced each of them to three months' imprisonment and fines of $100,000. On appeal, the Eighth Circuit upheld the sentences, deciding that jail time did not violate their constitutional rights to due process or the prohibition on cruel and unusual punishment. The case was watched closely. When the Supreme Court declined to hear the appeal, in May 2017, it was clear that the RCO doctrine was alive and well.

While the DeCoster appeal was pending, in 2016 a federal judge in Georgia sentenced Stewart Parnell, the owner and head of Peanut Corporation of America, to twenty-eight years in prison. A jury found Parnell guilty in 2014 of introducing adulterated food into interstate commerce after a 2009 salmonella outbreak that may have killed nine and sickened more than seven hundred people in forty-six states. Unlike the DeCoster case, this one did not rely on the RCO doctrine. These were felony convictions involving extensive proof that defendants had fabricated certifications claiming the peanut butter was safe even though tests indicated it was contaminated.[14] He was also convicted on many other counts, including conspiracy and obstruction of justice.[15] The judge also sentenced Parnell's brother Michael to twenty years in prison for his role in selling the tainted peanut butter to Kellogg's for use in its packaged crackers. Even a lower-level quality control employee received a five-year prison sentence in connection with her conviction for obstruction of justice. The company was small-time compared to Purdue Pharma, with just $25 million in annual sales, and it had gotten away with bad practices for years. At the time the criminal investigation began, Parnell was serving on the U.S. Department of Agriculture's Peanut Standards Board.

A GUILTY MIND

Given the power of the responsible corporate officer doctrine, it's no wonder that certain business interests wish to trim it back. In November 2015, the Republican-controlled House Judiciary Committee passed a measure that could greatly undermine laws intended to punish—and deter—white collar crime. If enacted, it would have also weakened the standard legal tools federal prosecutors have deployed for more than a century, including against legendary con men from Charles Ponzi to Bernie Madoff. Given the fast and furtive manner in which the provision was pushed forward, few legal experts had the opportunity to assess the impact these changes might have for law enforcement and for victims.

The language under consideration was vague, yet could have had a broad impact—and it is likely to reappear someday, so it is worth analyzing. In an instant and blanket fashion, the law would have eliminated the use of the RCO doctrine. It would also have made it more difficult to deploy the mail fraud and wire fraud statutes.

Fortunately, opponents vocally challenged the proposal, claiming it would damage public health and safety. The changes would also encourage business executives to remain willfully blind to criminal conduct at their enterprises and deliberately uninformed about how to comply with federal laws and regulations governing their industries. The Justice Department expressed strong opposition. Spokesman Peter Carr explained that it "would create confusion and needless litigation, and significantly weaken" laws such as "those that play an important role in protecting the public welfare, including protecting consumers from unsafe food and medicine."[16] Additionally, President Obama expressed his objections and threatened to veto it. Thankfully, it did not advance. A White House official had warned: "If the bill became law, a terrorist could only be found guilty for using a weapon of mass destruction if he specifically knew his victims were going to be U.S. nationals, a killer could only be found guilty of certain firearm crimes if he knew the gun traveled in interstate commerce, and a white-collar criminal could only be found guilty of bank fraud if he knew he was robbing a bank that was [insured by the FDIC]."[17]

What was particularly suspicious about this pro-corporate-criminal language was that it was attached to a progressive bill supported by people who had been fighting for decades to reform the criminal justice system to address racial inequality and mass incarceration of the least powerful in society. The overhaul was supposed to focus on expunging criminal records for juvenile offenders and reducing penalties for low-level, nonviolent drug offenses.

Most troublesome, though, was that the proposed changes were at odds with the prevailing excuse for not holding any high-level bankers criminally accountable for their role in the financial crisis. Namely, how hard it supposedly was to prove intentional conduct. Lurking behind the scenes were conservative groups, such as the Heritage Foundation, that were trying to leverage "sentencing reform" to achieve what they call *mens rea* (or "guilty mind") reform. They have argued that droves of "morally blameless" individuals are imprisoned when they "unwittingly" commit acts that later turn out to be criminal.[18] The timing was quite odd, law professor and *Why Not Jail?* author Rena Steinzor reflected at the time. "People die for preventable reasons every day in America and the vast majority of corporate managers responsible for such episodes escape even a hint of criminal charges," she wrote. "We don't have a white-collar overcriminalization problem in this country. We have an undercriminalization problem."[19]

‖‖

CHAPTER 10

TAX AND PUNISH

Around the time the FBI added Willie Sutton to the Ten Most Wanted Fugitives list in 1950, a reporter asked him why he robbed banks. Sutton famously responded, "Because that's where the money is." Years later, in his 1976 autobiography, Sutton claimed that he did not actually deliver that now legendary response. But, he added, if asked, he would have. "That's what almost anyone would say," he wrote. "It couldn't be more obvious."[1] When holding up banks and jewelry stores, Sutton brandished a submachine gun, but never fired a shot. The threat of force alone was enough to get what he wanted.[2]

The IRS, the Justice Department, and Congress could learn from Willie Sutton. The IRS should audit the rich, because that's where the money is. The DOJ should investigate and prosecute wealthy tax evaders, because that's where the crime is. And Congress should close loopholes for hedge fund managers and impose higher tax rates, including a wealth tax for the 1 percent. Because that's where the inequality is. This "follow the big money" approach when it comes to auditing is obvious even inside the government. The independent inspector general for the IRS recommended in a 2015 report that the IRS crack down on the highest of the high earners. To paraphrase the tax-lingo-laden report, when reviewing tax returns for those who earn more than $200,000 per year, auditors should spend much more of their time on the very highest-income tax filers. Specifically, people who earn $5 million or more per year annually.[3]

FOLLOW THE MONEY

Good advice, but the IRS failed to heed it. The agency was busy trying to survive budget cut after budget cut. Its 2019 budget was around $2 billion lower than in 2009. Along came layoffs, with 30,000 fewer employees at the IRS by 2020.[4] Fewer auditors meant fewer audits. The agency lost out on collecting at least $18 billion per year. If the goal is compliance and collecting revenue, the cuts were so very foolish. But that $18 billion is just what the IRS, and thus the U.S. Treasury, is losing due to budget cuts. In fact, the government is leaving so much more money on the table. There's something called the "tax gap." This is a calculation the IRS makes to figure out the difference between what it should be collecting each year and what it actually brings in through tax receipts. In 2018, the tax gap was as much as $800 billion.[5]

After adding it all up, investigative journalists Paul Kiel and Jesse Eisinger of ProPublica noted in 2018, "Corporations and the

wealthy are the biggest beneficiaries of the IRS' decay."[6] Unbelievably, audits of the top earners, including those who bring in more
than $5 million per year—the most cost-effective to audit—have
fallen by around 80 percent. Pressure is off the wealthy. As a result, the very lowest earners—those who bring in $20,000 or less
per year of personal income—are just as likely to be audited as the
top 1 percent.[7] But only about 3 percent of the annual tax gap is
owed by these low earners.

It's unfair having "two tax systems in this country," as U.S. senator Ron Wyden, an Oregon Democrat, put it in 2019. The IRS is
now "ignoring wealthy tax cheats while penalizing low-income
workers over small mistakes." Wyden is a member of the Senate
Committee on Finance, which oversees the IRS. Under the status
quo, the senator lamented, "while the wealthy now have an open
invitation to cheat, low-income taxpayers are receiving heightened
scrutiny because they can be audited far more easily. All it takes is
a letter instead of a team of investigators and lawyers."[8]

People who work at the IRS agree with the senator's assessment. It's much more difficult to audit the wealthy, and especially
those who are attempting to legally avoid or criminally evade
taxes. Auditing Americans with money in offshore tax havens can
be the most difficult and time-consuming. On average, it can take
three years to finish. Yet staff face pressure to hit their numbers in
terms of cases closed, not revenue collected. As one former employee explained, "If you're not churning out the exams, you have
to explain why you're not."[9] The agency is so understaffed that
it has fallen behind on the lowest of the low-hanging fruit—
collecting from people who file their returns but have not yet paid
what they owe. After ten years, the IRS can no longer pursue

these delinquent accounts. In 2017, $8.3 billion of the tax debt expired. *Poof.* Back in 2010, before the budget slashing began, only $540 million expired.

Former IRS commissioner John Koskinen is not a foolish man. He begged and pleaded for funding. But now he is gone. The new IRS commissioner, Charles Rettig, is more reticent. During an April 2019 hearing before the Senate Finance Committee, Senator Wyden asked Commissioner Rettig to come up with a plan within thirty days to change the double standard, a system that is "stacked in favor of the wealthy" but "against the most vulnerable." [10] A year later, no such report had been provided. [11]

In January 2020, the picture was even bleaker. Incensed by the fresh IRS report revealing audit rates were their lowest in forty years, [12] Senator Wyden said, "The bulk of tax avoidance and fraud comes from corporations, pass-through business and those at the top." This was no accident. It was "by design." The architects, he said, were Republicans, who "have been on a decade-long crusade to gut IRS enforcement." Frankly, this was a case of "allowing the wealthy and well-connected to steal from taxpayers with no consequences." [13]

One part of the solution would be funding the IRS at 2010 levels or better, stepping up audits, and imposing civil penalties. But this is not enough. Only with a higher probability of a criminal indictment and some prison time will tax evasion end. For that, the Department of Justice must bring prosecutions. Furthermore, the system as it is, even before we get to any kind of enforcement, already furthers tremendous inequality. And the recent tax changes make it even worse.

TAX THE RICH

Taxing the rich is very popular. The vast majority of Americans even support the simple statement "Tax the rich." The organizers of the Tax March learned this through a professional poll and through anecdotal encounters on a summer 2019 bus tour. I attended one. There a volunteer dressed as Monopoly Man stood in the shade at the edge of Military Park in Newark, New Jersey. He was a welcome addition to the small group of activists and curious passersby on a hot day in mid-July. Newark was stop number fourteen on the nationwide journey. The Tax the Rich tour took off in Miami and finished in Detroit. As the team traversed the country, they held rallies in and spoke with the residents of Jacksonville, Columbia, Charlotte, Washington D.C., Phoenix, Las Vegas, Des Moines, Milwaukee, Chicago, and Louisville. Attendees opposed the Tax Cuts and Jobs Act of 2017—also known, among the Tax March team, as the Trump Tax Scam.[14] This law, which provided major tax cuts for wealthy Americans and corporations, was signed into law when both houses of Congress and the presidency were under Republican control.

The Tax March group was initially formed in early 2017. Frustrated by the failure of the new president to share his tax returns with the public as he had promised during the campaign, I and other cofounders organized a march in Washington D.C. and also helped support and inspire gatherings of more than 120,000 people in more than 150 locations nationwide on Tax Day—April 15. Whether Donald Trump's tax returns will see the light of day now depends upon the justices of the U.S. Supreme Court.[15] During oral arguments that were held on May 12, 2020, by telephone and broadcast live to the public, it seemed that a majority would rule against Trump at least in the case he brought against New York district attorney Cy Vance. In that case, the president seeks to block Vance from obtaining from Trump's accounting firm eight years of his personal and corporate tax returns. The court is expected to issue an opinion in June, after this book goes to press. The bigger goal for the Tax March movement, though, is the aim of having the wealthy pay their fair share so we can have a society that serves all of us, not just the few at the top.

What a swindle. Promise tax breaks and prosperity for all. Instead, deliver trillions of dollars in cuts for billionaires and big business. The rest of us should not hold our breath waiting for that mythical trickle-down effect. It's not coming. Already, 72 percent of Americans believe their taxes either went up or stayed the same thanks to the so-called tax cuts, according to a poll conducted by the *Wall Street Journal* and NBC in spring of 2019. Only 17 percent believed their taxes will go down. The reality is that while the top 1 percent received on average $51,000 in tax savings, for low earners the cuts were so small as not to be noticed.[16]

The bill's champions promised the cuts would pay for themselves through economic growth. But they didn't.[17] The economy grew 2.9 percent in 2018, which was the same rate as in 2015,[18] and just 2.3 percent in 2019. Even before the coronavirus crash, growth was expected to slow over the decade to an average of 1.7 percent.[19] Despite these lackluster results, the Republicans keep moving the goalposts. The plan's architect, Congressman Kevin Brady of Texas, said it may take the full ten years to figure out whether it worked.[20]

Supporters also said that businesses would use the tax savings from the 2017 law to invest in employees. Again, they didn't.[21] Instead, businesses used the extra cash to buy back stock from shareholders. The first year set records of more than $1 trillion in stock buybacks. So much for promised spending.[22] That put cash in the hands of the investor class—it did not help put food on the table for workers. Republican lawmakers claimed the law would help the average American, but predictably, instead, it will raise taxes on 92 million middle-class Americans.

The 2017 tax giveaway was expected to cost around $1.9 trillion by 2027, according to the Congressional Budget Office. Imagine if we had directed that money to where the greatest need is, not the greatest greed. We could have provided affordable childcare and pre-K to all families for a decade. But that's not all. Child poverty would have been eliminated during that period of time. After doing both, we could have also raised teachers' wages in low-income area schools by $10,000, doubled the amount of government funding for climate science, invested $100 billion fighting the opioid epidemic, and directed $60 billion toward community colleges.[23] All of that for ten years. Instead, we are faced with tremendous budget cuts, forcing the slashing of vital programs we all value, and that was before the pandemic arrived.

Worse than that, tucked into the legislation was language to kill part of the Affordable Care Act (Obamacare). Now, according to the Congressional Budget Office, 13 million people would lose their health insurance.[24] For the Republicans, ripping away health insurance was a feature, not a bug. This was how they could justify giving their wealthy campaign donors the tax cut they demanded. Did they even blink an eye knowing that to justify this tax cut they needed to show that 10,000 extra people would die per year? Instead of voting no to prevent these deaths, the Republicans said the government would save money because with thousands dying early year after year, less would be paid out in Social Security benefits, for example.[25]

BACK AT THE TROUGH

For the large corporations that had already gained the most from the federal tax giveaway, it was not enough. In early 2018, before the tax cuts came into effect, corporate lobbyists descended on the Treasury Department demanding more. They targeted the parts of the law that made them pay a bit more. Even though they had a lower tax bill ahead, they wanted to pay even less. According to sharp investigative reporting by Jesse Drucker and Jim Tankersley of the *New York Times*, "The crush of meetings was so intense that some top Treasury officials had little time to do their jobs."[26]

Then came the coronavirus. In March 2020, the country faced the beginning of a major recession. For the week ending March 21, 3.3 million Americans filed for unemployment benefits. That was an all-time high. The highest number of claims filed previously had been in October 1982, with 695,000 jobless claims. Though that record level for March 21 was shocking, the following week was even more unbelievable, with 6.6 million additional filings. That was a total of 10 million people filing for unemployment benefits in just two weeks.

First in line for a bailout were the very corporations who, as part of the relief package, now have access to a slush fund of more than

$500 billion. Many of the firms on the ropes, including the airline industry, paid back billions of dollars to shareholders through stock buybacks when times were flush.

And even after trillions were poured in to prop up the financial markets and businesses through congressional and Federal Reserve actions, for the vast majority of Americans who depend on wages to survive, life got much worse. We reached 14.7 percent unemployment by early May—the highest it's been since 1940. By then, more than 36 million people had filed for unemployment in just eight weeks. Things were most dire for the lowest of earners. In May, Fed chairman Jerome Powell announced that an astonishing 40 percent of people living in households earning less than $40,000 per year lost a job in March. Yet, despite this bleak picture, Congressional Republicans said they were done. No more relief packages. All they sought was legal protection from lawsuits brought by employees and customers against businesses that opened up during the pandemic. Why are we not surprised?[27]

CLOSE THE LUCRATIVE LOOPHOLES

At some point soon, ideally as part of this recovery effort, we need to end the tax law inequities and close the very lucrative loopholes that give the 1 percent special advantages over the rest of us. Most people know about the unfair fact that wages are taxed at a much higher rate than profits earned on investments (known as capital gains). Even billionaire Warren Buffett rails against the reality that he pays a lower tax rate than his secretary does. Less familiar is something called the "carried-interest loophole." This concept may be obscure to some of us, but it's at the white-hot center of tax reform debates. In simple terms, this "loot" hole allows money managers to pay half the taxes they should on the huge cut of the profit they take from pooling together and investing other people's money. Instead of paying the top tax rate of 37 percent on everything they earn over around $520,000, they only pay 20 percent. Break that down to real numbers. Let's say a rich private fund manager clears $10.52 million for himself. He saves $1.7 million in personal taxes. But the numbers are so much bigger. The top twenty-five hedge fund managers in 2018 together earned $15.38 billion, or, on average, $615 million each.[28] Thanks to the loot hole, the public loses more than $2 billion in tax receipts from just twenty-five people. Altogether, there are 3,000 to 5,000 fund managers who benefit from this special treatment.[29]

Even candidate Trump promised to address it. On the campaign trail in 2015 and 2016, he regularly promised to close the loophole. "The hedge fund guys are getting away with murder. They're making a tremendous amount of money. They have to pay taxes." Yet as soon as he was elected, he surrounded himself with financiers, bankers, and money managers, many of whom made a killing using the carried-interest loophole.[30] He selected as a close adviser Stephen Schwarzman, the billionaire leader of Blackstone Group, one of the world's largest private equity fund firms. Years earlier, when the Obama administration was looking at carried interest, Schwarzman lashed out. Making moguls pay their fair share of taxes was "war," he insisted. "It's like when Hitler invaded Poland in 1939."[31] Though he would later apologize for drawing this distasteful analogy, Schwarzman was right in a sense.

The white men in his world had built a special realm, richer than kings, and they saw their own government as a hostile invader.

But with Trump in office, despite the noises he'd made to pretend he was a champion "of forgotten men and women of our country"[32] and that he would tax the "hedge fund guys," there were no worries for Wall Street. Treasury Secretary Steven Mnuchin, a loophole man himself, assured his fellow financiers at a conference in the first year of the administration, "I know this issue is incredibly important to everyone in this room."[33]

It's nice work if you can get it. Take over struggling companies, pay yourself big fees just for completing the purchase, then lay off workers, and have the company file for bankruptcy. Make out like bandits. And after that, still gain special tax treatment. Why? Because you throw around money gained this way and make sure Congress does not close this loophole. Special tax treatment should be justified by good policy reasons. Still waiting to hear one.

‖‖‖‖‖‖‖‖‖‖‖‖‖‖‖‖‖‖‖‖‖‖‖‖‖‖‖‖‖‖‖‖‖‖‖‖

CHAPTER 11

THE SIX FIXES

America, we have a big dirty money problem. The corporate crime, elite impunity, and public corruption disease did not infect us overnight, though. We've been exposed now for so very long that we are almost immune. Almost. If you still get angry when you see prosperous predators get away with it, we still have a chance to fight back. I'm ready to speak up about what's broken and promote specific, significant, and enduring fixes. At the end of this chapter, following these proposed solutions, I'll explain why and how you can join this effort. You don't need a law degree or a lobbyist's contact list to exert influence. There are more honest people in America who believe that when we get big money out of politics and when big businesses and the elite are made to obey the law, we are all safer and our society is more just.

In a nutshell, here's the problem. The extremely wealthy and well connected have incentives and opportunities for crime and corruption. Absolute power corrupts absolutely. Extreme wealth is criminogenic and members of the upper classes provide one another with a kind of mutually assured immunity. It's difficult for law enforcement with comparatively limited resources to intervene. Prosecutors also have insufficient incentives to pursue complex and time-consuming cases against respectable high-status individuals and business entities. And the tools they have to detect and punish offenders have been dulled by the courts. Furthermore, the urgency to prioritize white collar crime is low when it's hard for the public to see the victims. Our most powerful counterweights are whistleblowers and journalists. Yet they lack the protection and financial support they need. Finally, we have incomplete and inconsistent data available on the amount and nature of white collar crime and white collar offenders. So what are the corresponding solutions?

CLEANING UP THE MESS

First, we should create and fund a new division within the Justice Department to focus on detecting, prosecuting, convicting, and incarcerating big money criminals. This elite crime division should monitor the usual suspects so as to prevent crime where the incentives and opportunities are most prevalent. It's absurd that the same corporations face serious criminal or civil investigations and then reoffend again and again—often under the same leadership. Thus, a high priority of this new division should be to end the dependence on deferred prosecution and nonprosecution agreements. These DPAs and NPAs with large corporate offenders should not be allowed unless responsible high-level executives are prosecuted. If no one at the top is responsible, then the corporation itself if guilty should face criminal charges and a trial where witnesses testify and the public can learn of the misdeeds.

As Nobel laureates George Akerlof and Robert Shiller explain in their book *Phishing for Phools*, "If business people behave in the purely selfish and self-serving way that economic theory assumes, our free-market system tends to spawn manipulation and deception."[1] The only way to stop their behavior is through sure and painful enforcement. Take their money, take their liberty, set an example.

Success for prosecutors should be measured not by the number of cases closed, but instead by the scope of the harm and the number of victims helped by pursuing the matter. Implementation of this policy would recognize that white collar crime should be treated as seriously as organized crime. This division would have devoted funding, specially assigned attorneys, dedicated FBI agents, and support staff. It would focus on securing compliance with the law by bringing meaningful, complex cases against powerful offenders. It would take on large-scale firms where new and dangerous products and complicated regulations exist. It would also monitor marketing and new developments, and bring early cases to stave off emerging threats before they develop into industry practices. The division would work closely with devoted contacts within the enforcement divisions of the major federal administrative agencies. Instead of waiting for referrals, it would proactively research and anticipate businesses under stress that might choose to cut corners or engage in a race to the bottom.

Second, we need to empower and encourage law enforcement to take on those difficult and time-consuming cases involving elite offenders and large businesses. To do so, we must amend some of the federal laws that have been weakened by the courts. This includes our antibribery statute. The law prohibiting bribery of public officials must be updated to create an outright ban on any gift giving to or acceptance of gifts by members of Congress above a specific low-dollar threshold.

We also need to make it easier for law enforcement to trace money laundering, and make it harder for natural persons to hide behind shell companies formed in highly secretive jurisdictions, including Delaware. Toward this end, Congress should enact the Corporate Transparency Act, which has already passed in the House. It would require corporations, LLCs, and other business entities that appear to be shells (such as those that have few to no employees) to disclose, on an ongoing basis, their beneficial owners to the Treasury Department's Financial Crimes Enforcement Network (FinCEN). This will help detect money laundering and tax evasion schemes. In addition, federal prosecutors should be better trained in the use of the responsible corporate officer doctrine to hold criminally accountable those executives who are in a position to affect the health and safety of the public.

Third, we need to create more visibility and protections for victims of white collar crime. Toward this goal, we should create a nationwide registry for white collar criminal offenders. That way, before engaging in consumer or business transactions, ordinary people can consult the registry. This is similar to the concept of a sex offender registry, but given that white collar crime cases are typically prosecuted at the federal level, and offenders can live one place and use internet, mail, and telephone to target people across the country, it should be centralized.

In addition, Congress should amend the Crime Victims' Rights Act of 2004 to make it more accessible to people harmed by white collar crime. Surviving family members of those who got hooked on opioids because of OxyContin, for example, should be informed before any government settlement. On tax evasion, imagine the impact if, in a tax fraud sentencing, a voice were given to those who depend upon public funds, such as mayors, town governments, citizens, or school boards. In addition to a voice, victims also need social safety nets. We cannot expect everyone to be fully compensated by offenders through civil and criminal settlements. Everything from extended unemployment insurance to Medicare for All helps those who have lost their savings to fraudsters, or lost their jobs because they chose to leave a corrupt business or spoke out against its criminal practices and were fired.

Fourth, we need to protect and support both independent investigative journalists and whistleblowers. Independent journalists perform the difficult research that law enforcement under political pressure or other constraints cannot always perform. They shed light on major social problems and help rouse and rally the public to demand change. Yet they are under financial and physical threat. Congress should allocate funds to independent investigative journalism organizations that agree to share their research with newsrooms nationwide after initial publication so they can build on their work.

We also need to empower whistleblowers, not just protect them from retaliation. Presently, under the *qui tam* provisions of the False Claims Act, we give whistleblowers special standing to directly sue contractors that are defrauding the federal government; the government can then choose to intervene and take over the matter and the whistleblower receives a portion of the recovery. Congress should expand this to provide standing to whistleblowers for a wider range of white collar crimes. Also, Congress should ban forced arbitration for both employment and consumer legal disputes. This will give employees and consumers their day in court and let sunlight disinfect workplaces and businesses.

Fifth, we must restore funding to the IRS so it can recover money that goes uncollected due to understaffing. The agency must close the estimated $800 billion "tax gap"—the difference between what the IRS believes it is owed and the tax receipts it actually collects. In addition, with more staff, the IRS can avoid the problem of having to let so many delinquent accounts go uncollected due to expiration. Also, Congress should close the glaring loopholes in the tax code and also create a more equitable system, including a wealth tax, to help decrease the vast income inequality that makes so many of the uber-wealthy above the law in the first place.

And sixth, we need to improve data collection across all law enforcement agencies nationwide that report through the FBI's Uniform Crime Reporting system. We need to be able to track all criminal offenses, including designated white collar offenses, the income and assets of the alleged offenders, and the estimated financial losses involved. Further, there needs to be one centralized database to track to their final disposition the numbers and types of all civil charges and settlements by all federal agencies, even where these cases do not result in referrals for criminal prosecution by the Justice Department.

MEETING THE CHALLENGE

This book is just the beginning. To fight white collar crime, I am launching a website at the address BigDirtyMoney.com. There, in addition to staying current on high-profile legal matters, I will track the ongoing progress of the "Six Fixes" proposed here. The Big Dirty Money website will also provide up-to-date information on how to identify and contact your U.S. representatives and senators and state officials about the corporate and white collar crime problem we face. This website will showcase proposals, efforts, and successes of the many reformers, journalists, and whistleblowers who hope to stem corporate crime and public corruption and who seek an equitable tax system. This new space will also provide direction for victims on how to report incidents of fraud and other white collar predation. And, hopefully, it can be a destination for writers and policymakers who want to roll up their sleeves and get to work cleaning up the mess we are in.

A hundred years ago, progressive legal reformer Louis Brandeis wrote, "Sunlight is said to be the best of disinfectants; electric light the most efficient policeman."[2] But to clean up this white collar crime epidemic, we need more than vision. Today the crime is hiding in plain sight. Now we need to use our voices. As abolitionist Frederick Douglass proclaimed in 1857, "Power concedes nothing without a demand. It never did and it never will."[3] It's time to demand an end to this elite crime spree. We must act, and not just for us, but for the society that will be here generations to come. We owe it to our children and grandchildren. And we owe it to the people who have come before us, like journalist Daphne Caruana Galizia. The last two sentences of her final blog post were: "There are crooks everywhere you look now. The situation is desperate." May her memory be a call to action.

||||||||||||||||||||||||||||||||||||||||||||||||

CRIME AFTER TRUMP

On December 19, 2019, the U.S. House of Representatives voted to impeach Donald Trump on two grounds: abuse of office and obstruction of Congress. As expected, after a contentious trial in the Senate, the vote to convict failed mainly along partisan lines. Only Senator Mitt Romney from Utah broke with the Republican Party and voted to support one impeachment count to convict the president. To convict and remove a president from office, the Constitution requires two-thirds of the senators present to agree, and there was not even a simple majority willing to do so. When this book went to press, Trump, though permanently marred by the impeachment, was still in office, taking revenge on those who testified against him during House hearings, and he was perpetually campaigning for reelection.

I began writing this book just after the Mueller Report was

released in 2019, and finished in mid-May 2020. I finished during the presidential campaign drama and while we all tried to flatten the coronavirus curve, even as deaths from COVID-19 climbed, shifting from hope to despair and back. I expect the Trump administration will end before we have treatments or a vaccine. And the man himself will likely leave the White House long before we have a cure for our white collar crime epidemic. Regardless of the outcome of the November election, we have more work to do to make our country inhospitable to leaders like Donald Trump. If we continue to serve as a popular haven for global kleptocrats, maintain weak bribery prohibitions, allow big dirty money to flood our elections, secure implicit immunity for the upper class, allow corporate executives to commit crimes and walk away with no or very, very light sentences, we will continue to be the petri dish for another future corrupt, organized-crime-tied, friend-to-all-dictators, lying, cheating, megalomaniac American president. In the words of provocative opinion columnist Maureen Dowd, our "climate of confusion and cynicism allows Trump to prosper. He did not come to Washington to clean up the tainted system; he came to bathe in it."[1]

ACKNOWLEDGMENTS

My first boyfriend was a white collar criminal. Cranbrook, the Michigan prep school I attended as a day student, suspended him in the early spring of 1983, during his junior (and my sophmore) year. He refused to say why at first. In time, he confessed. The administration had caught him embezzling from the school store. He had a job there and siphoned off unspent balances of other boarding students' allowance accounts on candy. The Skittles he sometimes gave me after chemistry class may have been ill-gotten proceeds. Before he returned to campus later in the semester, to the dismay of my parents, I forgave him. My parents implored me to end the relationship. How could I trust him? they asked. Mom and Dad's point was, Cheaters cheat. My point was, He's tall, dark, and handsome and looks smashing in Brooks Brothers (hey, it was the eighties). I was roped in by his charm and attention.

But while on probation, he got caught smoking in his dorm room and that was it. Expulsion. Before that happened, foolishly, I stayed loyal to him until the day I spotted him walking through a downtown shopping area holding hands with another girl. Since then, white collar criminals and their repeated betrayals have fascinated me.

So I suppose he's the first person to thank for my exposure to this topic.

Then, early in my legal career, after a brief stint at a large corporate law firm in New York, in 1995, I took an in-house position as a marketing lawyer for a promising startup company in Connecticut. In three years, that dream job quite literally created nightmares. Senior management was engaged in accounting fraud, which was discovered and made public in early 1998 after a merger with a larger corporation based in New Jersey. In a single day, the stock price of the newly merged company, Cendant, dropped by more than 45 percent, shaving $14 billion off its market capitalization. Even after two deadlocked juries, the federal prosecutor tried a third time and convicted the chairman, who was sentenced to twelve years in prison. The president was also convicted and incarcerated. This event shook me. I was in my twenties, trusted these managers, and had no idea why they did this.

Fast-forward another decade to the global financial crisis of 2008. With my first book, *Other People's Houses*, I set out to explain the decades of deregulation that helped cause the crash. However, at the book launch in 2014, and then at every event that followed, audience members always posed this question: "Why didn't any bankers go to jail?" This bothered me. I had explained in the book that there was fraud at every link of the toxic mortgage supply chain. But I did not have a clear answer to that question. There was accounting fraud at the banks, so why did no bank executives go to prison? Why didn't the prosecutors even try? So I dug in to more research. This book, *Big Dirty Money*, is the result of that exploration.

I owe my deepest gratitude to my agent Jill Marr of Sandra Dijkstra Literary Agency for believing in my voice and connecting me with the incomparable Wendy Wolf, my editor at Viking. I am grateful for Wendy's vision and detailed editing work, particularly for the potent combination of red ink and fairy dust she applied to the manuscript. And extra thanks to the entire Viking team including Terezia Cicel, Nicholas LoVecchio, Sharon Gonzalez, Madeline Rohlin, Meighan Cavanaugh, Linda Friedner, Louise Braverman, Julia Rickard, Mary Stone, Alex Cruz-Jimenez, and Bridget Gilleran.

Before the pandemic, I toiled away at the Writers' Mill and benefited from kitchen conversations with colleagues there. I researched and wrote throughout the fall of 2019, while visiting at Harvard Law School, and am grateful for the faculty there whose ideas found their way into the book, including John Coates, Glenn Cohen, Martha Minow, and Matthew Stephenson. I am also thankful for the immensely helpful feedback offered by my new colleagues at the Western New England University School of Law when I workshopped the preface there in February of 2020. I am also always appreciative of the group at APPEAL, including Jamee Moudud, Martha McCluskey, and Frank Pasquale, who supported a panel on white collar crime at the 2019 conference. And much thanks to former colleague Michele Martinez Cambpell, who encouraged me to begin teaching a white collar crime course long ago. Through teaching, I've encountered many wonderful students over the years and thank them for their engagement, noting here those whose questions or own work assisted research into new areas, including Bailey Choudhury, Shekhinah Cluba, Rose Hirsch, Akash Singh, Kurt Walters, and Breanna Weaver.

No one composes on a blank slate. In addition to those many writers whose work is referenced in the book, I would also like to thank each of the following for the conversations we've had about their white collar crime or public corruption scholarship—William K. Black, Sam

Buell, June Carbone, Brandon Garrett, Ellen Podgor, Peter Henning, Rena Steinzer, and Zephyr Teachout. Writing in this area without having never worked as a prosecutor or even in the federal government is a daunting task, and therefore I relied on the writing, news appearances, lunch conversations, and classroom visits of numerous talented current and former public servants, including Brian Cohen, Bob Fiske, Ty Gellasch, Eli Honig, Renato Mariotti, Barb McQuade, Mimi Rocah, Joyce Vance, and Michael Zeldin.

Finally, thank you Michael for your love and patience, and also for the strong coffee and opinions.

NOTES

PREFACE: CRIME SCENE

1. Michael D. Shear and Maggie Haberman, "Trump Grants Clemency to Blagojevich, Milken and Kerik," *New York Times*, February 19, 2020, www.nytimes.com/2020/02/18/us/politics/trump-pardon-blagojevich -debartolo.html.

2. Derrick Bryson Taylor, Heather Murphy, and Mariel Padilla, "A Complete List of Trump's Pardons and Commutations," *New York Times*, February 19, 2020, www.nytimes.com/2020/02/18/us/politics/trump-pardons .html; Federal Bureau of Investigation, "Owner of Miami-Area Mental Health Company Sentenced to 35 Years in Prison for Orchestrating $205 Million Medicare Fraud Scheme," press release, December 8, 2011, https://archives.fbi.gov/archives/miami/press-releases/2011/owner-of -miami-area-mental-health-company-sentenced-to-35-years-in-prison -for-orchestrating-205-million-medicare-fraud-scheme-1.

3. Statement from the Press Secretary Regarding Executive Grants of Clemency, Whitehouse.gov, February 18, 2020, www.whitehouse.gov/briefings -statements/statement-press-secretary-regarding-executive-grants -clemency-2/.

4. Lenny Bernstein, Aaron C. Davis, Christopher Rowland, and Renae Merle, "Sacklers Could Hold On to Most of Personal Fortune in Proposed Purdue Settlement," *Washington Post*, August 3, 2019, www.washington post.com/health/sacklers-could-hold-on-to-most-of-personal-fortune -in-proposed-purdue-settlement/2019/08/31/4577f93a-cb71-11e9-a4f3 -c081a126de70_story.html.

5. Alex Morrell, "The OxyContin Clan: The $14 Billion Newcomer to Forbes 2015 List of Richest U.S. Families," *Forbes*, July 1, 2015, www.forbes.com /sites/alexmorrell/2015/07/01/the-oxycontin-clan-the-14-billion -newcomer-to-forbes-2015-list-of-richest-u-s-families/#6d8d5a9075e0.

6. Centers for Disease Control, National Center for Health Statistics, page last reviewed March 19, 2020, www.cdc.gov/drugoverdose/data/prescribing /overview.html.

7. Katherine Blunt and Russell Gold, "PG&E Knew for Years Its Lines Could Spark Wildfires, and Didn't Fix Them," *Wall Street Journal*, July 10, 2019, https://www.wsj.com/articles/pg-e-knew-for-years-its-lines-could -spark-wildfires-and-didnt-fix-them-11562768885; Kurtis Alexander, "Re- claiming Paradise Six Months After the Camp Fire, a Devastated Commu- nity Hopes to Rebuild—If It Can," *San Francisco Chronicle*, May 3, 2019, https://projects.sfchronicle.com/2019/rebuilding-paradise/; Priya Krishna- kumar and Jon Schleuss, "More than 18,000 buildings burned in North- ern California. Here's what that looks like from above," *Los Angeles Times*, December 10, 2018, www.latimes.com/projects/la-me-camp-fire-building -destruction-map/.

8. Jessica Dye, "Ex-GM Engineer DeGiorgio Acknowledges 'Mistakes' Made over Ignition Switch," Reuters, January 15, 2016, www.autonews.com /article/20160115/OEM11/160119769/ex-gm-engineer-degiorgio -acknowledges-mistakes-made-over-ignition-switch.

9. "GM Sacks 15 Workers in Fallout over Faulty Ignition Switches," NBC News, June 15, 2014, www.nbcnews.com/storyline/gm-recall/gm-sacks -15-workers-fallout-over-faulty-ignition-switches-n123331.

10. "GM Settles Criminal Case over Ignition Switches," CBS News, Sep- tember 17, 2015, www.cbsnews.com/news/gm-settles-criminal-case-over -ignition-switches/.

11. Trip Gabriel, "Ex-Governor of Virginia Is Indicted on Charges over Loans and Gifts," *New York Times*, January 21, 2014, www.nytimes.com/2014 /01/22/us/former-virginia-governor-and-his-wife-are-indicted.html.

12. University of Virginia, "Virginia Population Estimates," showed a population of 8,025,514 in 2010 and 8,326,289 in 2014, https://demographics .coopercenter.org/virginia-population-estimates. By comparison, the Virginia Department of Health, "Virginia Employment Demographic Profile," showed 3.8 million people employed in 2010 and 4.05 million in 2014. This is a 250,000 increase in employment compared to a more than 300,000 increase in population.

13. Matthew Goldstein, "Leon Cooperman's Hedge Fund Settles Insider Trading Case," *New York Times*, May 18, 2017, www.nytimes.com/2017 /05/18/business/dealbook/leon-cooperman-omega-advisors-insider -trading.html.

14. Securities and Exchange Commission, "SEC Charges Hedge Fund Manager Leon Cooperman with Insider Trading," press release, September 26, 2016, www.sec.gov/news/pressrelease/2016-189.html.

15. Wells Fargo, "Wells Fargo Reports Completion of Expanded Third-Party Review of Retail Banking Accounts, Paving Way to Complete Remediation Effort," press release, August 31, 2017, https://newsroom.wf.com/press -release/wells-fargo-reports-completion-expanded-third-party-review -retail-banking-accounts.

16. Stacy Cowley, "Wells Fargo Whistle-Blower Wins $5.4 Million and His Job Back," *New York Times*, April 3, 2017, www.nytimes.com/2017/04 /03/business/04-wells-fargo-whistleblower-fired-osha.html.

17. Renae Merle, "Wells Fargo CEO Steps Down in Wake of Sham Accounts Scandal," *Washington Post*, October 12, 2016, /www.washingtonpost.com /news/business/wp/2016/10/12/wells-fargo-ceo-to-retire-in-wake-of-sham -accounts-scandal/; Matt Krantz, "Wells Fargo CEO Stumpf Retires with $134M," *USA Today*, October 12, 2016, www.usatoday.com/story/money /markets/2016/10/12/wells-fargo-ceo-retires-under-fire/91964778/.

18. Nathan Bomey, "Ex-Wells Fargo CEO Banned from Banking, Must Pay $17.5M Fine for Role in Fake-Accounts Scandal," *USA Today*, January 23, 2020, www.usatoday.com/story/money/2020/01/23/wells-fargo-ex-ceo -john-stumpf-banned-banking-fined-17-5-m/4554673002/.

19. John Carreyrou, *Bad Blood: Secrets and Lies in a Silicon Valley Startup* (New York: Knopf, 2018).

20. Securities and Exchange Commission, "Theranos, CEO Holmes, and Former President Balwani Charged with Massive Fraud," press release, March 14, 2018, www.sec.gov/news/press-release/2018-41.

21. Nick Bilton, " 'She Never Looks Back,': Inside Elizabeth Holmes's Chilling Final Months at Theranos," *Vanity Fair*, February 21, 2019, www .vanityfair.com/news/2019/02/inside-elizabeth-holmess-final -months-at-theranos.

22. Shirin Ghaffary, "Here's What WeWork Is Giving Laid-Off Employees Who Aren't Named Adam Neumann," *Vox*, November 7, 2019, www.vox .com/recode/2019/11/7/20953930/wework-adam-neumann-severance -laid-off-employees-layoffs-buyout-unicorn-ipo; Eliot Brown, "WeWork Employee Options Underwater as Ex-CEO Reaps," *Wall Street Journal*, October 23, 2019, www.wsj.com/articles/wework-employees-feel-sting-as -ex-ceo-stands-to-reap-11571870011.

23. April Wall-Parker, "Measuring White Collar Crime," in *The Handbook of White-Collar Crime*, ed. Melissa L. Rorie (Hoboken, NJ: Wiley-Blackwell, 2020), 33.

24. Federal Bureau of Investigation, "FBI Releases Crime Statistics," press release, September 30, 2019, www.fbi.gov/news/pressrel/press-releases/fbi -releases-2018-crime-statistics; see also https://ucr.fbi.gov/crime-in-the.u.s /2018/crime-in-the-u.s.-2018/topic-pages/property-crime.

25. Wall-Parker, "Measuring White Collar Crime," 35.

26. Jeffrey Reiman and Paul Leighton, *The Rich Get Richer and the Poor Get Prison: Ideology, Class, and Criminal Justice*, 10th ed. (New York: Pearson, 2013), xix.

27. Jan Hoffman, "How Anti-Vaccine Sentiment Took Hold in the United States," *New York Times*, September 23, 2019, www.nytimes.com/2019 /09/23/health/anti-vaccination-movement-us.html; Jane O'Donnell, "Why Big Pharma Distrust Is Fueling the Anti-Vaxxer Movement and Playing a Role in the Measles Outbreak," *USA Today*, April 23, 2019, www.usato day.com/story/news/health/2019/04/23/vaccine-measles-big-pharma -distrust-conspiracy/3473144002/.

28. David Brown, "In 2000, Measles Had Been Officially 'Eliminated' in the U.S. Will That Change?," *Washington Post*, September 28, 2019, www .washingtonpost.com/health/in-2000-measles-had-been-officially -eliminated-in-the-us-will-that-change/2019/09/27/56ac487a-deed-11e9 -b199-f638bf2c340f_story.html.

29. Noah Higgins-Dunn, "Alex Jones to Stop Selling Coronavirus 'Treatment' Products," CNBC, March 12, 2020, www.cnbc.com/2020/03/12 /ny-attorney-general-orders-alex-jones-to-stop-selling-coronavirus-cures .html; Letter from Lisa Landau, Chief Health Care Bureau to Alex Jones,

re Cease and Desist Notification, March 12, 2020, https://ag.ny.gov/sites /default/files/jones_cease_and_desist_3.12.2020.pdf.

30. Zoe Prebble and John Prebble, "The Morality of Tax Avoidance," *Creighton Law Review* 43, no. 693 (2010): 724.

31. Wendy Sawyer and Peter Wagner, "Mass Incarceration: The Whole Pie 2020," *Prison Policy Initiative*, March 24, 2020, www.prisonpolicy.org /reports/pie2020.html.

32. Theresa Waldrop and Cheri Mossburg, "Police Detain Man Eating a Sandwich on a San Francisco Train Platform," CNN, November 11, 2019, www.cnn.com/2019/11/11/us/bart-san-francisco-man-detained-sandwich /index.html.

33. "Statement of United States Attorney John Brownlee on the Guilty Plea of the Purdue Frederick Company and Its Executives for Illegally Misbranding OxyContin," May 10, 2007, https://assets.documentcloud.org/documents /279028/purdue-guilty-plea.pdf.

34. Barry Meier, "In Guilty Plea, OxyContin Maker to Pay $600 Million," *New York Times*, May 10, 2007, www.nytimes.com/2007/05/10/business /11drug-web.html.

35. Joshua Melvin, "Number of homes destroyed in San Bruno explosion now at 38," *Mercury News*, December 17, 2010, www.mercurynews.com/2010 /12/17/number-of-homes-destroyed-in-san-bruno-explosion-now-at-38/; Katherine Blunt, "A Judge Wants to Control PG&E's Dividends Until It Reduces Risk of Fires," *Wall Street Journal*, March 31, 2019, www.wsj .com/articles/a-judge-wants-to-control-pg-es-dividends-until-it-reduces -risk-of-fires-11554049719.

36. Joel Rosenblatt, "PG&E Faces Strict Probation Judge After Massive Kincade Fire," *Bloomberg*, November 12, 2019, www.bloomberg.com/news /articles/2019-11-12/pg-e-faces-probation-judge-first-time-since-massive -kincade-fire.

37. Ivan Penn and Peter Eavis, "PG&E Will Plead Guilty to Involuntary Manslaughter in Camp Fire," *New York Times*, March 23, 2020, www .nytimes.com/2020/03/23/business/energy-environment/pge-camp-fire -manslaughter.html

38. Michael Liedtke, "PG&E to Use Wildfire Victims Fund to Pay for Past Crimes," Associated Press, March 27, 2020.

39. Press Release, Department of Justice, U.S. Attorney's Office, Southern District of New York, "Manhattan U.S. Attorney Announces Criminal Charges Against General Motors And Deferred Prosecution Agreement

With $900 Million Forfeiture," September 17, 2015, www.justice.gov
/usao-sdny/pr/manhattan-us-attorney-announces-criminal-charges
-against-general-motors-and-deferred.

40. Rebecca R. Ruiz, "Woman Cleared in Death Tied to G.M.'s Faulty Ignition Switch," *New York Times*, www.nytimes.com/2014/11/25/business
/woman-cleared-in-death-caused-by-gms-faulty-ignition-switch.html.

41. Micheline Maynard, "The $2 Billion Toll of GM's Defect Coverup,"
Forbes, September 17, 2015, www.forbes.com/sites/michelinemaynard/2015
/09/17/the-2-billion-toll-of-gms-defect-coverup/#56510fcc11cb.

42. Bill Vlasic, "G.M. Posts Record Profit of $9.7 Billion for 2015," *New York
Times*, February 3, 2016, www.nytimes.com/2016/02/04/business/gm
-general-motors-q4-earnings.html.

43. Stephanie Avakian, "Statement on Leon Cooperman Settling Insider
Trading Charges," Public Statement, SEC, May 18, 2017, www.sec.gov
/news/public-statement/statement-leon-cooperman-settling-insider
-trading-charges.

44. Matthew Goldstein, "Leon Cooperman's Hedge Fund Settles Insider
Trading Case," *New York Times*, May 18, 2017, www.nytimes.com/2017
/05/18/business/dealbook/leon-cooperman-omega-advisors-insider
-trading.html.

45. Jessica Bursztynsky, "Leon Cooperman Sees 'One More Leg' Higher Before the Bull Market Ends," CNBC, October 16, 2019, www.cnbc.com
/2019/10/16/cooperman-to-warren-sanders-stop-treating-billionaires
-as-criminals.html.

46. John Gapper, "How Steve Cohen Survived an Insider Trading Scandal,"
Financial Times, February 7, 2017, www.ft.com/content/efda2ca2-ec69
-11e6-930f-061b01e23655.

47. Peter Henning, "Can the S.E.C. Force Repayment of Ill-Gotten Gains?,"
New York Times, November 29, 2019, www.nytimes.com/2019/11/29/busi
ness/dealbook/sec-fraud-disgorgement.html.

48. Michael Corkery, "Wells Fargo Fined $185 Million for Fraudulently
Opening Accounts," *New York Times*, September 8, 2016, www.nytimes
.com/2016/09/09/business/dealbook/wells-fargo-fined-for-years-of
-harm-to-customers.html; Michael Corkery, "Wells Fargo Offers Regrets,
but Doesn't Admit Misconduct," *New York Times*, September 9, 2020,
www.nytimes.com/2016/09/10/business/dealbook/wells-fargo-apologizes
-but-doesnt-admit-misconduct.html.

49. Department of Justice, Office of Public Affairs, press release, "Justice Department Obtains $5.4 Million in Additional Relief to Compensate Servicemembers for Unlawful Repossessions by Wells Fargo Dealer Services," November 14, 2017, www.justice.gov/opa/pr/justice-department -obtains-54-million-additional-relief-compensate-servicemembers -unlawful.

50. Gretchen Morgenson, "Wells Fargo Forced Unwanted Auto Insurance on Borrowers," *New York Times*, July 27, 2017, www.nytimes.com/2017/07 /27/business/wells-fargo-unwanted-auto-insurance.html.

51. Renae Merle, "U.S. to Fine Wells Fargo $1 Billion," *Wall Street Journal*, April 19, 2018, www.washingtonpost.com/business/economy/regulators -planning-to-slap-wells-fargo-with-1-billion-fine/2018/04/19/ec1f58c6 -4415-11e8-ad8f-27a8c409298b_story.html; Matthew Goldstein, "Wells Fargo Pays $1 Billion to Federal Regulators," *New York Times*, April 20, 2018, www.nytimes.com/2018/04/20/business/wells-fargo-cfpb-penalty -regulators.html.

52. Scott Horsley, "Wells Fargo Paying $3 Billion to Settle U.S. Case over Fraudulent Customer Accounts," *All Things Considered*, NPR, February 21, 2020, www.npr.org/2020/02/21/808205303/wells-fargo-paying -3-billion-to-settle-u-s-case-over-illegal-sales-practices.

53. Department of Justice, "Wells Fargo Agrees to Pay $3 Billion to Resolve Criminal and Civil Investigations into Sales Practices Involving the Opening of Millions of Accounts Without Customer Authorization," press release, February 21, 2020, www.justice.gov/opa/pr/wells-fargo-agrees-pay-3-billion -resolve-criminal-and-civil-investigations-sales-practices.

54. Lenore Palladino, "What Wells Fargo's $40.6 Billion in Stock Buybacks Could Have Meant for Its Employees and Customers," Roosevelt Institute, November 7, 2018, https://rooseveltinstitute.org/what-wells-fargos -40-6-billion-stock-buybacks-could-have-meant-its-employees-and -customers/; Matt Egan, "Wells Fargo Has Splurged on Stock Buybacks Since Fake Accounts Scandal," CNN, January 14, 2019, www.cnn.com /2019/01/14/investing/wells-fargo-buybacks-earnings/index.html.

55. Kevin Wack, "Wells Fargo to Cut up to 26,000 Jobs Within Three Years," *American Banker*, September 20, 2018, www.americanbanker.com/news /wells-fargo-to-cut-up-to-10-of-workforce-within-three-years.

56. Kevin LaCroix, "WeWork, SoftBank, Neumann Hit with Shareholder Lawsuit," *D&O Diary*, November 10, 2019, www.dandodiary.com/2019

/11/articles/shareholders-derivative-litigation/wework-neumann-hit-with
-shareholder-lawsuit/.

57. Theron Mohamed, "A Former WeWork Employee Is Suing over Adam Neumann's $1.7 Billion Golden Parachute," *Markets Insider*, November 9, 2019,
www.markets.businessinsider.com/news/stocks/wework-ex-employee-sues
-adam-neumann-2-billion-leaving-deal-2019-11-1028675038.

58. Jennifer Gould Keil, "Ex-WeWork CEO Adam Neumann Flees NYC to
Escape 'Negative Energy': Pals," *New York Post,* December 17, 2019,
https://nypost.com/2019/12/17/ex-wework-ceo-adam-neumann-flees
-nyc-to-escape-negative-energy-pals/.

59. Kosaku Narioka, "SoftBank Says It Won't Buy WeWork Co-Founder
Neumann's Shares," *Wall Street Journal*, April 2, 2020, www.wsj.com
/articles/softbank-says-it-wont-buy-wework-co-founder-neumanns-shares
-11585812968.

60. Todd Haselton and Alex Sherman, "WeWork's Adam Neumann offered
package worth up to $1.7 billion to step down from board," CNBC,
October 23, 2019, www.cnbc.com/2019/10/22/weworks-adam-neumann
-to-get-200-million-to-leave-board-report-says.html.

61. Securities and Exchange Commission, "Theranos, CEO Holmes, and
Former President Balwani Charged with Massive Fraud," press release,
March 14, 2018, www.sec.gov/news/press-release/2018-41.

62. Reed Abelson, "Theranos Founder Elizabeth Holmes Indicted on Fraud
Charges," *New York Times*, June 15, 2018, www.nytimes.com/2018/06/
15/health/theranos-elizabeth-holmes-fraud.html; Department of Justice,
U.S. Attorney's Office, Northern District of California, "Theranos Founder
and Former Chief Operating Officer Charged In Alleged Wire Fraud
Schemes," press release, June 15, 2018, www.justice.gov/usao-ndca/pr
/theranos-founder-and-former-chief-operating-officer-charged-alleged
-wire-fraud-schemes.

63. Ethan Holmes, "Elizabeth Holmes' Theranos Case: Feds Claim Patient
Harms Related to HIV, Pregnancy," *Mercury News*, January 16, 2020,
www.mercurynews.com/2020/01/14/elizabeth-holmes-theranos-case
-feds-claim-patient-harms-related-to-hiv-pregnancy/.

64. *U.S. v. Holmes and Balwani*, U.S. District Court, Northern District of
California, Case No. 5:18-cr-00258-EJD, Order, February 11, 2020,
www.courtlistener.com/recap/gov.uscourts.cand.327949/gov.uscou
rts.cand.327949.330.0.pdf; Micah Maidenberg, "Theranos Trial's Judge

Narrows Case Against Founder Elizabeth Holmes," *Wall Street Journal*, February 12, 2020, www.wsj.com/articles/theranos-trial-judge-narrows -case-against-founder-elizabeth-holmes-11581540190.

65. See generally Anat Admati and Martin Hellwig, *The Bankers' New Clothes: What's Wrong with Banking and What to Do About It* (Princeton, NJ: Princeton University Press, 2013); and Jennifer Taub, *Other People's Houses: How Decades of Bailouts, Captive Regulators, and Toxic Bankers Made Home Mortgages a Thrilling Business* (New Haven, CT: Yale University Press, 2014).

66. Taub, *Other People's Houses*, 4.

67. CoreLogic, "United States Residential Foreclosure Crisis: Ten Years Later," March 2017, www.corelogic.com/research/foreclosure-report/national-fore closure-report-10-year.pdf.

68. Jesse Hamilton, "Banks Crushed Profit Record with $237 Billion in 2018, FDIC Says," *Bloomberg*, February 21, 2019, www.bloomberg.com/news /articles/2019-02-21/banks-crushed-profit-record-with-237-billion -in-2018-fdic-says.

69. Jennifer Taub, "Delays, Dilutions, and Delusions: Implementing the Dodd-Frank Act," in *Restoring Shared Prosperity: A Policy Agenda from Leading Keynesian Economists*, eds. Thomas Palley and Gustav Horn (AFL-CIO, Macroeconomic Policy Institute, and Friedrich-Ebert-Stiftung, 2013).

70. Kristinn Ingi Jónsson, "36 manns í samtals 96 ára fangelsi í hrunmálu-num [36 People in a Total of 96 Years in Prison in the Crash]," *Visir*, February 7, 2018, www.visir.is/g/2018180209183/36-manns-i-samtals-96 -ara-fangelsi-i-hrunmalunum.

71. Larissa Kyzer, "Former Kaupþing Bank CEO Convicted of Insider Fraud," *Iceland Review*, November 9, 2018, www.icelandreview.com/business /kaupthing-bank-ceo-convicted-insider-fraud/.

72. Sydney E. Ahlstrom, "Lord Acton's Famous Remarks," *New York Times*, March 13, 1974, www.nytimes.com/1974/03/13/archives/lord-actons-fa mous-remark.html.

73. Harry Manuel Shulman, "Cultural Aspects of Criminal Responsibility," *Journal of Criminal Law & Criminology* 43 (1952): 323–24, https://digi talcommons.law.yale.edu/fss_papers/4619/.

74. Ali Winston, "Medical Examiner Testifies Eric Garner Died of Asthma Caused by Officer's Chokehold," *New York Times*, May 15, 2019, www

.nytimes.com/2019/05/15/nyregion/eric-garner-death-daniel
-pantaleo-chokehold.html; Rebecca Davis O'Brien, "NYC Proceeds with
Cigarette Lawsuit After Garner Decision," *Wall Street Journal*, December 16, 2014, www.wsj.com/articles/nyc-proceeds-with-cigarette-lawsuit
-after-garner-decision-1418755857.

75. Steve Mullis, "'Profoundly Sorry' HSBC Reaches $1.98B Settlement in
Money Laundering Case," NPR, December 10, 2012, www.npr.org
/sections/thetwo-way/2012/12/10/166904724/reports-1-9-billion
-settlement-expected-in-hsbc-money-laundering-case.

76. Steve Slater and Matt Scuffham, "HSBC Says Swiss Scandal Has Brought
'Shame' on Bank," Reuters, February 23, 2015, www.reuters.com/article
/hsbc-results/hsbc-says-swiss-scandal-has-brought-shame-on-bank
-idINKBN0LR0WV20150223.

77. U.S. Department of Justice, Office of Public Affairs, press release, "HSBC
Holdings Plc Agrees to Pay More Than $100 Million to Resolve Fraud
Charges," January 18, 2018, www.justice.gov/opa/pr/hsbc-holdings-plc
-agrees-pay-more-100-million-resolve-fraud-charges; U.S. Department of Justice, Office of Public Affairs, press release, "Justice Department Announces
Deferred Prosecution Agreement with HSBC Private Bank (Suisse) SA,"
December 10, 2019, www.justice.gov/opa/pr/justice-department-announces
-deferred-prosecution-agreement-hsbc-private-bank-suisse-sa.

78. Tamar Frankel, *The Ponzi Scheme Puzzle: A History and Analysis of Con
Artists and Victims* (New York: Oxford University Press, 2012), 59–60.

79. Christopher M. Matthews and Katherine Blunt, "Ex-Enron CEO Skilling
Plans Second Act," *Wall Street Journal*, March 22, 2019, www.wsj.com
/articles/ex-enron-ceo-skilling-plots-second-act-11553282732.

80. Chloe Melas, "Lori Loughlin Shopping for Crisis Management Help,"
CNN, May 3, 2019, www.cnn.com/2019/05/02/entertainment/lori-loughlin
-mossimo-giannulli-crisis-management-pr/index.html.

81. Edwin Sutherland, *White Collar Crime* (New York: Dryden, 1949), 9.

82. *U.S. v. Fred C. Trump, Donald Trump, and Trump Management Inc.*, civil
action, no. No. 73 C 1529, consent order, June 10, 1975, www.clearing
house.net/chDocs/public/FH-NY-0024-0034.pdf.

83. Michael Kranish and Robert O'Harrow Jr., "Inside the Government's
Racial Bias Case against Donald Trump's Company, and How He
Fought It," *Washington Post*, January 23, 2016, www.washingtonpost.com
/politics/inside-the-governments-racial-bias-case-against-donald-trumps

-company-and-how-he-fought-it/2016/01/23/fb90163e-bfbe-11e5-bcda
-62a36b394160_story.html.

84. Charles Bagil, "Trump Paid Over $1 Million in Labor Settlement, Docu-
ments Reveal," *New York Times*, November 27, 2017, www.nytimes.com
/2017/11/27/nyregion/trump-tower-illegal-immigrant-workers-union
-settlement.html.

85. Richard Goldstruck, "Corruption and Racketeering in the New York
Construction Industry," Final Report to Governor Mario M. Cuomo,
New York State Organized Crime Task Force, 1989, www.ceic.gouv.qc.ca
/fileadmin/Fichiers_client/centre_documentaire/CEIC-R-3591_01.pdf.

86. Joseph P. Fried, "Head of L.I. Teamster Local Indicted in Rackets Inquiry," *New York Times*, January 14, 1982, www.nytimes.com/1982/01/14
/nyregion/head-of-li-teamster-local-indicted-in-rackets-inquiry.html.

87. Michael Rothfeld and Alexandra Berzon, "Donald Trump and the Mob,"
Wall Street Journal, September 1, 2016, www.wsj.com/articles/donald
-trump-dealt-with-a-series-of-people-who-had-mob-ties-1472736922.

88. Selwyn Raab, "Key Teamster Leader Is Convicted of Labor Racketeering by L.I. Jury," *New York Times*, October 9, 1982, www.nytimes.com
/1982/10/09/us/key-teamster-leader-is-convicted-of-labor-racketeering
-by-li-jury.html.

89. Selwyn Raab, "Cody Sentenced to Five-Year Term as Racketeer," *New
York Times*, December 2, 1982, www.nytimes.com/1982/12/02/nyregion
/cody-sentenced-to-5-year-term-as-a-racketeer.html.

90. Andrea Bernstein, *American Oligarchs: The Kushners, the Trumps, and the
Marriage of Money and Power* (New York: Norton, 2020); Dean Baquet,
"Trump Says He Didn't Know He Employed Illegal Aliens," *New York
Times*, July 13, 1990, www.nytimes.com/1990/07/13/nyregion/trump
-says-he-didn-t-know-he-employed-illegal-aliens.html.

91. Wayne Barrett, *Trump: The Greatest Show on Earth: The Deals, the Downfall, the Reinvention* (New York: Regan Arts, 2016), location 4138 in Kin-
dle version.

92. David Cay Johnston, "Just What Were Donald Trump's Ties to the Mob?"
Politico Magazine, May 22, 2016, www.politico.com/magazine/story/2016/05
/donald-trump-2016-mob-organized-crime-213910.

93. See generally David Cay Johnston, *The Making of Donald Trump* (New
York: Melville House, 2016); David Cay Johnston, "The Drug Trafficker
Donald Trump Risked His Casino Empire to Protect," *The Daily Beast*,

October 19, 2016, updated December 16, 2018, www.thedailybeast.com /the-drug-trafficker-donald-trump-risked-his-casino-empire-to-protect; Bernstein, *American Oligarchs*, 90.

94. Craig Unger, "Trump's businesses are full of dirty Russian money. The scandal is that it's legal," *Washington Post,* March 29, 2019, www.washing tonpost.com/outlook/trumps-businesses-are-full-of-dirty-russian-money -the-scandal-is-thats-legal/2019/03/29/11b812da-5171-11e9-88a1-ed34 6f0ec94f_story.html.

95. Dan Andrews, "Bulgari Firm Pleads Guilty to Tax Evasion," UPI, December 5, 1986, www.upi.com/Archives/1986/12/05/Bulgari-firm-pleads -quilty-to-tax-evasion/2090534142800/.

96. James Rowley, "Trump Agrees to Pay $750,000 Penalty to Settle Antitrust Lawsuit," Associated Press, April 5, 1988, www.apnews.com/54ea0d c590fc97d9e9e86c65336649a1.

97. Max J. Rosenthal, "The Trump Files: The Shady Way Fred Trump Tried to Save His Son's Casino," *Mother Jones*, September 26, 2016, www.moth erjones.com/politics/2016/09/trump-files-fred-trump-funneled-cash -donald-using-casino-chips/.

98. Michael Isikoff, "Trump challenged over ties to mob-linked gambler with ugly past," Yahoo News, March 7, 2016, www.yahoo.com/news/trump -challenged-over-ties-to-mob-linked-gambler-100050602.html

99. Securities and Exchange Commission, "SEC Brings First Pro Forma Financial Reporting Case: Trump Hotels Charged with Issuing Misleading Earnings Release," press release, January 16, 2002, www.sec.gov/news /headlines/trumphotels.htm.

100. Christina Binkley and Judith Burns, "SEC Brings Case Against Trump Hotels Alleging Improper Use of 'Pro Forma,'" *Wall Street Journal,* January 17, 2002, www.wsj.com/articles/SB101119802590296360.

101. Aaron Smith and Chris Isidore, "Trump Taj Mahal closes its doors in Atlantic City," CNN, October 10, 2016, https://money.cnn.com/2016/10 /10/news/companies/trump-taj-mahal-closed/; Russ Buettner and Charles V. Bagli, "How Donald Trump Bankrupted His Atlantic City Casinos, but Still Earned Millions," *New York Times*, www.nytimes.com/2016/06 /12/nyregion/donald-trump-atlantic-city.html.

102. "FinCEN Fines Trump Taj Mahal Casino Resort $10 Million for Significant and Long Standing Anti-Money Laundering Violations," press release, March 6, 2015, www.fincen.gov/news/news-releases/fincen-fines-trump -taj-mahal-casino-resort-10-million-significant-and-long.

103. Bill Chappell, "'Trump University' Documents Put On Display Aggressive Sales Techniques," NPR, May 31, 2016, www.npr.org/sections /thetwo-way/2016/05/31/480214102/trump-university-playbooks" -released-by-court-advise-being-courteous-to-media.

104. Steve Eder, "Donald Trump Agrees to Pay $25 Million in Trump University Settlement," *New York Times*, November 18, 2016, www.nytimes .com/2016/11/19/us/politics/trump-university.html.

105. Russ Buettner, Susanne Craig, and David Barstow, "11 Takeaways from the Time's Investigation into Trump's Wealth," *New York Times*, October 2, 2018, www.nytimes.com/2018/10/02/us/politics/donald-trump-wealth -fred-trump.html.

106. U.S. Department of Justice, Special Counsel Robert S. Mueller III, "Report on the Investigation into Russian Interference in the 2016 Presidential Election," March 2019, www.justice.gov/storage/report.pdf.

107. Jesse Eisinger, "Take home message from today: Imagine a world where white-collar crime, bank fraud, accounting fraud, and tax fraud were properly investigated & prosecuted. That's a world where 'President Trump' is an impossibility," Twitter, February 28, 2019, https://twitter .com/eisingerj/status/1100927669456330752.

CHAPTER I: DEFINING WHITE COLLAR CRIME

1. Gilbert Geis and Colin Goff, "Introduction to Edwin H. Sutherland," *White Collar Crime: The Uncut Version* (New Haven, CT: Yale University Press, 1983), xv, citing Howard Odum, "Edwin H. Sutherland," *Social Forces* 29, no. 3 (1951): 348–49.

2. Program of the Thirty-Fourth Annual Meeting of the American Sociological Society, the Benjamin Franklin Hotel, December 27, 28, and 29, 1939, www.asanet.org/sites/default/files/1939_annual_meeting_program _2.pdf.

3. Geis and Goff, "Introduction," ix.

4. Edwin H. Sutherland, "White-Collar Criminality," *American Sociological Review* 5, no. 1 (1940), 2.

5. Sutherland, "White-Collar Criminality," 1.

6. Sutherland, "White-Collar Criminality," 1–2.

7. Sutherland, "White-Collar Criminality," 2.

8. Sutherland, "White-Collar Criminality," 5.

9. Securities and Exchange Commission, "SEC Charges Former Country-wide Executives with Fraud: Former CEO Angelo Mozilo Additionally Charged with Insider Trading," press release, June 4, 2009, www.sec.gov/news/press/2009/2009-129.htm.

10. Gretchen Morgenson, "Case on Mortgage Official Is Said to Be Dropped," *New York Times,* February 19, 2011, www.nytimes.com/2011/02/20/business/20mozilo.html.

11. Gretchen Morgenson, "Lending Magnate Settles Fraud Case," *New York Times,* October 15, 2010, www.nytimes.com/2010/10/16/business/16countrywide.html; Securities and Exchange Commission, "Former Countrywide CEO Angelo Mozilo to Pay SEC's Largest-Ever Financial Penalty Against a Public Company's Senior Executive," press release, October 15, 2020, www.sec.gov/news/press/2010/2010-197.htm.

12. Morgenson, "Case on Mortgage Official Is Said to Be Dropped."

13. Sutherland, "White-Collar Criminality," 6–7.

14. Sutherland, "White-Collar Criminality," 7.

15. "T. J. Pendergast, 72, Dies in Kansas City," *New York Times,* January 27, 1945, www.timesmachine.nytimes.com/timesmachine/1945/01/27/88187801.pdf?pdf_redirect=true&ip=0.

16. Sutherland, "White-Collar Criminality," 8–9.

17. Sutherland, "White-Collar Criminality," 7–8.

18. Sutherland, "White-Collar Criminality," 11.

19. Sutherland, "White-Collar Criminality," 11.

20. "Hits Criminality in White Collars," *New York Times,* December 28, 1939, https://timesmachine.nytimes.com/timesmachine/1939/12/28/113086988.html?pageNumber=12.

21. "Poverty Belittled as Crime Factor: Sociologist Cites Frauds in Business," *Philadelphia Inquirer,* December 28, 1939.

22. Sutherland, "White-Collar Criminality," 1–12.

23. Thomas I. Emerson, "Book Review: *White Collar Crime,*" *Yale Law Journal* 59 (1950): 581–85.

24. Donald R. Cressey, "Foreword," in Edwin H. Sutherland, *White Collar Crime* (New York: Holt, Rinehart and Winston, 1961), fn 9, vii.

25. Sutherland, *White Collar Crime: The Uncut Version,* xxix.

26. Emerson, "Book Review: *White Collar Crime,*" 581–85.

27. Brian Eule, "Watch Your Words, Professor," *Stanford Magazine,* January/February 2015, www.stanfordmag.org/contents/watch-your-words-professor.

28. Edward A. Ross, *Sin and Society: An Analysis of Latter-Day Iniquity* (Boston: Houghton Mifflin, 1907), 48. Ross created the word by tacking on the Greek-derived suffix *-oid,* "having the form of; similar to," by analogy with *asteroid,* "starlike."

29. Ross, *Sin and Society,* 50.

30. Ross, *Sin and Society,* 51.

31. Ross, *Sin and Society,* 51.

CHAPTER 2: HARM BEYOND MEASURE

1. Wall-Parker, "Measuring White Collar Crime," 32–42.

2. Cynthia Barnett, "The Measurement of White-Collar Crime Using Uniform Crime Reporting (UCR) Data," U.S. Department of Justice, Federal Bureau of Investigation, Criminal Justice Information Services, 2000, 6, www.ucr.fbi.gov/nibrs/nibrs_wcc.pdf.

3. See Transactional Records Access Clearinghouse (TRAC), "White Collar Crime Prosecutions for October 2019," January 27, 2020 (showing the number of defendants charged federally for white collar offenses down from a peak of 1,000 per month in 2011 to 389 in October 2019), https://trac.syr.edu/tracreports/bulletins/white_collar_crime/monthlyoct19/fil/; Paul Healy and George Serafeim, "How to Scandal-Proof Your Company," *Harvard Business Review,* July–August 2019 ("fraud, bribery, embezzlement and money laundering are rampant"), https://hbr.org/2019/07/white-collar-crime.

4. Hobbes, "Golden Age of White Collar Crime."

5. David Gelles, "Fired Boeing C.E.O. Muilenburg Will Get More Than $60 Million," *New York Times,* January 10, 2020, www.nytimes.com/2020/01/10/business/boeing-dennis-muilenburg-severance.html.

6. David Shephardson, "New Boeing 737 MAX Documents Show 'Very Disturbing' Employee Concerns: U.S. House Aide," Reuters, December 24, 2019, www.reuters.com/article/us-boeing-737max/new-boeing-737-max-documents-show-very-disturbing-employee-concerns-u-s-house-aide-idUSKBN1YS1BS?utm_source=applenews.

7. Aaron Gregg, "Plane crash victims' families 'sickened' by fired Boeing CEO's $62 million payout," *Washington Post,* January 13, 2020, www.washingtonpost.com/business/2020/01/13/plane-crash-victims-families-sickened-by-fired-boeing-ceos-62-million-payout/.

8. Natalie Kitroeff and Michael S. Schmidt, "Federal Prosecutors Investigating Whether Boeing Pilot Lied to F.A.A.," *New York Times*, February 21, 2020, www.nytimes.com/2020/02/21/business/boeing-737-max-investigation.html.

9. Doha Madani, "Fyre Festival Organizer Billy McFarland Sentenced to 6 Years on Fraud Charges," NBC News, October 11, 2018, www.nbcnews.com/news/us-news/fyre-festival-organizer-billy-mcfarland-sentenced-6-years-fraud-charges-n919086.

10. Heran Mamo, "Fyre Festival's Andy King Is Thirsty No More in New Evian Water Ad Campaign," *Billboard*, January 17, 2020, www.billboard.com/articles/news/lifestyle/8548367/fyre-festival-andy-king-evian-water-ad.

11. Gary S. Becker, "Crime and Punishment: An Economic Approach," *Journal of Political Economy* 76, no. 2 (1968): 169–217, www.jstor.org/stable/1830482?seq=1.

12. Becker, "Crime and Punishment," 198.

13. Becker, "Crime and Punishment," 170, 172.

14. Becker, "Crime and Punishment," 199.

15. Becker, "Crime and Punishment," 193. Italics in original.

16. Becker, "Crime and Punishment," 194–195.

17. William K. Black, "Gary Becker's Imperialistic Blunders about Crime," *New Economic Perspectives*, June 19, 2014, https://neweconomicperspectives.org/2014/06/gary-beckers-imperialistic-blunders-crime.html.

18. Dorothy S. Lund and Natasha Sarin, "The Cost of Doing Business: Corporate Crime and Punishment Post-Crisis," Institute for Law and Economics, Research Paper No. 20-13, February 19, 2020, www.papers.ssrn.com/sol3/papers.cfm?abstract_id=3537245.

19. Michael L. Benson and Sally S. Simpson, *White-Collar Crime: An Opportunity Perspective* (New York: Routledge, 2018), 3.

20. Leslie Eaton, "Assault With a Fiscal Weapon; As Swindlers Branch Out, Victims Want to Be Heard," *New York Times*, May 25, 1999, www.nytimes.com/1999/05/25/business/assault-with-a-fiscal-weapon-as-swindlers-branch-out-victims-want-to-be-heard.html.

21. See, generally, Russell Mokhiber's *Corporate Crime Reporter*, www.corporatecrimereporter.com/.

22. David O. Friedrichs, "White Collar Crime: Definitional Debates and the Case for a Typological Approach," in *The Handbook of White-Collar Crime*, ed. Melissa L. Rorie (Hoboken, NJ: Wiley-Blackwell, 2020), 28.

23. Brian K. Payne, *White-Collar Crime: The Essentials*, 2nd ed. (Los Angeles: Sage, 2017), 26.

24. Payne, *White-Collar Crime*, 25, citing D. Weisburd, E. Waring, and E. Chayet, "Class, Status, and the Punishment of White-Collar Criminals," *Law and Social Inquiry* 15, no. 2 (1990): 353.

25. Barnett, "The Measurement of White-Collar Crime," 4.

26. Sutherland, *White Collar Crime*, 9.

27. Ellen S. Podgor and Lucian E. Dervan, "'White Collar Crime': Still Hazy After All These Years," *Georgia Law Review* 50, no. 3 (2015): 709, 711.

28. Payne, *White-Collar Crime*, 1.

29. Marshall Clinard, Richard Quinney, and John Wildeman, *Criminal Behavior Systems: A Typology* (Cincinnati: Anderson, 1994).

30. Podgor and Dervan, "'White Collar Crime,'" 712.

31. Catherine Rampell, "We're About to Hit a New Record Low for White-Collar Prosecutions," *Washington Post*, September 27, 2019, www.washingtonpost.com/opinions/2019/09/27/were-about-hit-new-record-low-white-collar-prosecutions/, citing "White Collar Prosecutions Hit All-Time Low in January 2019," TRAC Reports, https://trac.syr.edu/tracreports/crim/550/.

32. Transactional Records Access Clearinghouse, "About Us," trac.syr.edu/aboutTRACgeneral.html.

33. Office of the United States Attorneys, "Annual Statistical Reports," www.justice.gov/usao/resources/annual-statistical-reports.

34. Office of the United States Attorneys' Annual Statistical Report 2018, Table 1, Table 3A, www.justice.gov/usao/page/file/1199336/download.

35. Office of the United States Attorneys' Statistical Report, Fiscal Year 1992, 21-30, www.justice.gov/sites/default/files/usao/legacy/2009/07/31/STATISTICAL_REPORT_FISCAL_YEAR_1992.pdf.

36. Office of the United States Attorneys, "Annual Statistical Reports: Fiscal Year 2018," 12, Table 3A, www.justice.gov/usao/page/file/1199336/download.

37. Ben Conarck, "Trump Commutes Sentence of Miami Woman Doing 35 Years in Prison for Bilking Medicare," *Miami Herald,* February 18, 2020, www.miamiherald.com/news/politics-government/article240404271.html.

38. The Federal Bureau of Investigation, "Uniform Crime Reporting (UCR) Program," www.fbi.gov/services/cjis/ucr.

39. Barnett, "The Measurement of White-Collar Crime," 6.

40. Author-written survey and phone interviews with several federal prosecutors in summer 2019.

CHAPTER 3: CORPORATE CRIME WAVES AND CRACKDOWNS

1. Ben Protess, Robert Gebeloff, and Danielle Ivory, "Trump Administration Spares Corporate Wrongdoers Billions in Penalties," *New York Times*, November 3, 2018, www.nytimes.com/2018/11/03/us/trump-sec-doj-corporate -penalties.html.

2. Peter Stubley, "White-Collar Prosecutions and Corporate Fines Drop Under Trump," *Independent*, July 18, 2019, www.independent.co.uk/news /world/americas/trump-drop-white-collar-crime-prosecutions-fines -a9010441.html.

3. John F. Savarese, Partner Wachtell, Lipton, Rosen & Katz, "Why Compliance (Still) Matters," *Harvard Law School Forum on Corporate Governance*, July 28, 2019, www.corpgov.law.harvard.edu/2019/07/28/why-com pliance-still-matters/.

4. Rick Claypool, Taylor Lincoln, Michael Tanglis, and Alan Zibel, "Corporate Impunity," Public Citizen, July 2018, www.citizen.org/wp-content /uploads/migration/corporate-enforcement-public-citizen-report-july -2018.pdf.

5. Nathaniel Meyersohn, "Walmart Settles with US Government over International Bribery," CNN Business, June 20, 2019, www.cnn.com/2019 /06/20/business/walmart-bribery-mexico-brazil-fcpa-sec/index.html.

6. Protess, Gebeloff, and Ivory, "Trump Administration Spares Corporate Wrongdoers."

7. Department of Justice, Office of Public Affairs, "Walmart Inc. and Brazil-Based Subsidiary Agree to Pay $137 Million to Resolve Foreign Corrupt Practices Act Case," June 20, 2019, www.justice.gov/opa/pr/walmart-inc -and-brazil-based-subsidiary-agree-pay-137-million-resolve-foreign -corrupt.

8. Meyersohn, "Walmart Settles with US Government."

9. Walmart press release, "Walmart Reaches Agreements with the DOJ and the SEC to Resolve Their FCPA Investigations," June 20, 2019, www

.corporate.walmart.com/newsroom/2019/06/20/walmart-reaches
-agreements-with-the-doj-and-the-sec-to-resolve-their-fcpa-investigations.

10. Protess, Gebeloff, and Ivory, "Trump Administration Spares Corporate Wrongdoers."

11. Corporate Prosecution Registry, Legal Data Lab at the University of Virginia School of Law and Duke University School of Law, www.lib.law .virginia.edu/Garrett/corporate-prosecution-registry/about.html.

12. Protess, Gebeloff, and Ivory, "Trump Administration Spares Corporate Wrongdoers."

13. "Market Cap to Maximum Sentence: Booking Enron by the Numbers," *Wall Street Journal*, May 25, 2006, www.wsj.com/articles/SB114780 226218554397.

14. Bethany McLean and Peter Elkind, *The Smartest Guys in the Room: The Amazing Rise and Scandalous Fall of Enron* (New York: Penguin, 2003).

15. Department of Justice, press release, "Federal Jury Convicts Former Enron Chief Executives Ken Lay, Jeff Skilling on Fraud, Conspiracy and Related Charges," May 25, 2006, www.justice.gov/archive/opa/pr/2006/May/06 _crm_328.html.

16. "Timeline: Ken Lay and the Arc of Enron," NPR, July 5, 2006, www .npr.org/2006/07/05/5535821/timeline-ken-lay-and-the-arc-of-enron; Kate Murphy and Alexei Barrionuevo, "Fastow Sentenced to 6 Years," *New York Times*, September 27, 2006, www.nytimes.com/2006/09/27/business /27enron.html.

17. Matt Stevens and Matthew Haag, "Jeffrey Skilling, Former Enron Chief, Released After 12 Years in Prison," *New York Times*, February 22, 2019, www.nytimes.com/2019/02/22/business/enron-ceo-skilling-scandal.html.

18. Jennifer Bayot, "Ebbers Sentenced to 25 Years in Prison for $11 Billion Fraud," *New York Times*, July 13, 2005, www.nytimes.com/2005/07/13 /business/ebbers-sentenced-to-25-years-in-prison-for-11-billion-fraud.html.

19. Harrison Smith, "Bernard Ebbers, WorldCom CEO convicted in historic fraud scandal, dies at 78," *Washington Post*, February 3, 2020, www.wash ingtonpost.com/local/obituaries/bernard-ebbers-worldcom-ceo -convicted-in-historic-fraud-scandal-dies-at-78/2020/02/03/91c8cfe4 -4696-11ea-8124-0ca81effcdfb_story.html.

20. Lorraine Mirabella, "Rise and Fall of Rite Aid Chief," *Baltimore Sun*, May 28, 2004, www.baltimoresun.com/news/bs-xpm-2004-05-28-0405280 087-story.html.

21. Dan Frosch, "Ex-Chief at Qwest Found Guilty of Insider Trading," *New York Times,* April 20, 2007, www.nytimes.com/2007/04/20/technology /20qwest.html; U.S. Attorney's Office, Colorado, press release, "Former Qwest Chief Executive Officer Joseph Nacchio Sentenced to 72 Months in Prison for Insider Trading," July 27, 2007, www.justice.gov/archive /usao/co/news/2007/July07/7_27_07.html.

22. Associated Press, "Ex-Cendant Chairman Sentenced for Fraud," *New York Times,* January 18, 2007, www.nytimes.com/2007/01/18/business /18cendant.html.

23. David Von Drehle, *Triangle: The Fire That Changed America* (New York: Atlantic Monthly Press, 2003).

24. "Exxon Valdez Oil Spill," History.com, August 21, 2018, www.history .com/topics/1980s/exxon-valdez-oil-spill.

25. Peter Liebhold, "What You May Not Know About the Triangle Shirtwaist Factory Fire," National Museum of American History, September 5, 2018, https://americanhistory.si.edu/blog/triangle.

26. U.S. Department of Labor, About Us, History, "The New York Factory Investigating Commission," www.dol.gov/general/aboutdol/history/mono -regsafepart07.

27. David Von Drehle, "No, History Was Not Unfair to the Triangle Shirt-waist Factory Owners," *Washington Post,* December 20, 2018, www.wash ingtonpost.com/opinions/no-history-was-not-unfair-to-the-triangle -shirtwaist-factory-owners/2018/12/20/10fb050e-046a-11e9-9122 -82e98f91ee6f_story.html.

28. Timothy Egan, "Court Overturns Conviction of Exxon Valdez's Cap-tain," *New York Times,* June 11, 1992, www.nytimes.com/1992/07/11/us /court-overturns-conviction-of-exxon-valdez-s-captain.html; Kim Mur-phy, "Exxon Valdez Victims Finally Getting Payout," *Seattle Times,* De-cember 7, 2008, www.seattletimes.com/seattle-news/exxon-valdez-victims -finally-getting-payout/.

29. "Whitney Goes Free on Parole," *New York Times,* July 9, 1941, https://timesmachine.nytimes.com/timesmachine/1941/07/09/87640390 .pdf.

30. John Steele Gordon, "Before Madoff, We Had Schuyler and Whitney," *Barron's,* August 10, 2009, www.barrons.com/articles/SB1249694514655 16129?tesla=y.

31. Securities and Exchange Commission, "Former Countrywide CEO An-gelo Mozilo to Pay SEC's Largest-Ever Financial Penalty Against a Public

Company's Senior Executive," press release, October 15 2010, www.sec
.gov/news/press/2010/2010-197.htm.

32. Securities and Exchange Commission, "SEC Charges Former Countrywide Executives with Fraud," press release, June 4, 2009, www.sec.gov
/news/press/2009/2009-129.htm.

33. Nick Werle, "Prosecuting Corporate Crime When Firms Are Too Big to
Jail: Investigation, Deterrence, and Judicial Review," *Yale Law Journal*
128, no. 5 (March 2019), www.yalelawjournal.org/note/prosecuting-cor
porate-crime-when-firms-are-too-big-to-jail.

34. Department of Justice, press release, "HSBC Holdings Plc Agrees to Pay
More Than $100 Million to Resolve Fraud Charges," January 18, 2018,
www.justice.gov/opa/pr/hsbc-holdings-plc-agrees-pay-more-100-million
-resolve-fraud-charges.

35. U.S. Department of Justice, Office of Public Affairs, press release, "Justice
Department Announces Deferred Prosecution Agreement with HSBC
Private Bank (Suisse) SA," December 10, 2019, www.justice.gov/opa/pr
/justice-department-announces-deferred-prosecution-agreement-hsbc
-private-bank-suisse-sa.

36. Offices of Representative Pramila Jayapal and Senator Elizabeth Warren,
"Rigged Justice 2.0: Government of the Billionaires, by the Billionaires,
and for the Billionaires," May 14, 2019, 8, www.warren.senate.gov/imo
/media/doc/Rigged%20Justice%20Report.pdf.

37. James A. Cox, "Bilboes, Brands, and Branks: Colonial Crimes and Punishments," *Colonial Williamsburg Journal*, Spring 2003, www.history.org
/foundation/journal/spring03/branks.cfm.

38. Cox, "Bilboes, Brands, and Branks."

39. Lawrence Friedman, *Crime and Punishment in American History* (New
York: Basic Books, 1994), 113.

40. Charles Doyle, "Qui Tam: The False Claims Act and Related Federal
Statutes," Congressional Research Service, August 6, 2009, https://fas
.org/sgp/crs/misc/R40785.pdf.

41. Adam Winkler: *We the Corporations: How American Businesses Won Their
Civil Rights* (New York: Norton, 2018), 3–4.

42. Friedman, *Crime and Punishment*, 109.

43. Friedman, *Crime and Punishment*, 40.

44. Friedman, *Crime and Punishment*, 41–42.

45. Friedman, *Crime and Punishment*, 109.

46. Friedman, *Crime and Punishment*, 114.

47. Tom Mueller, *Crisis of Conscience: Whistleblowing in an Age of Fraud* (New York: Riverhead, 2019), 15.

48. Doyle, "Qui Tam," 5.

49. Friedman, *Crime and Punishment,* 116.

50. Friedman, *Crime and Punishment,* 104.

51. Friedman, *Crime and Punishment,* 105.

52. *Standard Oil Company of New Jersey v. U.S.,* 221 U.S. 1 (1911).

53. 212 U.S. 481 (1909).

54. Adolf A. Berle and Gardiner C. Means, *The Modern Corporation and Private Property* (New York: Harcourt, Brace & World, 1932).

55. Joel Seligman, "A Brief History of Delaware's General Incorporation Laws of 1899," *Delaware Journal of Corporation Law* 1, no. 2 (1976).

56. Delaware Code, Title 8, §102(b)(7).

57. Taub, *Other People's Houses,* 40–41.

58. Francis T. Cullen, Gray Cavender, William J. Maakestad, and Michael L. Benson, *Corporate Crime Under Attack: The Fight to Criminalize Business Violence,* 2nd ed. (New York: Routledge, 2006), 40.

59. "Love Canal Follow-Up Health Study," Division of Environmental Health Assessment, Center for Environmental Health, New York State Department of Health for the U.S. Department of Health and Human Services, Agency for Toxic Substances and Disease Registry, October 2008, www .health.ny.gov/environmental/investigations/love_canal/docs/report _public_comment_final.pdf.

60. Eckardt C. Beck, "The Love Canal Tragedy," *EPA Journal,* January 1979, https://archive.epa.gov/epa/aboutepa/love-canal-tragedy.html.

61. "Love Canal Follow-Up Health Study," 55.

62. Carl Zimmer, "Answers Begin to Emerge on How Thalidomide Caused Defects," *New York Times,* March 15, 2010, www.nytimes.com/2010/03 /16/science/16limb.html?pagewanted=all.

63. Sydney Lupkin, "Pharmaceutical Company Grunenthal Apologizes 50 Years After Drug Pulled Off Market," ABC News, September 1, 2012, https://abcnews.go.com/Health/drug-manufacturer-apologizes-thalidomide -victims/story?id=17135262.

64. Maria Pleyte, "White Collar Crime in the Twenty-First Century: Interview with Professor John Poulos," *UC Davis Business Law Journal,* blog, December 1, 2003, www.blj.ucdavis.edu/archives/vol-4-no-1/white-collar -crime-in-the-twenty-first-century.html.

65. Kenneth Mann, *Defending White-Collar Crime: A Portrait of Attorneys at Work* (New Haven, CT: Yale University Press, 1985), 19.

66. Mann, *Defending White-Collar Crime*, 21.

67. Memorandum from Lewis F. Powell Jr. to Eugene B. Sydnor Jr., August 23, 1971, www.scholarlycommons.law.wlu.edu/cgi/viewcontent.cgi?article =1000&context=powellmemo.

68. Powell Memo, 2–3.

69. Powell Memo, 3.

70. Powell Memo, 6.

71. Powell Memo, 11.

72. Powell Memo, 25.

73. Taub, *Other People's Houses,* 106.

74. Joshua Holland, "Hundreds of Wall Street Execs Went to Prison During the Last Fraud-Fueled Bank Crisis," Bill Moyers, September 17, 2013, www.billmoyers.com/2013/09/17/hundreds-of-wall-street-execs-went-to -prison-during-the-last-fraud-fueled-bank-crisis/.

75. 15 U.S. Code §7246.

76. "For David Polk, Dodd-Frank Pays," *The American Lawyer,* December 2010, www.davispolk.com/files/uploads/Articles/For.Davis.Polk.Dodd -Frank.Pays.AmLaw.dec10.pdf.

77. Jesse Eisinger, "Why Only One Top Banker Went to Jail for the Financial Crisis," *New York Times,* April 30, 2014, www.nytimes.com/2014/05/04 /magazine/only-one-top-banker-jail-financial-crisis.html.

78. Laura Noonan, Cale Tilford, Richard Milne, Ian Mount and Peter Wise, "Who went to jail for their role in the financial crisis?," September 20, 2018, *Financial Times,* https://ig.ft.com/jailed-bankers/.

79. Jiayang Fan, "The Accused," *New Yorker,* October 5, 2015, www.new yorker.com/magazine/2015/10/12/the-accused-jiayang-fan.

80. James C. McKinley Jr., "Abacus Bank Found Not Guilty of Mortgage Fraud and Other Charges," *New York Times,* June 4, 2015, www.nytimes .com/2015/06/05/nyregion/abacus-bank-found-not-guilty-of-mortgage -fraud-and-other-charges.html.

81. PBS, *Frontline,* Season 2017, Episode 15, "Abacus: Small Enough to Jail," www.pbs.org/video/abacus-small-enough-to-jail-suqmxe/.

82. Jason M. Breslow, "Lanny Breuer: Financial Fraud Has Not Gone Unpunished," PBS, *Frontline,* January 22, 2013, www.pbs.org/wgbh/frontline /article/lanny-breuer-financial-fraud-has-not-gone-unpunished/.

83. Jed S. Rakoff, "The Financial Crisis: Why Have No High-Level Executives Been Prosecuted?," *New York Review of Books*, January 9, 2014, www .nybooks.com/articles/2014/01/09/financial-crisis-why-no-executive -prosecutions/.

84. Susan Page, "Ben Bernanke: More Execs Should Have Gone to Jail for Causing Great Recession," *USA Today*, October 4, 2015, www.usatoday .com/story/news/politics/2015/10/04/ben-bernanke-execs-jail-great -recession-federal-reserve/72959402/.

85. Amicus brief of the Chamber of Commerce of the United States in Support of Petitioner in *Jeffrey K. Skilling v. United States*, December 2009, www.americanbar.org/content/dam/aba/publishing/preview/publiced _preview_briefs_pdfs_09_10_08_1394_PetitionerAmCuCoC.pdf.

86. Amicus briefs in *United States v. Vorley* and *United States v. Bases*; see www.chamberlitigation.com/cases/issue/securities-law-capital-markets -corporate-governance/dodd-frank-act.

87. Max de Haldevang and Heather Timmons, "One of the US's Greatest Gifts to the Global Economy Is Under Threat from Trump," *Quartz*, March 13, 2017, https://qz.com/927217/one-of-the-worlds-best-weapons -against-bribery-and-corruption-is-under-threat-from-trump/.

88. De Haldevang and Timmons, "One of the US's Greatest Gifts."

89. Oversight of the U.S. Department of Justice, Full Committee Hearing, March 6, 2013, www.judiciary.senate.gov/meetings/oversight-of-the-us -department-of-justice-2013-03-06.

90. Rod J. Rosenstein, "Remarks at the American Conference Institute's 35th International Conference on the Foreign Corrupt Practices Act," Oxon Hill, Maryland, November 29, 2018, www.justice.gov/opa/speech/dep uty-attorney-general-rod-j-rosenstein-delivers-remarks-american -conference-institute-0.

91. Dylan Tokar, "The Department of Justice Is Turning Back the Clock on Corporate Accountability," *Nation*, March 6, 2019, www.thenation.com /article/financial-crisis-justice-department-corporate-prosecutions-yates -memo/.

92. Sharon LaFraniere, "Mueller, in First Comments on Russia Inquiry, Declines to Clear Trump," *New York Times*, May 29, 2019, www.nytimes .com/2019/05/29/us/politics/mueller-special-counsel.html.

CHAPTER 4: VICTIMS IN THE SHADOWS

1. Katharine Q. Seelye, Julie Turkewitz, Jack Healy, and Alan Blinder, "How Do You Recover after Millions Watch You Overdose?," *New York Times*, December 11, 2018, www.nytimes.com/2018/12/11/us/overdoses-youtube -opioids-drugs.html.

2. J. M. Olejarz, "Understanding White-Collar Crime," *Harvard Business Review*, November 2016, https://hbr.org/2016/11/understanding-white -collar-crime.

3. See, e.g., Eugene Soltes, *Why They Do It: Inside the Mind of the White-Collar Criminal* (New York: Public Affairs, 2016); John Carreyrou, *Bad Blood: Secrets and Lies in a Silicon Valley Startup* (New York: Knopf, 2018); Diana B. Henriques, *The Wizard of Lies: Bernie Madoff and the Death of Trust* (New York: St. Martin's, 2017).

4. Hazel Croall, "What Is Known and What Should Be Known About White-Collar Crime Victimization?," in *The Oxford Handbook of White-Collar Crime*, eds. Shanna R. Van Slyke, Michael L. Benson, and Francis Cullin (New York: Oxford University Press, 2016), 59–77.

5. Croall, "What Is Known," 61.

6. Wall-Parker, "Measuring White Collar Crime," 38.

7. Payne, *White-Collar Crime*, 243.

8. Payne, *White-Collar Crime*, 38–39.

9. Environmental Protection Agency, "The Benefits and Costs of the Clean Air Act from 1990 to 2020," March 2011, 14, www.epa.gov/sites /production/files/2015-07/documents/summaryreport.pdf.

10. Rodney Huff, Christian Desilets, and John Kane, "The 2010 National Public Survey on White Collar Crime," National White Collar Crime Center, 2010, www.nw3c.org/docs/research/2010-national-public-survey -on-white-collar-crime.pdf.

11. Huff, Desilets, and Kane, "2010 National Public Survey," 14, Figure 1.

12. Michael R. Rand, "Criminal Victimization, 2008," Bureau of Justice Statistics, Bulletin, September 2009, Table 1, www.bjs.gov/content/pub/pdf /cv08.pdf.

13. Croall, "What Is Known," 66–67.

14. Forti and Visconti, "From Economic Crime to Corporate Violence," 66.

15. Seelye, Turkewitz, Healy, and Blinder, "How Do You Recover After Millions Have Watched You Overdose?"

16. Centers for Disease Control and Prevention, "Overview of the Drug Overdose Epidemic: Behind the Numbers," December 19, 2018 (revised), www.cdc.gov/drugoverdose/data/index.html.

17. Lindsey Bever and Peter Holley, "Mother Captured in 'Heartbreaking' Overdose Video Charged with Child Endangerment," *Washington Post,* November 30, 2016, www.washingtonpost.com/news/true-crime/wp/2016 /11/30/mother-captured-in-heartbreaking-overdose-video-charged -with-child-endangerment/?utm_term=.90cf071cac4a.

18. Seelye, Turkewitz, Healy, and Blinder, "How Do You Recover?"

19. Emily Langer, "Raymond Sackler, Philanthropist and Maker of OxyContin, Dies at 97," *Washington Post,* July 21, 2017, www.washingtonpost .com/local/obituaries/raymond-sackler-philanthropist-and-maker -of-oxycontin-dies-at-97/2017/07/21/5c1306dc-6e1a-11e7-96ab-5f38 140b38cc_story.html.

20. Christina Marinelli, "Stories in Stone: How an Egyptian Temple Tells Its Story," *Metropolitan Museum of Art,* blog, April 12, 2017, www .metmuseum.org/blogs/metkids/2017/temple-of-dendur.

21. Jared S. Hopkins, "OxyContin Made the Sacklers Rich. Now It's Tearing Them Apart," *Wall Street Journal,* July 13, 2019, www.wsj.com/articles /oxycontin-made-the-sacklers-rich-now-its-tearing-them-apart -11562990475.

22. Jillian Sackler, "Stop Blaming My Late Husband, Arthur Sackler, for the Opioid Crisis," *Washington Post,* April 11, 2019, www.washingtonpost .com/opinions/stop-blaming-my-late-husband-arthur-sackler-for-the -opioid-crisis/2019/04/11/5b8478a4-5c89-11e9-a00e-050dc7b82693 _story.html.

23. Art Van Zee, "The Promotion and Marketing of OxyContin: Commercial Triumph, Public Health Tragedy," *American Journal of Public Health* 99, no. 1 (February 2009): 221–27, citing "OxyContin Marketing Plan, 2002," Purdue Pharma, Stamford, Connecticut, 2002.

24. Patrick Radden Keefe, "The Family That Built an Empire of Pain," *New Yorker,* October 23, 2017, www.newyorker.com/magazine/2017/10/30 /the-family-that-built-an-empire-of-pain.

25. Linda Searing, "The Big Number: 50 million adults experience chronic pain," *Washington Post,* October 21, 2018, www.washingtonpost.com /national/health-science/the-big-number-50-million-adults-experience -chronic-pain/2018/10/19/30831828-d2e0-11e8-83d6-291fcead2ab1 _story.html.

26. Van Zee, "The Promotion and Marketing of OxyContin," citing "New Drug Application for OxyContin," Purdue Pharma, Stamford, Connecticut, December 1995.

27. Van Zee, "The Promotion and Marketing of OxyContin," citing General Accounting Office, Publication GAO-04-110, December 2003.

28. Scott Higham, Sari Horwitz, and Steven Rich, "76 Billion Opioid Pills: Newly Released Federal Data Unmasks the Epidemic," *Washington Post,* July 16, 2019, www.washingtonpost.com/investigations/76-billion-opioid -pills-newly-released-federal-data-unmasks-the-epidemic/2019/07/16 /5f29fd62-a73e-11e9-86dd-d7f0e60391e9_story.html?utm_term =.3ba117973cd2.

29. "Prescription Drugs: OxyContin Abuse and Diversion and Efforts to Address the Problem," General Accounting Office, Publication GAO-04-110, December 2003, www.govinfo.gov/content/pkg/GAOREPORTS -GAO-04-110/html/GAOREPORTS-GAO-04-110.htm.

30. Van Zee, "The Promotion and Marketing"; Janelle Lawrence, "Opioid Patient Worth $200,000 a Year to Purdue, State Says," *Bloomberg,* August 2, 2019, www.bloomberg.com/news/articles/2019-08-02/sacklers-are -massachusetts-ag-s-opioid-scapegoat-lawyer-says.

31. See "Statement of United States Attorney John Brownlee."

32. Barry Meier, "In Guilty Plea, OxyContin Maker to Pay $600 Million," *New York Times,* May 10, 2007, www.nytimes.com/2007/05/10/business /11drug-web.html.

33. Keefe, "The Family That Built an Empire of Pain."

34. Meier, "In Guilty Plea."

35. Andrew Lloyd Webber and Tim Rice, "The Money Kept Rolling In (and Out)," *Evita,* 1977.

36. General Accounting Office, Publication GAO-04-110.

37. "Oxycontin and Addiction," Substance Abuse Healthy Library, January 20, 2016, citing "Statement of John B. Brown, III, Acting Administrator Drug Enforcement Administration Before the United States House of Representatives Committee on Appropriations Subcommittee for the Departments of Commerce, Justice, State, the Judiciary and Related Agencies," March 20, 2003, www.comhs.org/about-us/newsroom/health -library/2016/01/20/oxycontin-and-addiction.

38. General Accounting Office, Publication GAO-04-110.

39. Van Zee, "The Promotion and Marketing of OxyContin," citing T. Cicero, J. Inciardi, and A. Muñoz, "Trends in Abuse of OxyContin and

Other Opioid Analgesics in the United States: 2002–2004," *Journal of Pain* 6, no. 10 (2005): 662–72.

40. Carl Hiaasen, "How Many People Died from Opioids While Scott and Florida Lawmakers Coddled Big Pharma?," *Miami Herald,* August 2, 2019, www.miamiherald.com/opinion/opn-columns-blogs/carl-hiaasen /article233462847.html.

41. See "Statement of United States Attorney John Brownlee."

42. See "Statement of United States Attorney John Brownlee."

43. This criminal charge involved three separate sections of the law: 21 U.S.C. §§331(a), 352(a), and 333(a)(1).

44. Meier, "In Guilty Plea, OxyContin Maker to Pay $600 Million."

45. See "Statement of United States Attorney John Brownlee."

46. Hamish Bowles, "Wild-at-Heart," *Vogue,* October 2013, https://archive .vogue.com/article/2013/10/wild-at-heart.

47. Oli Coleman, "Sacklers Fleeing NYC Following Family's OxyContin Scandal," Page Six, *New York Post,* May 20, 2019, https://pagesix.com /2019/05/20/sacklers-fleeing-nyc-following-familys-oxycontin-scandal/.

48. "Opioid Summaries by State," National Institute on Drug Abuse, May 2019 (revised), www.drugabuse.gov/drugs-abuse/opioids/opioid-summaries -by-state.

49. Centers for Disease Control and Prevention, "Prescription Opioid Data," June 27, 2019 (revised), www.cdc.gov/drugoverdose/data/prescribing .html.

50. Sara Randazzo, "Purdue Pharma Hit with Fresh Round of Opioid Law- suits," *Wall Street Journal,* May 16, 2019, www.wsj.com/articles/purdue -pharma-hit-with-fresh-round-of-opioid-lawsuits-11558028971?mod =article_inline.

51. Martha Bebinger, "Purdue Pharma Agrees to $270 Million Opioid Settle- ment with Oklahoma," NPR, March 26, 2019, www.npr.org/sections /health-shots/2019/03/26/706848006/purdue-pharma-agrees-to-270 -million-opioid-settlement-with-oklahoma; Jan Hoffman, "Purdue Pharma and Sacklers Reach $270 Million Settlement in Opioid Lawsuit," *New York Times,* March 26, 2019, www.nytimes.com/2019/03/26/health/opioids-pur due-pharma-oklahoma.html.

52. See First Amended Complaint, *Commonwealth of Massachusetts v. Pur- due Pharma,* January 31, 2019, www.assets.documentcloud.org/documents /5715954/Massachusetts-AGO-Amended-Complaint-2019-01-31 .pdf.

53. Higham, Horwitz, and Rich, "76 Billion Opioid Pills."

54. Sara Randazzo, "Purdue Pharma in Talks with Justice Department to Resolve Criminal, Civil Probes," *Wall Street Journal*, September 6, 2019, www.wsj.com/articles/purdue-pharma-in-talks-with-justice-department-to-resolve-criminal-civil-probes-11567792243.

55. "Purdue OxyContin Settlement Would Rank Among Largest in Pharma History," Reuters, September 11, 2019, www.reuters.com/article/us-purdue-pharma-settlement-history-fact/purdue-oxycontin-settlement-would-rank-among-largest-in-pharma-history-idUSKCN1VW2KL.

56. Jan Hoffman, "Purdue Pharma Tentatively Settles Thousands of Opioid Cases," *New York Times*, September 11, 2019, updated September 13, 2019, www.nytimes.com/2019/09/11/health/purdue-pharma-opioids-settlement.html?module=inline.

57. Associated Press, "North Carolina Among 25 States To Reject Purdue Pharma Settlement," WFAE, September 14, 2019, www.wfae.org/post/north-carolina-among-25-states-reject-purdue-pharma-settlement#stream/0.

58. Maura Healey, "Why I and Other Attorneys General Are Saying No to Purdue Pharma's Settlement," *Washington Post,* September 16, 2019, www.washingtonpost.com/opinions/why-im-rejecting-the-purdue-pharma-settlement/2019/09/16/1f86e94c-d8b5-11e9-ac63-3016711543fe_story.html.

59. Mike Spector and Tom Hals, "OxyContin Maker Purdue Pharma Is 'Pharma Co X' in U.S. Opioid Kick-Back Probe," Reuters, January 28, 2020, www.reuters.com/article/us-purdue-pharma-investigation-opioids-e/exclusive-oxycontin-maker-purdue-is-pharma-co-x-in-us-opioid-kickback-probe-sources-idUSKBN1ZR2RY.

60. Laura Strickler, "N.Y. AG: We Found $1 Billion in Sackler Wire Transfers, Purdue Pharma Owners Are 'Lowballing' Opioid Victims," NBC News, September 14, 2019, www.nbcnews.com/news/us-news/n-y-ag-we-found-1-billion-sackler-wire-transfers-n1054401.

61. Amy Woodyatt, "Louvre Removes Sackler Family Name from Museum Walls amid Opioid Controversy," CNN, July 18, 2019, www.cnn.com/style/article/sackler-family-louvre-intl-scli/index.html.

62. Victoria Stapley Brown, "The Met Is Re-evaluating Its Gift Acceptance Policy in Wake of Sackler Lawsuits," *Art Newspaper,* January 21, 2019, www.theartnewspaper.com/news/the-met-is-re-evaluating-its-gift-policy-in-wake-of-sackler-lawsuits.

63. Elizabeth Harris, "The Met Will Turn Down Sackler Money amid Fury over the Opioid Crisis," *New York Times*, May 15, 2019, www.nytimes .com/2019/05/15/arts/design/met-museum-sackler-opioids.html.

64. Cassandra Cross, "No Laughing Matter: Blaming the Victim of Online Fraud," *International Review of Victimology* 21, no. 2 (March 2015).

65. "Weight Loss Scams," AARP, April 19, 2019, www.aarp.org/money /scams-fraud/info-2019/weight-loss.html.

66. Daniela Porat and Patricia Callahan, "Evenflo, Maker of the 'Big Kid' Booster Seat, Put Profits over Child Safety," ProPublica, February 6, 2020, www.propublica.org/article/evenflo-maker-of-the-big-kid-booster-seat -put-profits-over-child-safety.

67. Department of Justice, *Roles, Rights, and Responsibilities: A Handbook for Fraud Victims Participating in the Federal Criminal Justice System*, 1998.

68. DOJ, *Roles, Rights, and Responsibilities.*

69. Taub, *Other People's Houses.*

CHAPTER 5: MUTUALLY ASSURED IMMUNITY FOR THE UPPER CLASS

1. Richard E. Farley, "Whatever Happened to Ivan Boesky?," *Town & Country,* November 9, 2016, www.townandcountrymag.com/society/money -and-power/a8525/ivan-boesky/.

2. John Homans, "Ivan the Terrible," *New York*, March 30, 2012, www .nymag.com/news/features/scandals/ivan-boesky-2012-4/; Bryan Burrough, "Hunting for Ivan Boesky," *Vanity Fair*, January 1993, www.vanityfair .com/news/1993/01/ivan-boesky-199301.

3. Bob Greene, "A $100 Million Idea: Use Greed for Good," *Chicago Tribune*, December 15, 1986, www.chicagotribune.com/news/ct-xpm-1986 -12-15-8604030634-story.html.

4. Martin Crustinger, "Ivan Boesky, Risk Arbitrager, Penalized $100 Million by SEC," Associated Press, November 15, 1986, https://apnews.com /f57e5758b375d2451bb23454f91f01fd.

5. James Sterngold, "Boesky Sentenced to 3 Years in Jail in Insider Scandal," *New York Times*, December 19, 1987, www.nytimes.com/1987/12/19 /business/boesky-sentenced-to-3-years-in-jail-in-insider-scandal.html.

6. "Boesky's Plea on Sentencing," *New York Times*, December 17, 1987, www.nytimes.com/1987/12/17/business/boesky-plea-on-sentencing.html;

Glenn Kessler, "Lompoc Prison, AKA 'Club Fed West,' Awaits Boesky," *Washington Post,* March 24, 1988, www.washingtonpost.com/archive/busi ness/1988/03/24/lompoc-prison-aka-club-fed-west-awaits-boesky /5ed43dcb-12af-4eb0-a73e-4526a5e736eb/.

7. Kurt Eichenwald, "Six Guilty of Stock Conspiracy," *New York Times,* August 1, 1989, www.nytimes.com/1989/08/01/business/six-guilty-of-stock -conspiracy.html.

8. Kurt Eichenwald, "Milken Defends 'Junk Bonds' as He Enters His Guilty Plea," *New York Times,* April 25, 1990, www.nytimes.com/1990/04/25 /business/milken-defends-junk-bonds-as-he-enters-his-guilty-plea.html.

9. Edward Wyatt, "Stratton Oakmont Executives Admit Stock Manipulation," *New York Times,* September 24, 1999, www.nytimes.com/1999/09 /24/business/stratton-oakmont-executives-admit-stock-manipulation.html.

10. 21 U.S. 642 (1997).

11. See, e.g., Hollie Silverman and A. J. Willingham, "A Judge Who Was Lenient on a Teen Accused of Rape Because He Came from a 'Good Family' Is Getting Threats," CNN, July 9, 2019, www.cnn.com/2019/07/09/us/judge -threatened-after-teen-rape-leniency/index.html; Associated Press and *USA Today,* "Judge Who Gave Stanford Rapist Brock Turner Lenient Sentence in Sexual Assault Case Is Ousted from Job by Voters," *South China Morning Post,* June 7, 2018, www.scmp.com/news/world/united-states-canada /article/2149614/judge-aaron-persky-who-gave-brock-turner-lenient.

12. German Lopez, "Brock Turner Loses Appeal of Sexual Assault Conviction," *Vox,* August 9, 2018, www.vox.com/identities/2018/8/9/17670322 /brock-turner-stanford-judge-persky-sexual-assault.

13. Cris Barrish, "Judge Said Du Pont Heir 'Will Not Fare Well' in Prison," *News Journal* (Delaware), March 28, 2014, www.delawareonline.com /story/news/crime/2014/03/28/sunday-preview-du-pont-heir-stayed -prison/7016769/.

14. Dana Ford, "Texas Teen Ethan Couch Gets 10 Years' Probation for Driving Drunk, Killing 4," CNN, www.cnn.com/2013/12/11/us/texas-teen -dwi-wreck/index.html.

15. Sarah Kaplan and Sarah Larimer, "'Affluenza' Teen Ethan Couch Captured in Mexico with His Mother," *Washington Post,* December 30, 2015, www.washingtonpost.com/news/morning-mix/wp/2015/12/29/reports -affluenza-teen-ethan-couch-has-been-detained-in-mexico/.

16. Stephen Young, "Affluenza Mom Tonya Couch's Bail Revoked. Again," *Dallas Observer,* www.dallasobserver.com/news/tonya-couchs-bail-revoked

-11652385; Claire Z. Cardona, "A History of Texas 'Affluenza Teen' Ethan Couch and His Family's Troubles with the Law," *Dallas Morning News*, August 2018, www.dallasnews.com/news/crime/2018/08/22/history-texas -affluenza-teen-ethan-couch-familys-troubles-law.

17. Lloyd Brumfield and Tom Steele, "Ethan Couch Released from Jail After 'Weak Positive' Drug Test Result," *Dallas Morning News*, January 3, 2020, www.dallasnews.com/news/2020/01/03/ethan-couch-released-from-jail -after-weak-positive-drug-test-result/.

18. Alan Feuer, "What the Jury's Note Could Mean for the Weinstein Deliberations," *New York Times*, February 21, 2020, www.nytimes.com/2020 /02/21/nyregion/harvey-weinstein-trial-jury.html.

19. Ronan Farrow, "Harvey Weinstein's Army of Spies," *New Yorker*, November 6, 2017, www.newyorker.com/news/news-desk/harvey-weinsteins-army -of-spies.

20. "Transcript: Donald Trump's Taped Comments About Women," October 8, 2016, *New York Times*, www.nytimes.com/2016/10/08/us/donald-trump -tape-transcript.html.

21. Megan Twohey and Jodi Kantor, "Weinstein and His Accusers Reach Tentative $25 Million Deal," *New York Times*, December 11, 2019, www .nytimes.com/2019/12/11/us/harvey-weinstein-settlement.html.

22. Rebecca Rosenberg, "Harvey Weinstein: I Deserve Pat on Back When It Comes to Women," Page Six, *New York Post*, December 15, 2019, https:// pagesix.com/2019/12/15/harvey-weinstein-i-deserve-pat-on-back -when-it-comes-to-women/.

23. Jan Ransom, "Harvey Weinstein's Stunning Downfall: 23 Years in Prison," *New York Times*, March 12, 2020, www.nytimes.com/2020/03 /11/nyregion/harvey-weinstein-sentencing.html.

24. Paul Tharp, "Sins of the Father—Grubman Finds Tony Prep Schools Unkind to Kinder," *New York Post*, March 7, 2003, https://nypost.com/2003 /03/07/sins-of-the-father-grubman-finds-tony-prep-schools-unkind -to-kinder/.

25. Alia Wong, "The Cutthroat World of Elite Public Schools," *Atlantic*, December 4, 2014, www.theatlantic.com/education/archive/2014/12/the -cutthroat-world-of-elite-public-schools/383382/.

26. Nikole Hannah-Jones, "Choosing a School for My Daughter in a Segregated City," *New York Times*, June 9, 2016, www.nytimes.com/2016/06 /12/magazine/choosing-a-school-for-my-daughter-in-a-segregated-city .html.

27. David Kleinbard, "The $1.7 Trillion Dot.Com Lesson," CNN Money, November 9, 2000, https://money.cnn.com/2000/11/09/technology/over view/.

28. Amy Feldman and Joan Caplin, "Is Jack Grubman the Worst Analyst Ever?," *Money Magazine*, April 25, 2002, https://money.cnn.com/2002 /04/25/pf/investing/grubman/.

29. *Securities and Exchange Commission v. Jack Grubman*, Complaint, April 28, 2003, www.sec.gov/litigation/complaints/comp18111b.htm.

30. Emily Nelson and Laurie P. Cohen, "Why Grubman Was So Keen to Get His Twins into the Y," *Wall Street Journal*, November 15, 2002, www.wsj .com/articles/SB1037311252116524828.

31. *SEC v. Jack Grubman.*

32. Charles Gasparino and Paul Beckett, "How John Reed Lost the Reins of Citigroup to His Co-Chairman," *Wall Street Journal*, April 14, 2000, www.wsj.com/articles/SB955666053711760021.

33. Memorandum from Jack B. Grubman to Sanford I. Weill, "AT&T and the 92nd Street Y," November 5, 1999, available at www.pbs.org/wgbh /pages/frontline/shows/wallstreet/wcom/92memo.html.

34. Gretchen Morgenson and Patrick McGeehan, "Wall St. and the Nursery School: A New York Story," *New York Times*, November 14, 2002, www .nytimes.com/2002/11/14/business/wall-st-and-the-nursery-school-a-new -york-story.html.

35. Randall Smith and Deborah Solomon, "Ebber's Exit Pinches Grubman, WorldCom's Biggest Cheerleader," *Wall Street Journal*, May 3, 2002, www.wsj.com/articles/SB1020374960801957120.

36. Reuters, "WorldCom Restates Profits by $74.4 Billion for 2 Years," *New York Times*, March 13, 2004, www.nytimes.com/2004/03/13/business /worldcom-restates-profits-by-74.4-billion-for-2-years.html.

37. Stephen Davis, Jon Lukomnik, and David Pitt-Watson, *The New Capitalists: How Citizen Investors Are Reshaping the Corporate Agenda* (Boston: Harvard Business School Press, 2006).

38. Feldman and Caplin, "Is Jack Grubman the Worst Analyst Ever?"

39. Michael Rubinkam (Associated Press), "Analyst Is Under a Harsher Light," *Los Angeles Times*, August 12, 2002, www.latimes.com/archives /la-xpm-2002-aug-12-fi-grubman12-story.html.

40. Janet Guyon, "Jack Grubman Is Back. Just Ask Him," *Fortune,* May 16, 2005, https://money.cnn.com/magazines/fortune/fortune_archive/2005 /05/16/8260134/index.htm.

41. Securities and Exchange Commission et al., "Ten of Nation's Top Investment Firms Settle Enforcement Actions Involving Conflicts of Interest Between Research and Investment Banking," joint press release, April 28, 2003, www.sec.gov/news/press/2003-54.htm.

42. Securities and Exchange Commission, "Questions and Answers Regarding the Distribution Funds in the Analysts Cases," August 19, 2003, www.sec.gov/news/press/globaldistqa.htm.

43. Stephen Labaton, "Wall Street Settlement: The Overview," *New York Times*, April 29, 2003, www.nytimes.com/2003/04/29/business/wall-street-settlement-overview-10-wall-st-firms-reach-settlement-analyst.html.

44. William H. Donaldson, "Speech by SEC Chairman: Prepared for Delivery at SEC Press Conference Regarding Global Settlement," Securities and Exchange Commission, April 28, 2003, www.sec.gov/news/speech/spch042803whd.htm.

45. Taub, *Other People's Houses,* x.

46. Michiyo Nakamoto and David Wighton, "Citigroup Chief Stays Bullish on Buy-Outs," *Financial Times*, July 9, 2007, www.ft.com/content/80e2987a-2e50-11dc-821c-0000779fd2ac.

47. Associated Press, "Regulators Finalize $1.4 Billion Wall St. Settlement," *New York Times*, April 28, 2003, www.nytimes.com/2003/04/28/business/regulators-finalize-14-billion-wall-st-settlement.html; Kathleen Day and Ben White, "SEC Probes Wall Street Executives," April 25, 2003, *Washington Post*, www.washingtonpost.com/archive/business/2003/04/25/sec-probes-wall-street-executives/98ee0c90-1b35-4a1c-9ae0-380d51e05605/.

48. Bob Connors, "Cops Bust Homeless Woman for Sending Child to School," NBC Connecticut, April 17, 2011, www.nbcconnecticut.com/news/local/Cops-Bust-Homeless-Woman-for-Sending-Child-to-School-120004374.html.

49. John Nickerson, "Bridgeport Woman Arrested for Registering Son in Norwalk School," *Stamford Advocate*, April 16, 2011, www.stamfordadvocate.com/policereports/article/Bridgeport-woman-arrested-for-registering-son-in-1340009.php.

50. Melissa Korn and Jennifer Levitz, "Another Parent Is Charged in College-Admissions Cheating Scheme," *Wall Street Journal*, December 9, 2019, www.wsj.com/articles/another-parent-is-charged-in-college-admissions-cheating-scheme-11575924695?mod=article_inline.

51. Daniel Golden and Doris Burke, "The Unseen Victims of the 'Varsity Blues' College Admissions Scandal," *New Yorker*, October 8, 2019, www.newyorker.com/books/page-turner/the-unseen-student-victims-of-the-varsity-blues-college-admissions-scandal.

52. U.S. Attorney's Office, District of Massachusetts, "Investigations of College Admissions and Testing Bribery Scheme," February 21, 2020 (updated), www.justice.gov/usao-ma/investigations-college-admissions-and-testing-bribery-scheme.

53. Joey Garrison, "Judge Sentences Ex-CEO to Longest Prison Term in College Admissions Scandal, Decries 'Appalling' Actions," *USA Today*, February 7, 2020, www.usatoday.com/story/news/nation/2020/02/07/college-admission-scandal-former-financier-doug-hodge-serve-xx-months-prison-most-so-far-parents-ple/4689485002/.

54. Golden and Burke, "The Unseen Victims."

55. U.S. Attorney, "Investigations of College Admissions and Testing Bribery Scheme."

56. Danny Hakim and William K. Rashbaum, "Governor Eliot Spitzer of New York is Linked to Prostitution Ring," *New York Times*, March 10, 2008, www.nytimes.com/2008/03/10/world/americas/10iht-10york.10884445.html; "How Spitzer Got Stung," CBS, March 11, 2008, www.cbsnews.com/news/how-spitzer-got-stung/.

57. James C. McKinley Jr., "Woman Accused of Blackmailing Eliot Spitzer Accepts Plea Deal," *New York Times*, October 2, 2007, www.nytimes.com/2017/10/02/nyregion/eliot-spitzer-blackmail-plea-deal.html.

58. Jane Mayer and Ronan Farrow, "Four Women Accuse New York's Attorney General of Physical Abuse," *New Yorker*, May 7, 2018, www.newyorker.com/news/news-desk/four-women-accuse-new-yorks-attorney-general-of-physical-abuse.

59. Bernstein, *American Oligarchs*, 198–99.

60. Andrew Prokop, "Trump Has Known About Eric Schneiderman Allegations for Years, Court Filing Reveals," *Vox*, May 11, 2018, www.vox.com/2018/5/11/17345298/trump-schneiderman-cohen-blackmail.

61. Josh Gerstein, "Lawyer Says He Took Schneiderman Abuse Allegations to Trump Attorney," *Politico*, May 11, 2018, www.politico.com/story/2018/05/11/eric-schneiderman-accusations-trump-583887.

62. "Wall Street Legend Sandy Weill: Break Up the Big Banks," CNBC, July 25, 2012, updated April 29, 2014, www.cnbc.com/id/48315170; Katrina

Brooker, "Citi's Creator, Alone with His Regrets," *New York Times*, January 2, 2010, www.nytimes.com/2010/01/03/business/economy/03weill.html? pagewanted=3&ref=business.

63. Winkler, *We the Corporations*, 173.

CHAPTER 6: FORGIVENESS FOR THE FORTUNATE

1. Martha Minow, *When Should Law Forgive?* (New York: Norton, 2019), 3.
2. Minow, *When Should Law Forgive?*, 1.
3. Minow, *When Should Law Forgive?*, 7.
4. John L. Hess, "Bergman Given 4 Months," *New York Times*, June 18, 1976, https://timesmachine.nytimes.com/timesmachine/1976/06/18/76402825 .pdf.
5. *United States v. Bergman*, 416 F. Supp. 496 (S.D.N.Y. 1976).
6. U.S. Sentencing Commission, *Inter-District Differences in Federal Sentencing Practices: Sentencing Practices Across Districts from 2005–2017*, January 2020, www.ussc.gov/sites/default/files/pdf/research-and-publications /research-publications/2020/20200122_Inter-District-Report.pdf.
7. Matt Zapotosky, Lynh Bui, Tom Jackman, and Devlin Barrett, "Manafort convicted on 8 counts; mistrial declared on 10 others," *New York Times*, August 21, 2018, www.washingtonpost.com/world/national-security /manafort-jury-suggests-it-cannot-come-to-a-consensus-on-a-single -count/2018/08/21/a2478ac0-a559-11e8-a656-943eefab5daf_story.html.
8. *United States v. Paul J. Manafort Jr.*, Plea agreement, September 13, 2018, www.justice.gov/file/1094151/download.
9. Darren Samuelsohn and Josh Gerstein, "Mueller: Guidelines call for Manafort to get up to 24.5 years in prison for Virginia convictions," *Politico*, February 15, 2019, www.politico.com/story/2019/02/15/mueller -manafort-sentencing-1173314.
10. Miles Parks and Ryan Lucas, "Paul Manafort, Former Trump Campaign Chairman, Sentenced to Just Under 4 Years," *Morning Edition*, NPR, March 7, 2019, www.npr.org/2019/03/07/701045248/paul-manafort-former -trump-campaign-chairman-sentenced-to-just-under-4-years.
11. Sharon LaFraniere and Alan Blinder, "Manafort's 47 Months: A Sentence That Drew Gasps from Around the Country," *New York Times*, March 8, 2019, www.nytimes.com/2019/03/08/us/politics/manafort-sentencing-ellis.html.

12. Virginia Heffernan, "How Could Anyone Think Paul Manafort Lived an 'Otherwise Blameless' Life?," *Los Angeles Times*, March 9, 2019, www .latimes.com/opinion/op-ed/la-oe-heffernan-manafort-sentence-guilt -20190309-story.html.

13. "Ex-Trump Campaign Chairman Paul Manafort Released from Prison to Home Confinement," *Wall Street Journal*, May 13, 2020, www.wsj.com /articles/ex-trump-campaign-chairman-paul-manafort-released-to-home -confinement-11589375414.

14. Joseph Goldstein and Nate Schweber, "Man's Death After Chokehold Raises Old Issue for the Police," *New York Times*, July 18, 2014, www .nytimes.com/2014/07/19/nyregion/staten-island-man-dies-after-he -is-put-in-chokehold-during-arrest.html?smid=pl-share.

15. John Marzulli, Rocco Parascandola, and Thomas Tracy, "NYPD No. 3's Order to Crack Down on Selling Loose Cigarettes Led to Chokehold Death of Eric Garner," *New York Daily News*, August 7, 2014, www .nydailynews.com/new-york/nyc-crime/wife-man-filmed-chokehold -arrested-article-1.1893790.

16. Ali Winston, "Medical Examiner Testifies Eric Garner Died of Asthma Caused by Officer's Chokehold," *New York Times*, May 15, 2019, www .nytimes.com/2019/05/15/nyregion/eric-garner-death-daniel-pantaleo -chokehold.html.

17. Michael R. Sisak, "NYPD Officer Says He Inflated Charge Against Eric Garner," Associated Press, May 22, 2019, https://apnews.com/ce589240f b884eceab7eaba2bfdff9e2.

18. New York Consolidated Laws, Tax Law–Tax §1814, Cigarette and Tobacco Products Tax, https://codes.findlaw.com/ny/tax-law/tax-sect-1814.html.

19. "Prices of Cigarettes by State," Fair Reporters, March 25, 2019, http:// fairreporters.net/health/prices-of-cigarettes-by-state/.

20. Joseph Goldstein, "A Cigarette for 75 Cents, 2 for $1: The Brisk, Shady Sale of 'Loosies,'" *New York Times*, April 11, 2011, www.nytimes.com /2011/04/05/nyregion/05loosie.html.

21. Chris Francescani, "Loose Cigarette Arrests in NYC Drop in Year After Eric Garner's Death," *Wall Street Journal*, July 15, 2015, www.wsj.com /articles/loose-cigarette-arrests-in-nyc-drop-in-year-after-eric-garners -death-1436992014.

22. Mark Morales, David Shortell, and Eric Levenson, "Prosecutors Say They Could Not Prove NYPD Officer Acted Willfully in Eric Garner's Death,"

CNN, July 16, 2019, www.cnn.com/2019/07/16/us/eric-garner-death-five
-years-later/index.html.

23. Emily Saul and Lia Eustachewich, "AG Barr Made Decision to Not Bring
Charges Against Eric Garner Cop," *New York Post,* July 16, 2019, https://
nypost.com/2019/07/16/ag-barr-made-decision-to-not-bring-charges
-against-eric-garner-cop-official/.

24. U.S. Attorney's Office, Eastern District of New York, "Statement by
United States Attorney Richard P. Donoghue," July 16, 2019, www.justice
.gov/usao-edny/pr/statement-united-states-attorney-richard-p-donoghue.

25. Gina Daidone and Kaja Whitehouse, "Pension Official Pleads Guilty to
Sex-and-Drug-Fueled Corruption," *New York Post*, November 8, 2017,
https://nypost.com/2017/11/08/pension-official-pleads-guilty-to-sex-and
-drug-fueled-corruption/.

26. Justin Baer, "Former New York Pension-Fund Executive Sentenced to 21
Months in Prison," *Wall Street Journal*, July 12, 2018, www.wsj.com
/articles/former-new-york-pension-fund-executive-sentenced-to-21
-months-in-prison-1531429910.

27. Nate Raymond and David Ingram, "N.Y. Pension Fund Manager, Brokers
Charged in Pay-to-Play Scheme," Reuters, December 21, 2016, www
.reuters.com/article/us-new-york-corruption-pensionfund-idUSKB
N14A1M3.

28. U.S. Attorney's Office, Southern District of New York, "Former Portfolio
Manager at the New York State Common Retirement Fund Charged in
'Pay-for-Play' Bribery Scheme," December 21, 2017, press release, www
.justice.gov/usao-sdny/pr/former-portfolio-manager-new-york-state
-common-retirement-fund-charged-pay-play-bribery.

29. U.S. Attorney's Office, Southern District of New York, "Former Managing Director at New York Broker-Dealer Sentenced in 'Pay-to-Play' Bribery Scheme Involving Public Pension Fund," press release, September 29,
2017, www.justice.gov/usao-sdny/pr/former-managing-director-new-york
-broker-dealer-sentenced-pay-play-bribery-scheme.

30. Brendan Pierson, "Ex-N.Y. Brokerage Executive Avoids Prison for Pension
Bribe Scheme," Reuters, September 29, 2017, www.reuters.com/article
/legal-us-new-york-corruption-pensions/ex-n-y-brokerage-executive
-avoids-prison-for-pension-bribe-scheme-idUSKCN1C42PP.

31. Anisa Kundu, "UC Berkeley Hires Deborah Kelley, Guilty of Committing Fraud, as Major Gifts Assistant," *Daily Californian,* July 17, 2018,

www.dailycal.org/2018/07/17/uc-berkeley-hires-deborah-kelley-guilty
-committing-fraud-major-gifts-assistant/.

32. Kenneth Mann, Stanton Wheeler, and Austin Sarat, "Sentencing the White-Collar Offender," *American Criminal Law Review* 17 (1980): 482, 486, 490.

33. Mann, Wheeler, and Sarat, "Sentencing the White-Collar Offender," 500.

34. Associated Press, "Guilty Plea in Fraud Case Tied to New York Pension," *New York Times*, December 4, 2009, www.nytimes.com/2009/12/04 /nyregion/04pension.html; New York State Office of the Attorney General, "Cuomo Announces Felony Guilty Plea by Former Comptroller Alan Hevesi in Pay-to-Play Pension Fund Kickback Scheme," press release, October 7, 2010, https://ag.ny.gov/press-release/cuomo-announces-felony-guilty-plea-former-comptroller-alan-hevesi-pay-play-pension.

35. Associated Press, "Guilty Plea in Fraud Case Tied to New York Pension."

36. Karen Freifeld, "LA Money Manager Gets No Jail in NY Corruption Case," Reuters, November 26, 2012, www.reuters.com/article/newyork -pension-broidy/la-money-manager-gets-no-jail-in-ny-corruption-case -idUSL1E8MQ4KJ20121126; Kara Scannell, "Former Trump inaugural fundraiser probed by federal prosecutors in New York," CNN, July 8, 2019, www.cnn.com/2019/07/08/politics/elliott-broidy-federal-investigation /index.html.

37. David A. Graham, "Trump's Vision of Lawless Order," *Atlantic*, July 29, 2017, www.theatlantic.com/politics/archive/2017/07/trump-long-island-ms -13/535317/.

38. Melissa Etehad, "Joe Arpaio, Former Sheriff in Arizona, Is Found Guilty of Criminal Contempt," *Los Angeles Times*, July 31, 2017, www.latimes .com/nation/la-na-joe-arpaio-verdict-20170706-story.html.

39. See Department of Justice, "Pardons Granted by President Trump," www.justice.gov/pardon/pardons-granted-president-donald-trump; Julie Hirschfeld Davis and Maggie Haberman, "Trump Pardons Joe Arpaio, Who Became Face of Crackdown on Illegal Immigration," *New York Times*, August 25, 2017, www.nytimes.com/2017/08/25/us/politics/joe -arpaio-trump-pardon-sheriff-arizona.html.

40. James F. McCarty, "West Virginia Federal Prison in the Mountains Houses Cuyahoga County's Corruption Convicts," *Cleveland Plain Dealer*, June 20, 2011, www.cleveland.com/countyincrisis/2011/06/west _virginia_federal_prison_i.html.

41. Federal Bureau of Prisons, FCI Morgantown, www.bop.gov/locations /institutions/mrg/.

42. Sam Taxy, Julie Samuels, and William Adams, "Drug Offenders in Federal Prison: Estimates of Characteristics Based on Linked Data," U.S. Department of Justice, Office of Justice Programs, Bureau of Justice Statistics, October 2015 (data from FY 2012), www.bjs.gov/content/pub /pdf/dofp12.pdf.

43. Federal Sentencing Commission, "Mandatory Minimum Penalties for Drug Offenses in the Criminal Justice System," October 2017, 18, Figure 3, www.ussc.gov/research/research-reports/mandatory-minimum-penalties -drug-offenses-federal-system.

44. Federal Bureau of Prisons, "Inmate Statistics: Based on Prior Month's Data," retrieved May 13, 2020, www.bop.gov/about/statistics/statistics _inmate_offenses.jsp.

45. Wendy Sawyer and Peter Wagner, "Mass Incarceration: The Whole Pie 2020," Prison Policy Initiative, March 24, 2020, www.prisonpolicy.org /reports/pie2020.html.

CHAPTER 7: WHISTLEBLOWERS AND JOURNALISTS

1. "Daniel Ellsberg Explains Why He Leaked The Pentagon Papers," *Fresh Air*, NPR, January 19, 2018, first aired December 4, 2017, www.npr.org /2018/01/19/579101965/daniel-ellsberg-explains-why-he-leaked-the -pentagon-papers.

2. Bob Woodward and Carl Bernstein, "Break-In Memo Sent to Ehrlichman," *Washington Post*, June 13, 1973, www.washingtonpost.com/politics/break -in-memo-sent-to-ehrlichman/2012/06/04/gJQAKsRCJV_story.html.

3. David Von Drehle, "FBI's No. 2 Was 'Deep Throat': Mark Felt Ends 30-Year Mystery of the *Post*'s Watergate Source," *Washington Post*, June 1, 2005, www.washingtonpost.com/politics/fbis-no-2-was-deep-throat-mark -felt-ends-30-year-mystery-of-the-posts-watergate-source/2012/06 /04/gJQAwseRIV_story.html.

4. "Nation: Poisoned by Plutonium," *TIME*, March 19, 1979, www.content .time.com/time/subscriber/article/0,33009,947011-1,00.html; Katharine Q. Seelye, "Kitty Tucker, 75, Who Raised Awareness of the Silkwood Case, Dies," *New York Times*, April 11, 2019, www.nytimes.com/2019/04 /11/obituaries/kitty-tucker-dead.html.

5. Jennifer Latson, "The Nuclear-Safety Activist Whose Mysterious Death Inspired a Movie," *TIME*, November 13, 2014, www.time.com/3574931 /karen-silkwood/.

6. Daniel Burnham, "A.E.C. Finds Evidence Supporting Charges of Health Hazards at Plutonium Processing Plant in Oklahoma," *New York Times*, January 8, 1975, www.nytimes.com/1975/01/08/archives/aec-finds-evidence -supporting-charges-of-health-hazards-at.html.

7. Lisa A. Goldstein, "Karen Silkwood: Nuclear Power Activist," *Women Whistle Blowers*, December 20, 2018, www.womenwhistleblowers.com /main/2018/12/20/karen-silkwood-nuclear-power-activist/.

8. Sherron Watkins, "Please Reconsider Proposed Amendments to the SEC Whistleblower Program," letter to the SEC Chairman and Commissioners, August 15, 2019, www.sec.gov/comments/s7-16-18/s71618-190087.htm.

9. Comment letter from Americans for Financial Reform Education Fund, September 18, 2018, www.sec.gov/comments/s7-16-18/s71618-4373288 -175491.pdf.

10. Amendments to the SEC's Whistleblower Program Rules, 83 Fed. Reg. 34,702 (proposed July 20, 2018), www.govinfo.gov/app/details/FR-2018 -07-20/2018-14411.

11. Sheryl Gay Stolberg and Nicholas Fandos, "From Afar, Congress Moves to Oversee Trump Coronavirus Response," *New York Times*, April 2, 2020, www.nytimes.com/2020/04/02/us/politics/coronavirus-congress -oversight-trump.html.

12. Susan Fowler, "Reflecting on One Very, Very Strange Year at Uber," February 19, 2017, www.susanjfowler.com/blog/2017/2/19/reflecting-on-one -very-strange-year-at-uber.

13. Margaret Jane Radin, *Boilerplate: The Fine Print, Vanishing Rights, and the Rule of Law* (New Jersey: Princeton University Press, 2013).

14. Alexander J.S. Colvin, "The Growing Use of Mandatory Arbitration," *Economic Policy Institute,* April 6, 2018, www.epi.org/publication/the -growing-use-of-mandatory-arbitration-access-to-the-courts-is-now -barred-for-more-than-60-million-american-workers/.

15. Nancy M. Modesitt, Janie F. Schulman, and Daniel P. Westman, *Whistleblowing: The Law of Retaliatory Discharge*, 3rd ed. (Arlington, VA: Bloomberg BNA, 2015); and 2017 cumulative supplement (current through August 2017).

16. Monica Navarro and J. Marc Vezina, *What Is . . . Qui Tam?* (Chicago: American Bar Association, 2015), 1.

17. Navarro and Vezina, *What Is?*, 50.

18. Doyle, "Qui Tam," 1.

19. Doyle, "Qui Tam," 28. See *Vermont Agency of Natural Resources v. United States ex rel. Stevens*, 529 U.S. 765, 774 (2000). The injury to the United States establishes standing under the FCA for the relator.

20. Riva D. Atlas, "John M. Gravitt, 61, a Pioneer in Lawsuits by Whistle-Blowers," *New York Times*, March 1, 2001, www.nytimes.com/2001/03/01/business/john-m-gravitt-61-a-pioneer-in-lawsuits-by-whistle-blowers.html.

21. James Helmer, *False Claims Act: Whistleblower Litigation* (Arlington, VA: Bloomberg BNA, 2017), 2.

22. Helmer, *False Claims Act*, 4.

23. Helmer, *False Claims Act*, 5–6.

24. Helmer, *False Claims Act*, v, 9.

25. Michael Sainato, "Wells Fargo Employees Say Little Has Changed Since Fake Accounts Scandal," *Guardian*, January 4, 2019, www.theguardian.com/business/2019/jan/04/wells-fargo-fake-accounts-scandal-employees.

26. Gretchen Morgenson, "Ex-Credit Suisse Exec Says She Was Fired and Harassed When She Wouldn't Bend Accounting Rules," NBC News, December 11, 2019, www.nbcnews.com/business/corporations/ex-credit-suisse-exec-says-she-was-fired-harassed-when-n1100046?cid=sm_npd_nn_tw_ma.

27. See, e.g., Taub, *Other People's Houses*, 165.

28. "56 Journalists Killed in 2018/Motive Confirmed," Committee to Protect Journalists, https://cpj.org/data/killed/2018/?status=Killed&motiveConfirmed%5B%5D=Confirmed&type%5B%5D=Journalist&start_year=2018&end_year=2018&group_by=location.

29. Merrit Kennedy, "Montana's Gianforte Pleads Guilty, Won't Serve Jail Time in Assault on Journalist," NPR, June 12, 2017, www.npr.org/sections/thetwo-way/2017/06/12/532613316/montanas-gianforte-pleads-guilty-wont-serve-jail-time-in-assault-on-journalist.

30. Ben Jacobs, "'This Needs to Stop': *Guardian* Reporter Ben Jacobs' Statement to Court," *Guardian*, June 12, 2017, www.theguardian.com/us-news/2017/jun/12/ben-jacobs-greg-gianforte-sentence-free-press.

31. Timothy Williams and Amy Harmon, "Maryland Shooting Suspect Had Long-Running Dispute with Newspaper," *New York Times*, June 29, 2018, www.nytimes.com/2018/06/29/us/jarrod-ramos-annapolis-shooting.html.

32. Benjamin Weiser and Ali Watkins, "Cesar Sayoc, Who Mailed Pipe Bombs to Trump Critics, Is Sentenced to 20 Years," *New York Times*, August 5, 2019, www.nytimes.com/2019/08/05/nyregion/cesar-sayoc-sentencing-pipe-bombing.html.

33. Eli Rosenberg, "Trump Admitted He Attacks Press to Shield Himself from Negative Coverage, Lesley Stahl Says," *Washington Post*, May 22, 2018, www.washingtonpost.com/news/the-fix/wp/2018/05/22/trump-admitted-he-attacks-press-to-shield-himself-from-negative-coverage-60-minutes-reporter-says/.

34. Shane Harris, Greg Miller, and Josh Dawsey, "CIA Concludes Saudi Crown Prince Ordered Jamal Khashoggi's Assassination," *Washington Post*, November 16, 2018, www.washingtonpost.com/world/national-security/cia-concludes-saudi-crown-prince-ordered-jamal-khashoggis-assassination/2018/11/16/98c89fe6-e9b2-11e8-a939-9469f1166f9d_story.html.

35. Christina Maza, "'Get Rid of Them': Donald Trump and Vladimir Putin Bond over Dislike of Journalists and 'Fake News,'" *Newsweek*, June 28, 2019, www.newsweek.com/donald-trump-vladimir-putin-fake-news-press-freedom-1446490.

36. Terry Gross, "Ronan Farrow: 'Catch and Kill' Tactics Protected Both Weinstein and Trump," *Fresh Air*, NPR, October 15, 2019, www.npr.org/2019/10/15/770249717/ronan-farrow-catch-and-kill-tactics-protected-both-weinstein-and-trump.

37. "Daphne Caruana Galizia Killed as Vehicle Blows Up in Bidnija," *Malta Independent*, October 16, 2017, www.independent.com.mt/articles/2017-10-16/local-news/Person-dies-as-vehicle-goes-up-in-flames-in-Bidnija-6736180314.

38. "Murder in Paradise: The Death of a Crusading Journalist Rocks Malta," *Economist*, October 21, 2017, www.economist.com/europe/2017/10/21/the-death-of-a-crusading-journalist-rocks-malta.

39. Matthew Caruana Galizia, "Fighting for Justice for My Murdered Mother," BBC, May 2, 2019, www.bbc.com/news/world-48093331.

40. Caruana Galizia, "Fighting for Justice."

41. Stephen Grey, "The Silencing of Daphne," Reuters, April 17, 2018, www.reuters.com/investigates/special-report/malta-daphne/.

42. Grey, "Silencing of Daphne."

43. Chris Scicluna and Stephen Grey, "Police Investigating Murder of Malta Journalist Arrest Local Businessman," Reuters, November 20, 2019, www

.reuters.com/article/us-malta-daphne/police-investigating-murder
-of-malta-journalist-arrest-local-businessman-idUSKBN1XU0TQ.

44. Rachel Donadio, "A Tiny Island Exposes Europe's Failures," *Atlantic*,
December 5, 2019, www.theatlantic.com/international/archive/2019/12
/daphne-caruana-galizia-malta/602923/.

45. Scicluna and Grey, "Police Investigating Murder of Malta Journalist."

46. Luke Harding, "Panama Papers Investigation Wins Pulitzer Prize," *Guardian*,
April 11, 2017, www.theguardian.com/world/2017/apr/11/panama-papers
-investigation-wins-pulitzer-prize.

47. Marisa Taylor and Kevin G. Hall, "Have an Offshore? Maybe You're Feel-
ing Indigestion," McClatchyDC, April 6, 2016, www.mcclatchydc.com
/news/nation-world/national/article70402327.html.

48. Eric Lipton and Julie Creswell, "Panama Papers Show How Rich United
States Clients Hid Millions Abroad," *New York Times*, June 6, 2016,
www.nytimes.com/2016/06/06/us/panama-papers.html?hp&action
=click&pgtype=Homepage&clickSource=story-heading&module=first
-column-region&region=top-news&WT.nav=top-news&_r=0&fbclid=
IwAR1Act-1JIYxEdyAwSsH_y2gkmYsMoWuqvbUVfE-uaqJOVjy
fCuRAAFIzQE.

49. "About the Investigation," International Consortium of Investigative Journalists, www.icij.org/investigations/panama-papers/pages/panama-papers
-about-the-investigation/.

50. Michael Hudson, "Panama Papers Wins Pulitzer Prize," International
Consortium of Investigative Journalists, April 7, 2017, www.icij.org/blog
/2017/04/panama-papers-wins-pulitzer-prize/.

51. Will Fitzgibbon, "First American Charged with Panama Papers Crimes
Appears in Court," Panama Papers, ICIJ, January 29, 2019, www.icij.org
/investigations/panama-papers/first-american-charged-with-panama
-papers-crimes-appears-in-court/.

52. Department of Justice, U.S. Attorney's Office, "Four Defendants Charged
in Panama Papers Investigation," Southern District of New York, press release, December 4, 2018, www.justice.gov/usao-sdny/pr/four-defendants
-charged-panama-papers-investigation.

53. Department of Justice, Office of Public Affairs, press release, "U.S. Accountant Pleads Guilty in Panama Papers Investigation," February 28,
2020, www.justice.gov/opa/pr/us-accountant-pleads-guilty-panama-papers
-investigation.

54. Department of Justice, "Four Defendants Charged."

CHAPTER 8: A CONTAGION OF PUBLIC CORRUPTION

1. "Senate Health Committee Announces Briefing to Update Senators on Coronavirus," January 23, 2020, www.help.senate.gov/chair/newsroom /press/senate-health-committee-announces-briefing-to-update-senators -on-coronavirus.
2. Aaron Blake, "Timeline: Trump's efforts to downplay the coronavirus threat," *Washington Post*, March 31, 2020, www.washingtonpost.com /politics/2020/03/12/trump-coronavirus-timeline/.
3. Robert Faturechi and Derek Willis, "Senator Dumped Up to $1.7 Million of Stock After Reassuring Public About Coronavirus Preparedness," *ProPublica*, March 19, 2020, www.propublica.org/article/senator-dumped-up -to-1-7-million-of-stock-after-reassuring-public-about-coronavirus -preparedness.
4. Karl Evers-Hillstrom, "Senate Intel Chair Unloaded Stocks in Mid-February before Coronavirus Rocked Markets," ProPublica, March 19, 2020, www.opensecrets.org/news/2020/03/burr-unloaded-stocks-before -coronavirus/.
5. Chris Marquette, "DOJ Examining Sen. Richard Burr for Stock Dump," *Roll Call*, March 30, 2020, www.rollcall.com/2020/03/30/doj-examining -sen-richard-burr-for-stock-dump/.
6. Lachlan Markay, William Bredderman, Sam Brodey, "Sen. Kelly Loeffler Dumped Millions in Stock After Coronavirus Briefing," *Daily Beast*, March 19, 2020, updated March 20, 2020, www.thedailybeast.com/sen-kelly -loeffler-dumped-millions-in-stock-after-coronavirus-briefing?ref=scroll.
7. Lisette Voytko, "Senator Loeffler Discloses Additional Millions In Stock Sales, Inflaming Insider Trading Suspicions," *Forbes*, April 1, 2020, www .forbes.com/sites/lisettevoytko/2020/04/01/sen-loeffler-dumped -19-million-in-shares-after-coronavirus-intel-briefing/#28dc60a76d03.
8. David Leonhardt, "They. Sold. Their. Stock. They Could Have Made a Difference, But They Made a Profit," *New York Times*, March 20, 2020, www.nytimes.com/2020/03/20/opinion/burr-loeffler-stocks-coronavirus .html.
9. Del Quentin Wilber and Jennifer Haberkorn, "FBI Serves Search Warrant on Senator in Investigation of Stock Sales Linked to Coronavirus," May 13, 2020, *Los Angeles Times,* www.latimes.com/politics/story/2020-05-13 /fbi-serves-warrant-on-senator-stock-investigation.

10. Matthew Stephenson, "Corruption and Democratic Institutions: A Review and Synthesis," in *Greed, Corruption, and the Modern State: Essays in Political Economy*, eds. Susan Rose-Ackerman and Paul Lagunes (Cheltenham, UK: Edward Elgar, 2015), 92–133.

11. Zephyr Teachout, *Corruption in America: From Benjamin Franklin's Snuff Box to Citizens United* (Cambridge: Harvard University Press, 2014).

12. Scott Rasmussen, "Voters Rate Political Corruption as America's Biggest Crisis," Real Clear Politics, April 25, 2019, www.realclearpolitics.com /articles/2019/04/25/voters_rate_political_corruption_as_americas _biggest_crisis_140156.html.

13. Melanie Zenona, Kyle Cheney, and Josh Gerstein, "Prosecutors: Rep. Duncan Hunter Used Campaign Funds to Pursue Affairs," *Politico*, June 25, 2019, www.politico.com/story/2019/06/25/duncan-hunter-campaign -funds-affairs-1382197.

14. Neil Vigdor, "Duncan Hunter Sentenced to 11 Months in Prison for Stealing Campaign Funds," *New York Times*, March 17, 2020, www .nytimes.com/2020/03/17/us/duncan-hunter-sentencing.html.

15. *United States v. Sun-Diamond Growers of California*, 526 U.S. 398 (1999).

16. Joan Biskupic, "Court Narrows Gifts Law in Espy Ruling," *Washington Post*, April 28, 1999, www.washingtonpost.com/wp-srv/national/longterm /supcourt/stories/court042899.htm.

17. Biskupic, "Court Narrows."

18. *United States v. McDonnell*, 136 S. Ct. 2355 (2016).

19. *Buckley v. Valeo*, 424 U.S. 1 (1976).

20. *Buckley*, 424 U.S. at 45.

21. *Buckley*, 424 U.S. at 19.

22. *Federal Election Commission v. Wisconsin Right to Life, Inc.*, 551 U.S. 449 (2007).

23. 599 F.3d 686 (D.C. Cir. 2010).

24. 567 U.S. 516 (2012).

25. Bob Biersack, "McCutcheon Decision: Add Some More Zeroes to That Check," OpenSecrets, April 2, 2014, www.opensecrets.org/news/2014/04 /mccutcheon-decision-add-some-more-z/.

26. 138 S. Ct. 2448 (2018).

27. Alana Semuels, "Is This the End of Public-Sector Unions in America?," *Atlantic*, June 27, 2018, www.theatlantic.com/politics/archive/2018/06/janus -afscme-public-sector-unions/563879/.

28. *Janus v. AFSCME*, 138 S. Ct. 2448 (2018).

29. *Bluman v. Federal Election Commission*, 800 F. Supp. 2d 281, 290 (D.D.C. 2011).

30. 565 U.S. 1104 (2012).

31. Karl Evers-Hillstrom and Raymond Arke, "Following *Citizens United*, Foreign-Owned Corporations Funnel Millions into US Elections," Open-Secrets, March 22, 2019, www.opensecrets.org/news/2019/03/citizens-united-foreign-owned-corporations-put-millions-in-us-elections/.

32. Federal Election Commission, "FEC Remains Open for Business, Despite Lack of Quorum," September 11, 2019, www.fec.gov/updates/fec-remains-open-business-despite-lack-quorum/.

33. Congressional Research Service, "Federal Election Commission: Membership and Policymaking Quorum, In Brief," updated April 3, 2020, www.fas.org/sgp/crs/misc/R45160.pdf.

34. Sharon LaFraniere, Benjamin Weiser and Maggie Haberman, "Prosecutors Say Trump Directed Illegal Payments During Campaign," *New York Times*, December 7, 2018, www.nytimes.com/2018/12/07/nyregion/michael-cohen-sentence.html.

35. Karl Evers-Hillstrom, "Trump FEC Pick Offers Mixed Messages on Donor Disclosure," OpenSecrets, March 10, 2020, www.opensecrets.org/news/2020/03/trey-trainor-confirmation-hearing/.

36. Biography of James E. Trainor via Akerman LLP via Internet Archive, ProPublica, https://projects.propublica.org/trump-town/staffers/james-e-trainor-iii.

37. Zach Montellaro, "Senate clashes over fate of embattled election watchdog," *Politico*, March 10, 2010, www.politico.com/news/2020/03/10/senate-clashes-federal-election-watchdog-125094.

38. "Undercover in New York," Global Witness, January 31, 2016, www.globalwitness.org/shadyinc/.

39. "Anonymous, Inc., Part I," *60 Minutes*, CBS, www.cbs.com/shows/60_minutes/video/gx7ay0DIRgcqYOSpVU90j89KsHvWdVJB/anonymous-inc-part-i/.

40. Edward Robinson, "Corruption Fighter Gooch Tackles Abusive Shell Companies," *Bloomberg*, September 11, 2014, www.bloomberg.com/news/articles/2014-09-11/corruption-fighter-gooch-tackles-abusive-shell-companies.

41. Cyrus R. Vance Jr., "It's Time to Eliminate Anonymous Shell Companies," *Reuters*, October 9, 2012, http://blogs.reuters.com/great-debate/2012/10/09/its-time-to-eliminate-anonymous-shell-companies/.

42. Sheldon Whitehouse, "Whitehouse, Grassley Introduce Title Act to Curb Proliferation of Anonymous Shell Corporations in US," press release, June 18, 2019, www.whitehouse.senate.gov/news/release/whitehouse-grassley -introduce-title-act-to-curb-proliferation-of-anonymous-shell-corpora-tions-in-us.

43. House Judiciary Committee, Combating Kleptocracy hearing, June 19, 2019, video available at www.judiciary.senate.gov/meetings/combating -kleptocracy-beneficial-ownership-money-laundering-and-other-reforms.

44. Senate Committee on the Judiciary "Combatting Kleptocracy: Beneficial Ownership, Money Laundering, and Other Reforms," June 19, 2019, www.judiciary.senate.gov/meetings/combating-kleptocracy-beneficial -ownership-money-laundering-and-other-reforms.

45. Financial Crimes Enforcement Network, "FinCEN Takes Aim at Real Estate Secrecy in Manhattan and Miami," press release, January 13, 2016, www.fincen.gov/sites/default/files/news_release/20160113.pdf.

46. Nicholas Nehamas and Rene Rodriguez, *Miami Herald*, July 18, 2018, updated July 20, 2018, www.miamiherald.com/news/business/real-estate -news/article213797269.html.

47. Financial Crimes Enforcement Network, press release, "FinCEN Renews Real Estate 'Geographic Targeting Orders' to Identify High-End Cash Buyers in Six Major Metropolitan Areas, February 23, 2017, www.fincen .gov/news/news-releases/fincen-renews-real-estate-geographic-targeting -orders-identify-high-end-cash.

48. Financial Crimes Enforcement Network, press release, "FinCEN Reissues Real Estate Geographic Targeting Orders and Expands Coverage to 12 Metropolitan Areas," November 15, 2018, www.fincen.gov/news/news -releases/fincen-reissues-real-estate-geographic-targeting-orders-and -expands-coverage-12.

49. Final Vote Results for Roll Call 577, H.R. 2513, October 19, 2019.

50. H.R.2513, Corporate Transparency Act of 2019, www.congress.gov/bill /116th-congress/house-bill/2513/text.

51. Louise Russell-Prywata, "To Be Effective, Public Company Ownership Registries Must Be Linked," *Global Anticorruption Blog*, November 1, 2018, https://globalanticorruptionblog.com/2018/11/01/guest-post-to-be -effective-public-company-ownership-registries-must-be-linked/.

52. Russell-Prywata, "To Be Effective, Public Company Ownership."

CHAPTER 9: SUSPICIOUS MINDS

1. Margaret Heffernan, *Willful Blindness: Why We Ignore the Obvious at Our Peril* (New York: Bloomsbury, 2011), 1, citing the transcript in *U.S. v. Lay* in the Southern District of Texas, Houston Division, May 2006; Paul Pendergraft, "Enron Judge Brings No-Nonsense Approach to Bench," NPR, February 2, 2006, www.npr.org/templates/story/story.php?storyId= 5186649; *United States v. Skilling* (Fifth Circuit, 2009), p. 25, fn 19, www .justice.gov/sites/default/files/criminal-vns/legacy/2010/04/26/01-06 -09skilling.pdf.

2. Mary Flood, "Enron Jurors Must Discern Intent of Skilling, Lay," *Houston Chronicle*, April 2, 2006, www.chron.com/business/enron/article/Enron -jurors-must-discern-intent-of-Skilling-Lay-1525773.php.

3. Flood, "Enron Jurors Must Discern Intent."

4. Justice Manual, Criminal Resource Manual 901-999, "Knowingly and Willfully," www.justice.gov/archives/jm/criminal-resource-manual-910-know ingly-and-willfully.

5. *United States v. Yermian*, 468 U.S. 63 (1984).

6. *United States v. Dotterweich*, 320 U.S. 277, 284 (1943).

7. *Dotterweich*, at 283.

8. *Dotterweich*, at 280.

9. *Dotterweich*, at 286.

10. *Morissette v. United States*, 342 U.S. 246 (1952).

11. *United States v. Park*, 421 U.S. 658, 672 (1975).

12. *Park*, at 673–674.

13. Michael W. Peregrine, "The 'Responsible Corporate Officer Doctrine' Survives to Perplex Corporate Boards," *Harvard Law School Forum on Corporate Governance and Financial Regulation*, July 5, 2017, https:// corpgov.law.harvard.edu/2017/07/05/the-responsible-corporate-officer -doctrine-survives-to-perplex-corporate-boards/.

14. Department of Justice, "Former Peanut Company President Receives Largest Criminal Sentence in Food Safety Case," press release, September 21, 2015, www.justice.gov/opa/pr/former-peanut-company-president-receives- largest-criminal-sentence-food-safety-case-two.

15. Department of Justice, Office of Public Affairs, press release, "Former Peanut Company President Receives Largest Criminal Sentence in Food

Safety Case; Two Others also Sentenced for Their Roles in Salmonella-Tainted Peanut Product Outbreak," September 21, 2015, www.justice .gov/opa/pr/former-peanut-company-president-receives-largest-criminal -sentence-food-safety-case-two.

16. "Conyers Cooglatte Mens Rea Reform Deal in the Works in the House Judiciary Committee," *Corporate Crime Reporter*, November 13, 2015, www.corporatecrimereporter.com/news/200/conyers-goodlatte-mens-rea -reform-deal-in-the-works/?fbclid=IwAR1_3xS-CqtGFuO--e1r-rS8Eoiw Amm9T0jxSR8Y2t5skXClUu2OlSEKqmU.

17. Zach Carter, "White House Comes Out against Effort to Block White Collar Crime Prosecutions," *Huffington Post*, November 19, 2015, www .huffpost.com/entry/white-collar-crime-white-house-response_n _564dd06be4b00b7997f95240.

18. John G. Malcolm, "The Pressing Need for Mens Rea Reform," The Heritage Foundation, Legal Memorandum No. 160, September 1, 2015, http:// thf_media.s3.amazonaws.com/2015/pdf/LM160.pdf.

19. Rena Steinzor, "Federal White Collar Crime: Six Case Studies Drawn from Ongoing Prosecutions to Protect Public Health, Worker and Consumer Safety, and the Environment," Center for Progressive Reform, Issue Alert No. 1507, November 2015, https://cpr-assets.s3.amazonaws.com /documents/Steinzor_Federal_Crimes_1507_Final.pdf.

CHAPTER 10: TAX AND PUNISH

1. Willie Sutton and Edward Linn, *Where the Money Was* (New York: Viking, 1976), 120.

2. Peter Duffy, "Willie Sutton, Urbane Scoundrel," *New York Times*, February 17, 2002, www.nytimes.com/2002/02/17/nyregion/city-lore-willie -sutton-urbane-scoundrel.html.

3. Treasury Inspector General for Tax Administration, "Improvements Are Needed in Resource Allocation and Management Controls for Audits of High-Income Taxpayers," Audit Report 2015-30-078, September 18, 2015, www.treasury.gov/tigta/auditreports/2015reports/201530078fr.html.

4. Internal Revenue Service, "IRS Budget and Workforce," January 3, 2020 (updated), www.irs.gov/statistics/irs-budget-and-workforce; also see Richard Rubin, "IRS Personal Income-Tax Audits Drop to Lowest Level in Decades," *Wall Street Journal*, January 6, 2010, www.wsj.com/articles

/irs-personal-income-tax-audits-drop-to-lowest-level-in-decades-11578352541.

5. Paul Kiel, "Lawmakers Just Confronted the IRS over Tax Audits That Target the Poor," ProPublica, April 10, 2019, www.propublica.org/article/lawmakers-to-irs-commissioner-charles-rettig-system-stacked-for-the-rich.

6. Paul Kiel and Jesse Eisinger, "How the IRS Was Gutted," ProPublica, December 11, 2018, www.propublica.org/article/how-the-irs-was-gutted.

7. Paul Kiel, "It's Getting Worse: The IRS Now Audits Poor Americans at About the Same Rate as the Top 1%," ProPublica, May 30, 2019, www.propublica.org/article/irs-now-audits-poor-americans-at-about-the-same-rate-as-the-top-1-percent.

8. Kiel, "It's Getting Worse."

9. Kiel and Eisinger, "How the IRS Was Gutted."

10. Kiel, "Lawmakers Just Confronted the IRS."

11. Kiel, "Lawmakers Just Confronted the IRS."

12. Rubin, "IRS Personal Income-Tax Audits Drop."

13. Senate Committee on Finance, "Wyden Statement on Lowest IRS Audit Rates in 40 Years," press release, January 7, 2020, www.finance.senate.gov/ranking-members-news/wyden-statement-on-lowest-irs-audit-rates-in-40-years_-.

14. Ryan Thomas, "Americans Still Hurting from GOP Tax Scam, Want Corporations and the Wealthy to Pay Fair Share," press release, Tax March, April 15, 2019, https://taxmarch.org/americans-still-hurting-from-gop-tax-scam-want-corporations-and-the-wealthy-to-pay-fair-share/.

15. Amy Howe, "Justices to Take Up Battle over Trump Financial Documents," *Scotus Blog*, December 13, 2019, www.scotusblog.com/2019/12/justices-to-take-up-battle-over-trump-financial-documents/.

16. John Harwood, "Few Americans Think They're Getting a Trump Tax Cut: NBC/WSJ Poll," CNBC, April 8, 2019, www.cnbc.com/2019/04/05/few-americans-think-theyre-getting-a-trump-tax-cut-nbcwsj-poll.html.

17. Joseph Zeballos-Roig, "These 7 Charts Show Trump's Tax Cuts Still Haven't Been the Economic 'Rocket Fuel' He Promised, 2 Years After the Fact," *Markets Insider*, December 22, 2019, https://markets.businessinsider.com/news/stocks/7-charts-showing-trump-tax-cuts-not-economic-rocket-fuel-2019-12-1028780773.

18. Scott Horsley, "After 2 Years, Trump Tax Cuts Have Failed to Deliver on GOP's Promises," *All Things Considered*, NPR, December 20, 2019, www

.npr.org/2019/12/20/789540931/2-years-later-trump-tax-cuts-have
-failed-to-deliver-on-gops-promises.

19. Scott Horsley, "U.S. Economic Growth Slowed in 2019 to 2.3%," NPR, January 30, 2020, www.npr.org/2020/01/30/800985774/u-s-economy -slowed-in-2019-to-2-3.

20. Heather Long, "GOP Leader Concedes Tax Cuts May Not Pay for Themselves as 2019 Deficit Grows," *Washington Post,* June 11, 2019, www .washingtonpost.com/business/2019/06/11/gop-leader-concedes-tax-cuts -may-not-pay-themselves-deficit-grows/.

21. Kiel and Eisinger, "How the IRS Was Gutted."

22. Matt Egan, "Corporate America Gives Out a Record $1 Trillion in Stock Buybacks," CNN, December 17, 2018, www.cnn.com/2018/12/17/invest ing/stock-buybacks-trillion-dollars/index.html.

23. Galen Hendricks and Daniella Zessoules, "What We Could Have Had for $1.9 Trillion," Center for American Progress, June 20, 2019, www.ameri canprogress.org/issues/economy/news/2019/06/20/471209/1-9-trillion/.

24. Peter Sullivan, "CBO: ObamaCare Fix Would Not Make Up for Mandate Repeal, *The Hill,* November 29, 2017, https://thehill.com/policy/health care/362352-cbo-obamacare-fix-would-not-make-up-for-mandate-repeal.

25. Brett Samuels, "Larry Summers: 10,000 People Will Die Annually from GOP Tax Bill," *The Hill,* December 4, 2017, https://thehill.com/policy/healthcare /363152-larry-summers-10000-people-will-die-annually-from-gop-tax-bill.

26. Jesse Drucker and Jim Tankersley, "How Big Companies Won New Tax Breaks from the Trump Administration," *New York Times*, December 30, 2019, www.nytimes.com/2019/12/30/business/trump-tax-cuts-beat-gilti .html?smid=nytcore-ios-share.

27. Kimberly Amadeo and Somer G. Anderson, "Unemployment Rate by Year Since 1929 Compared to Inflation and GDP," The Balance, May 8, 2020, https://www.thebalance.com/unemployment-rate-by-year-3305506; Jerome H. Powell, "Current Economic Issues," at the Peterson Institute for International Economics, Washington, D.C. (via webcast), May 13, 2020, www.federalreserve.gov/newsevents/speech/powell20200513a.htm.

28. Liz Moyer, "Four Hedge Fund Managers Top $1 Billion in Pay as the Industry Rebounds," CNBC, May 30, 2018, www.cnbc.com/2018/05/30 /four-hedge-fund-managers-top-1-billion-in-pay.html.

29. Morris Pearl, with Sam Quigley, *How to Think Like a Patriotic Millionaire* (Washington D.C.: Strong Arm Press, 2018) 56.

30. Jeff Guo, "Trump Said Hedge Funders Were 'Getting Away with Murder.' Now He Wants One to Help Run the Economy," *Washington Post*, November 30, 2016, www.washingtonpost.com/news/wonk/wp/2016/11/30/trump-said-hedge-funders-were-getting-away-with-murder-now-he-wants-one-to-help-run-the-economy/.

31. Michael J. De La Merced, "Schwarzman's Unfortunate War Analogy," *New York Times*, August 16, 2010, https://dealbook.nytimes.com/2010/08/16/schwarzmans-unfortunate-war-analogy/.

32. Alexander Burns, "Donald Trump Rode to Power in the Role of the Common Man," *New York Times*, November 9, 2016, www.nytimes.com/2016/11/09/us/politics/donald-trump-wins.html.

33. Renae Merle, "What Is 'Carried Interest' and Why It Matters in the New GOP Tax Bill," *Washington Post,* November 7, 2017, www.washingtonpost.com/news/business/wp/2017/11/07/what-is-carried-interest-and-why-it-matters-in-the-new-gop-tax-bill/.

CHAPTER 11: THE SIX FIXES

1. George A. Akerlof and Robert J. Shiller, *Phishing for Phools: The Economics of Manipulation and Deception* (Princeton, NJ: Princeton University Press, 2015), vii.

2. Louis D. Brandeis, *Other People's Money: And How the Bankers Use It* (New York: F. A. Stokes, 1914), 92.

3. Frederick Douglass, West India Emancipation Speech, August 3, 1857, https://rbscp.lib.rochester.edu/4398.

EPILOGUE: CRIME AFTER TRUMP

1. Maureen Dowd, "Trump's Bad. Sadly, He's Not Alone," *New York Times*, December 14, 2019, www.nytimes.com/2019/12/14/opinion/sunday/trump-afghanistan-report-boeing.html.

INDEX